Social Justice in Schools

The Guilford Practical Intervention in the Schools Series

Kenneth W. Merrell, Founding Editor
Sandra M. Chafouleas, Series Editor

www.guilford.com/practical

This series presents the most reader-friendly resources available in key areas of evidence-based practice in school settings. Practitioners will find trustworthy guides on effective behavioral, mental health, and academic interventions, and assessment and measurement approaches. Covering all aspects of planning, implementing, and evaluating high-quality services for students, books in the series are carefully crafted for everyday utility. Features include ready-to-use reproducibles, appealing visual elements, and an over-sized format. Recent titles have Web pages where purchasers can download and print the reproducible materials.

Recent Volumes

Social and Emotional Learning in the Classroom,
Second Edition: Promoting Mental Health and Academic Success
Barbara A. Gueldner, Laura L. Feuerborn, and Kenneth W. Merrell

Responding to Problem Behavior in Schools,
Third Edition: The Check-In, Check-Out Intervention
Leanne S. Hawken, Deanne A. Crone, Kaitlin Bundock, and Robert H. Horner

School-Based Behavioral Assessment, Second Edition:
Informing Prevention and Intervention
*Sandra M. Chafouleas, Austin H. Johnson, T. Chris Riley-Tillman,
and Emily A. Iovino*

Child and Adolescent Suicidal Behavior, Second Edition:
School-Based Prevention, Assessment, and Intervention
David N. Miller

School Supports for Students in Military Families
Pamela Fenning

Safe and Healthy Schools, Second Edition: Practical Prevention Strategies
Jeffrey R. Sprague and Hill M. Walker

Clinical Interviews for Children and Adolescents,
Third Edition: Assessment to Intervention
Stephanie H. McConaughy and Sara A. Whitcomb

Executive Function Skills in the Classroom:
Overcoming Barriers, Building Strategies
Laurie Faith, Carol-Anne Bush, and Peg Dawson

The RTI Approach to Evaluating Learning Disabilities, Second Edition
*Joseph F. Kovaleski, Amanda M. VanDerHeyden, Timothy J. Runge,
Perry A. Zirkel, and Edward S. Shapiro*

Effective Bullying Prevention: A Comprehensive Schoolwide Approach
Adam Collins and Jason Harlacher

Social Justice in Schools: A Framework for Equity in Education
Charles A. Barrett

Social Justice in Schools

A Framework for Equity in Education

CHARLES A. BARRETT

Foreword by Ivory A. Toldson

THE GUILFORD PRESS
New York   London

Copyright © 2023 The Guilford Press
A Division of Guilford Publications, Inc.
370 Seventh Avenue, Suite 1200, New York, NY 10001
www.guilford.com

Printed in the United States of America

This book is printed on acid-free paper.

Last digit is print number: 9   8   7   6   5   4   3   2   1

Library of Congress Cataloging-in-Publication Data

Names: Barrett, Charles A. (Psychologist), author.
Title: Social justice in schools : a framework for equity in education /
    Charles A. Barrett ; foreword by Ivory A. Toldson.
Description: New York : The Guilford Press, 2023. | Series: The Guilford
    practical intervention in the schools series | Includes bibliographical
    references and index.
Identifiers: LCCN 2023004437 | ISBN 9781462552146 (paperback) |
    ISBN 9781462552153 (hardcover)
Subjects: LCSH: Social justice and education—United States. | Educational
    equalization—United States. | Minority students—United States. |
    School psychology—United States. | BISAC: PSYCHOLOGY / Psychotherapy /
    Child & Adolescent | EDUCATION / Educational Policy & Reform / General
Classification: LCC LC192.2 .B37 2023 | DDC 370.11/5—dc23/eng/20230207
LC record available at https://lccn.loc.gov/2023004437

To my nieces and nephews—

*That you would grow up in a world that affords you
access to the opportunities you deserve.*

That you would live in places and spaces that embrace who you are.

*That you would fulfill the dreams that live inside of you,
becoming the promise of our ancestors.*

About the Author

Charles A. Barrett, PhD, NCSP, a district-level administrator in Virginia, practiced as a school psychologist for 13 years at the elementary and secondary levels. He serves as an adjunct lecturer at several universities, where he is actively involved in the training and development of future school psychologists. Dr. Barrett was named School Psychologist of the Year by the Virginia Academy of School Psychologists and received the Rookie of the Year Award from the National Association of School Psychologists (NASP). His past leadership positions within NASP include co-chair of the Social Justice Task Force and African American Subcommittee, chair of the Multicultural Affairs and Social Justice Committees, and Virginia Delegate to the NASP Leadership Assembly. Dr. Barrett serves on the editorial boards of *School Psychology Review* and *School Psychology.* He is a frequent speaker and workshop presenter for educators, families, and community organizations. His website is *www.charlesbarrett.org*.

Foreword
Social Justice in Schools:
Setbacks and Setups

THE SETBACK: ANTI-CRT LEGISLATIONS

When I was an 11th grader, I felt immense discomfort when my U.S. history teacher taught us that slavery was a "system of a different time" and many enslaved people, "slaves" in her words, "had good relationships with their 'slave masters.'" Her lesson caused me so much angst that I became combative. Because of my confrontational behavior, the teacher sent me to the principal's office to be disciplined. I was humiliated and ashamed that I had been disruptive in class, but I was also angry. My parents instilled in me a love of learning and a respect for educators. They also taught me to be proud of my Black heritage.

So, when my history teacher minimized the experiences of my enslaved ancestors, I could not stay silent. However, these intense feelings of "discomfort" among students of color are ignored in the recent spate of anti-critical race theory (CRT) bills, aimed at protecting White people from feeling discomfort about the atrocities of some of their ancestors. Like most African Americans, I can trace my lineage back to the same racist enslavers whose crimes many lawmakers are trying to minimize through anti-CRT legislation.

My great-great-great-grandfather was a White enslaver in Kentucky, who raped an enslaved African woman on his plantation. She gave birth to my great-great grandfather,

Granderson Conn. Conn's White half-siblings taught him to read after his enslaver father moved his children—including those conceived of rape—to North Louisiana. Conn became free as a young adult and volunteered to fight for the Union Army in the Civil War. After the war, he returned to Louisiana and had a daughter (my great-grandmother) who had a son named John Henry Scott (my grandfather). My grandfather became a civil rights activist and father to many children, including my mother, civil rights activist Johnita Scott.

School should be a place where we can examine our past and pave the way for a more just future. However, the recent trend of anti-CRT legislation is a step backward. But, as my story shows, African Americans have been living with the consequences of slavery and racism since its inception. We cannot move forward if we do not deal with the harsh realities of our past. Charles A. Barrett's *Social Justice in Schools: A Framework for Equity in Education* can help educators see the importance of social justice in schools and the need to prepare all students for a more just future.

THE SETUP: SOCIAL JUSTICE IN SCHOOLS

Education is at the heart of social justice, and nowhere is this more evident than in our schools. Over the years, classrooms have become increasingly diverse, and educators have been tasked with creating a learning environment that promotes equity and inclusion for all students. As a result, we have seen a steady rise in initiatives and programs designed to ensure that everyone receives an equitable education.

This book provides teachers, administrators, parents, and other stakeholders with an invaluable resource that outlines specific steps they can take to promote social justice within their school environment. It focuses on challenging systems of privilege and implicit bias while empowering families through educational initiatives. The book also encourages educators to form a professional identity that reflects the values they believe in when it comes to social justice.

In addition, this book explores the concept of intersectionality—the idea that different aspects of identity intersect to create unique experiences of discrimination—which is essential for understanding issues related to race, gender, sexuality, disability status, and socioeconomic backgrounds. Practical strategies are provided for each topic, so readers can apply strategies immediately in their classrooms.

Overall, *Social Justice in Schools* provides a comprehensive framework for promoting equity and inclusion within educational settings. It goes beyond mere numbers by focusing on the children, families, schools, and communities we serve. By arming educators with effective tools and resources for implementing social justice practices into their everyday teaching practice, we can be sure that everyone has access to quality education regardless of their background or circumstances.

SUMMARY AND CONCLUSIONS

In the late 20th century, a person could not imagine a video phone beyond the dual-function stationary box with analog cables. Individuals had yet to conceive of the internet, wireless connectivity, global positioning systems, and digital media of the present. With no conception of the future, *naïve realism* prevented society from comprehending a video phone that would comprise a wireless device small enough to fit in a pocket. Naïve realism is also the reason that so many people who want racial justice in the United States have difficulty perceiving or believing it.

Our current economic, educational, and political systems are analogous to televisions, radios, and local-area network phones in the 1980s—using these systems to eradicate institutional racism will appear far-fetched from a myopic perspective. However, if we take a step back, it is easier to see that our systems are at an inflection point. We can use the power of data and the concepts in this book to create social justice in schools and other institutions.

Social Justice in Schools masterfully situates social justice within the larger context of society. The book is also important because it offers concrete recommendations for how to operationalize social justice in schools. The recommendations are based on the latest research and practice, and they are designed to help educators create more equitable learning environments for all students. The book provides a much-needed resource for educational administrators, policymakers, and practitioners who are committed to social justice in schools. It is an essential read for anyone who wants to understand how social justice can be operationalized in education.

Advancing a framework for equity in public education is important because a framework can help education systems move beyond rhetoric. A social justice framework can also provide a shared language and understanding of concepts like "privilege" and "implicit bias," which are often misunderstood. A social justice framework can also help us unpack the ways in which racism and other forms of oppression operate in education, and how they are connected to larger systems of inequality. As the book notes, it is important to understand social justice from a systems perspective, rather than an individual perspective. We must see social justice as something that happens (or does not happen) in schools because of the structures and systems in place, rather than because of individual teachers or administrators. We must also recognize that social justice is not a zero-sum game—in other words, one group's gain does not have to come at the expense of another group.

IVORY A. TOLDSON, PhD
Director, Education Innovation and Research, NAACP
Professor of Counseling Psychology, Howard University
Editor-in-Chief, *Journal of Negro Education*

Preface

As a proud product of public schools, I deeply believe in the power and potential of American public education. Despite its imperfections, public schools are one of the few places in which children from all backgrounds and walks of life can learn together, grow together, and truly develop the academic, social, emotional, and behavioral skills to be successful and productive citizens in an ever-changing and interconnected global society. But as anyone who has worked in public education knows, the mixing and commingling of children, families, and staff from different races, ethnicities, socioeconomic statuses, belief systems, and a host of other backgrounds is not always easy. In fact, it's often messy.

As you read about concepts and constructs that are relevant to social justice and achieving equitable outcomes, one of the most important realities and implications for practice is often overlooked and unspoken: Social justice work is messy work. Advancing equity and working to increase equitable outcomes is inconvenient. It's uncomfortable. Have you ever led your staff during a discussion about a sensitive or contentious topic? How about transitioning your school district or department through a significant reorganization? Have you tried to get 20 exuberant first graders to decide on which game they were going to play during recess? If so, you've already experienced the challenge of including, quite literally, many voices. If you've done any of these things, you are well acquainted with the importance of meeting and listening—and likely doing a lot more listening than anything else—followed by meeting again (and again) and listening even more to develop trust and build consensus.

Throughout *Social Justice in Schools*, you'll see that social justice is about learning and growing, which is inevitably unpleasant. These growing pains, however, are not only purposeful, but they're also filled with promise. Like adolescents who are experiencing developmental changes that will transition them from childhood to adulthood, many of their growing pains—whether physical, social, or emotional—are simply the result of being too big for where they were, yet too small for where they are going. And so it is with social justice: When individuals, schools, and school districts commit to challenging the systems and structures that create and perpetuate inequities, the growing pains that they encounter signify that they are on their way to where they have never been before. Between what is familiar and what is unfamiliar, they have left the safety of what is known to pursue the promise of the unknown.

So, as you're becoming (learning and growing), embrace the process. In all of its messiness and uneasiness, embrace the process, being careful to celebrate how far you've already come but also looking forward to where you can be. Having outgrown what is comfortable, embrace the temporary discomfort, knowing that you are on the path that leads to infinite positive possibilities.

More than my contribution to scholarship in psychology and education, *Social Justice in Schools* is my challenge to an institution that can rise above its current flaws to more effectively meet the needs of all children, all families, all schools, and all communities.

Let's get started.

Acknowledgments

I gratefully acknowledge the following individuals for their assistance in the preparation of this volume:

Julianna Carpenter, PhD, Education Specialist, Region 17 Education Service Center, and Adjunct Faculty, Texas Tech University, Lubbock, Texas

Sandra M. Chafouleas, PhD, Series Editor, The Guilford Practical Intervention in the Schools Series

Worokya Duncan, EdD, Head of Upper School, The Cathedral School, New York, New York

Natalie Graham, Editor, School Psychology and Literacy, The Guilford Press

Gabrielle Hicks, PhD, Postdoctoral Scholar, Center on Education and Training for Employment, The Ohio State University, Columbus, Ohio

Danielle Larson, MTS, Private Educator, Cleveland, Tennessee

Lottie Spurlock, MEd, Director of Equity, Loudoun County Public Schools, Ashburn, Virginia

Ayanna Troutman, MEd, School Psychology Graduate Student, University of Florida, Gainesville, Florida

Ronald A. Wilson, MBA, Pastor, Kings Chapel Church of God in Christ, Southampton, New York

Contents

CHAPTER 1

Social Justice
A Framework for Equity in Public Education

If we are genuinely serious about embracing social justice, we must transform our thinking. Social justice is not a condiment that is added to a sandwich or dressing that is placed over a salad. It is not something that gives flavor to our work after it's complete, but it is the work itself. Social justice is an essential ingredient that is baked into the process of whatever we are preparing for children.

Of all my professional roles, I am most proud to be a school psychologist. More than anything else, my experiences as a practitioner inform my graduate teaching, consulting, speaking, and writing. Having served real children and families who attend real schools in real communities has given me tremendous insight into the stubborn inequities that plague public education. But as I detail throughout this book, inequity is a result—it's a by-product, an outcome, of what we (educators, school systems) have or have not done, even unintentionally, for children.

In *How to Be an Antiracist*, Ibram X. Kendi provides a succinct definition, a non-definition, and concrete examples of racial equity and racial inequity. First, the non-definition: "racial inequity is when two or more racial groups are not standing on approximately equal footing" (Kendi, 2019, p. 18). As an example, in 2014, the number of individuals (by race) who were living in owner-occupied homes was 71% for White families, 45% for Latinx[1] families, and 41% for Black families. These disparate outcomes show that White families were almost twice as likely as Black families to own their homes. On

---

[1] Although it is an imperfect term, throughout this book, *Latinx* is used to refer to Hispanic individuals.

the other hand, the definition: "racial equity is when two or more racial groups are standing on relatively equal footing" (Kendi, 2019, p. 18). Using the same home ownership example, there should be relatively similar numbers of families across racial groups living in their own homes. In schools, inequity is often referred to as *disproportionality*—**the extent to which a certain group is represented in a category** (e.g., Black students receiving suspensions or expulsions; English learners [ELs] who are identified with a specific learning disability [SLD]; Latinx students who are eligible for the gifted program) **and differs from an agreed-upon benchmark** (e.g., White (or all other) students receiving suspensions or expulsions; White (or all other) students who are identified with SLD; White (or all other) students who are eligible for the gifted program). For many schools and school districts, disproportionate outcomes exist in at least one area (e.g., special education eligibility, suspension/expulsion [discipline], gifted identification). But as Kendi implied in his example above, an individual's race/ethnicity should not predict their likelihood of owning a home. Similarly, students' race/ethnicity, family socioeconomic status (SES), English proficiency, or any other demographic characteristic should not predict outcomes in the previously mentioned categories. When inequities (disproportionality) exist in schools, educators must investigate the factors (reasons) that contribute to such outcomes. More than an outcome, disproportionality is an opportunity to interrogate the policies and practices that lead to some students remaining in the margins of a high-quality education system while their peers excel.

Without oversimplifying or reducing social justice to a checklist of practices or begrudgingly viewing it as yet another thing to do, the primary answer to *Why am I writing this book?* is to give all educators—PreK–12 teachers, building administrators (e.g., assistant principals and principals), central office leaders (e.g., superintendents, assistant superintendents, special education directors, student services directors, chief equity officers), and mental health providers (e.g., school counselors, school psychologists, and school social workers)—a framework for how to think about social justice in schools and practical suggestions for embedding socially just practices into their day-to-day roles and responsibilities. In speaking to teachers, administrators, and policymakers about how socially just practices lead to equitable outcomes, they ultimately want to know three things: First, what is social justice? Second, why is it important for my respective role? Third, how do I engage in socially just practices to increase equitable outcomes for students, families, schools, and communities? These questions are answered throughout this book.

ABOUT THIS BOOK

Who Should Read This Book?

Everyone who cares about children. One of the biggest truths about social justice is that it is fundamentally about how systems and structures differentially affect people based on their intersecting identities. As a result, social justice requires everyone's commitment to shift the ways that unjust practices lead to negative outcomes for children. Whether you're a general education, special education, or EL teacher, *Social Justice in Schools* provides insight and helpful perspectives to better understand your students and families. For school-based mental health providers, this book explores how significant contextual factors (events happening around students) affect children's social, emotional, and behavioral functioning. For principals and central office administrators, it highlights the critical role of policy in promoting positive outcomes for children. Whether you're new to the profession or a veteran educator, this book will reinforce truths that you've known for a long time, give you language to navigate challenging situations, or demystify what social justice is and how it's relevant to equity in public education.

What Is This Book Trying to Convey?

We often teach children to look for the *main idea*. What is the main idea of *Social Justice in Schools*? The purpose of this text is to show as concretely as possible how educators can actively work toward promoting (increasing) equitable outcomes for all students. Additionally, the book challenges educators to think broadly about the world in which they (and their students) live and the contributing factors to children's difficulties. Over the course of eight chapters, readers are invited to critique their personal philosophical orientation to serving students and encouraged to commit themselves to ongoing professional learning to ultimately become more responsive to their students and families.

When Should I Read This Book?

Best described as a guide for practitioners, *Social Justice in Schools* is well suited for lifelong learners in their various roles as educators. Whether you read this book before each school year or assign it to your teachers, staff, departments, or professional learning communities as a shared book study, reading and rereading about these principles and concepts throughout your career will be time well spent. For graduate students, this book may be a required or recommended text or a resource to support your studies.

Where Does This Book Fit into My Professional Practice?

This is perhaps the easiest question to answer: This book belongs at the center of your (our) professional practice. Consider the following statement: *If we are genuinely serious about embracing social justice, we must transform our thinking. Social justice is not a condiment that is added to a sandwich or dressing that is placed over a salad. It is not something that gives flavor to our work after it's complete, but it is the work itself. Social justice is an essential ingredient that is baked into the process of whatever we are preparing for children.* So, rather than viewing social justice as separate from our teaching, our leadership, our counseling, our assessment, or our policymaking, because social justice is the work itself, it needs to be infused into all of these activities.

How Will This Book Help Me in My Academic Journey or Professional Practice?

When reading portions of this book, you might be encouraged because your practice is consistent with social justice. At other times, you will be challenged to revisit and revise your approach so that you can more effectively promote positive outcomes for children. Whatever it is for you on any given day, remember: It's OK as long as you're committed to making the necessary changes (i.e., challenging yourself and systems) that are in the best interest of children.

FEATURES OF *SOCIAL JUSTICE IN SCHOOLS*

What Can I Expect While Reading This Book?

To facilitate an engaging, interactive, and effective learning experience, the following text features have been included in each of the chapters. First, key vocabulary and their definitions are in **boldface type**. These terms are some of the most essential concepts to help you understand each chapter's content. If you are previewing the chapters, making a list of the key terms can be an effective strategy to expose yourself, your students, or your colleagues to the major points that will be covered in more detail.

To emphasize the active role that educators play in promoting social justice, Chapters 2 through 7 are titled using the following phrase: "Social Justice Is About. . . ." Next, and taken from Barrett (2018), a challenge statement highlights the content of the chapter. Further, learning outcomes are included to frame readers' expectations. Whether you use *Social Justice in Schools* in graduate courses or as a book study in professional learning communities, these objectives can be helpful for structuring lessons or small-group discussions about each chapter.

For school psychologists, not only does the book support the most recently adopted strategic goal (social justice) of the National Association of School Psychologists (NASP; 2017), but it is also aligned with the NASP Model for Comprehensive and Integrated School Psychological Services (Practice Model; NASP, 2020). But irrespective of discipline, *Social Justice in Schools* highlights the importance of all educators using data to inform decisions; consulting and collaborating with families, schools, and communities; implementing schoolwide practices to promote learning and safe and supportive environments; and providing evidence-based academic interventions, instructional supports, and mental and behavioral health services. As many professions and their respective associations have been more explicit about their commitment to social justice, *Social*

Justice in Schools shows how educators can embrace and embed these principles into all aspects of their professional practice.

Because some of the concepts can seem abstract, vignettes, scenarios, and case examples are included throughout the book to illustrate key principles. Though some of these examples are taken from real life, identifying information has been changed to protect the anonymity of students, families, schools, communities, and professionals. To be inclusive of all readers, particularly those who are nonbinary or whose gender identity is neither masculine nor feminine, *they/them/their* pronouns are used when referring to a single individual.

Last, *Discussion Questions* and *Resources for Professional Learning* have been included at the end of most chapters to inspire personal reflection, small-group discussion, and further learning. Given the nature of the content, it is important that readers allow themselves time to process the information, sometimes wrestle with their discomfort, and record their reactions while learning to think in new ways. This is an essential aspect of learning that is often overlooked, especially for adult students. The *Resources for Professional Learning* section includes books, articles, websites, and activities (e.g., links to lesson plans) that can reinforce key ideas previously presented in the chapter and be helpful to individuals, classes, schools, or small-group professional learning communities. In sum, the Questions and Resources are designed to facilitate active engagement with the material rather than passively receiving information.

SOCIAL JUSTICE IN SCHOOLS: A BRIEF OVERVIEW

In Chapter 2, readers are introduced to ecological systems theory (Bronfenbrenner, 1977) and the importance of developing a comprehensive understanding of students to make the most appropriate educational decisions. The chapter discusses how social justice is fundamentally about systems and structures leading to differential outcomes for students, families, schools, and communities.

Chapter 3 focuses on the importance of educators challenging themselves and their colleagues when their actions are inconsistent with social justice or socially just practices. Two real-world examples are provided that include sample language for responding to colleagues when their behavior is unintentionally harmful to students, and several principles are highlighted to show why the responses are necessary through the lens of social justice. School-based policies and practices that need to be disrupted and dismantled because they are not aligned with social justice and because they reinforce educational inequities are also reviewed. Last, the chapter addresses terms that are commonly used in psychology and education, including reframing language to be more consistent with social justice.

To encourage self-reflection, Chapter 4 focuses on the importance of educators understanding three foundational constructs—privilege, implicit bias, and intersectionality—and their relationship to inequities in public education. Though not always comfortable to discuss, these concepts are essential to developing a social justice paradigm that ultimately leads to equitable outcomes. Because the concepts can be relatively complex, vignettes and personal reflections are used to clearly articulate and illustrate them.

Chapter 5 discusses using a multimethod and multi-informant assessment approach to more accurately understand students' performance. References to assessing children's cognitive abilities, academic achievement, and social, emotional, and behavioral functioning highlight the importance of considering contextual factors (e.g., limited English proficiency, race/ethnicity, rater characteristics) that can influence their performance on traditional (standardized) instruments with implications for special education (e.g., SLD, other health impairment) and gifted eligibility. Lessons from the COVID-19 pandemic are highlighted to show how educators can think broadly (systemically) and creatively about meeting the needs of their students.

Chapter 6 focuses on educators developing a deep understanding of the students, families, and communities they serve. Using contemporary history (the polarizing 2016 presidential election, the highly publicized murders of several African Americans throughout 2020) and an interdisciplinary example from a pediatrician who studies the relationship between police violence, equity, and child health outcomes, the chapter shows how children's behavioral symptoms can be functionally related to, and sometimes better explained by, events that are happening around them (e.g., exposure to national crises or chronic community violence). Because the terms are frequently misunderstood, the chapter includes a brief discussion of what Black Lives Matter means in principle and the difference between making political statements on behalf of students and families and partisan alignment.

Because empowering families to be their children's most informed and effective advocates is central to social justice, Chapter 7 discusses the importance of educators intentionally creating school communities that are genuinely inclusive. Similar to Chapter 4, anecdotes are used to explain the differences between diversity, inclusion, and equity.

Chapter 8 provides a challenge to all educators. With an explicit focus on advocacy, policy, and systems change, the NASP Exposure Project—a multiyear, national initiative designed to address critical workforce shortages in school psychology and increase the number of racially and ethnically minoritized (REM)[2] individuals in the field—is highlighted as an effective strategy to promote diversity, which is necessary but not sufficient for inclusion or equity. Though the chapter cautions against looking for prescriptive

---

[2]As is discussed in Chapter 3, this book intentionally uses systems-centered language. For example, except for direct quotations that used other terms, when referring to non-White individuals as a collective group, *racially and ethnically minoritized* (REM) is used rather than *minority* or *minorities*. For more information about using systems-centered language, please read Barrett (2021a).

(checklist) approaches to tackling educational inequities, it provides practical suggestions for how individuals can collaboratively advance systems change in schools and school districts.

Chapter 9, the most autobiographical section of the book, encourages readers to reflect upon their lived experiences and how they have shaped their professional identities. From recognizing significant events that have informed their perspectives and approaches to serving children, families, schools, and communities to tracing their growth and development as social justice–oriented educators, readers will be challenged to think about their core values and how they align with infusing socially just practices into their respective professional roles.

Social Justice Is About Systems

Assess contextual variables to rule out alternative explanations for children's performance.

Social justice is a way of thinking about student functioning and informs how we practice as educators.

LEARNING OUTCOMES

After reading this chapter, you should be able to . . .

1. Define ecological systems theory (Bronfenbrenner, 1977).
2. Explain the relationship between ecological systems theory and social justice in schools.
3. Define social justice (NASP, 2017) and explain its essential components.
4. Explain why social justice is relevant to all educators and equity in public education.

CHAPTER OVERVIEW

In Chapter 2 you will learn about ecological systems theory (Bronfenbrenner, 1977) and how educators can use it to understand their students and make the most appropriate decisions. The chapter also explains how social justice is fundamentally about systems and structures that lead to differential outcomes for students, families, schools, and communities. Implications for educators using a broad systems orientation to fully understand children's performance are discussed.

INTRODUCTION

As a school psychologist, I was trained as a scientist-practitioner. Developing an appreciation for evidence-based approaches to serve students has been invaluable in my career as a practitioner, graduate educator, and central office administrator supporting school-based clinicians. As I've written before (Barrett, 2018), while I was completing my graduate studies at Lehigh University, my professors reinforced a central theme throughout my coursework: "What is the research question?" In other words, what problem are you trying to solve? In research, having a clear and well-articulated question is foundational to everything that follows—the literature that is reviewed, the participants who are recruited for a particular study, as well as the study design and its methodology. Similarly, for school psychologists, the research question (i.e., the reason for referral or referral question) informs subsequent practices (e.g., the instruments used to evaluate a student, the informant behavior rating scales that are administered, the types of observations that are conducted in which settings). When evaluating a student for whom the referral concerns are related to attention-deficit/hyperactivity disorder (ADHD), the behavior rating scales, interview questions, and types of observations that are completed are likely different from those for a student who is suspected of having an SLD, which is also different from those given for a student being assessed for an autism spectrum disorder (ASD). For teachers, the research question (i.e., the nature of the student's academic difficulty) determines their instructional and intervention approaches. For example, students whose reading weaknesses stem from fluency (reading smoothly and at an acceptable rate) are supported differently than students whose challenges are related to decoding (hearing and blending sounds to read unknown words) or comprehension (understanding what they are reading).

But not only is the research question essential, the theoretical framework from which educators operate is equally important. In fact, in many ways the research question (what we are trying to answer or the problem that we are trying to solve) is born out of the theoretical framework (how we view, conceptualize, or think about children's functioning). In psychology, there are several schools of thought or philosophical orientations that inform the work of school-based mental health providers. Some, for example, subscribe to a strict behaviorist perspective in the tradition of B. F. Skinner or John Watson—only focusing on what is observable and quantifiable (measurable). When a child leaves their classroom, a behaviorally oriented school psychologist would seek to understand the environmental conditions that preceded (antecedents) and followed (consequences) the target behavior (leaving the classroom without permission). After observing the student for a period of time and interviewing the child, their teachers, and parents/guardians, the school psychologist could determine that the student elopes (leaves the classroom) when asked to complete challenging academic tasks. As a result, the behavioral explanation (i.e., the function of the behavior) is that eloping allows the child to escape (avoid) academic tasks that are too difficult. An intervention, therefore, would focus on either teaching the child a socially acceptable way to escape such situations (e.g., raising their hand and asking for a break) or more appropriately matching the academic assignments to their developmental or instructional level.

Another orientation that school-based practitioners can embrace is the cognitive-behaviorist approach, which focuses on the relationship between a person's thoughts and their behavior. For example, after receiving their latest exam grade, a high school student struggles with depressive thoughts or issues of self-worth. From a cognitive-behavioral perspective, the school counselor helps the student to reframe their maladaptive thinking by highlighting their strengths and stellar grades in other subjects. Over time, the student learns to shift their thought patterns (cognitive restructuring) by accepting that they have many strengths/skills in other areas or classes, which also helps to elevate their mood and self-perceptions.

And though it's less popular in contemporary practice, those who are influenced by Sigmund Freud's psychoanalytic theory might view an adolescent male's aggressive tendencies as stemming from his relationship with his mother. In other words, this theoretical position suggests that there is a significant correlation between how an individual has resolved various psychosexual stages during the earliest years of life and their behavior as an adolescent or adult. Taken together, a person's theoretical orientation shapes how they think about students' difficulties and how they practice in their respective discipline.

ECOLOGICAL SYSTEMS THEORY AND SOCIAL JUSTICE

Having reviewed the relationship between a theoretical orientation and understanding student functioning, in this section I provide a brief overview of ecological systems theory (Bronfenbrenner, 1977) and how it is applicable to social justice. Fictitious vignettes are included to highlight how the framework's key principles are relevant to school-based practice. To learn more about the theory, interested readers are referred to Rosa and Tudge (2013).

According to Bronfenbrenner, psychologists should adopt a more sophisticated and nuanced approach to understanding human development by appreciating the broader contextual and environmental influences that shape human behavior. Dissatisfied with overly simplistic methods that only included observing individuals in a given setting, the Russian-born developmental psychologist asserted that a fuller and more complete understanding "requires examination of multiperson systems of interaction not limited to a single setting and must take into account aspects of the environment beyond the immediate situation containing the subject" (Bronfenbrenner, 1977, p. 514). **Ecological systems theory** is based on the following definition by Bronfenbrenner (Definition 1; D_1): **"The ecology of human development is the scientific study of the progressive, mutual accommodation, throughout the lifespan, between a growing human organism and the changing immediate environments in which it lives, as this process is affected by rela-**

tions obtaining within and between these immediate settings, as well as the larger social contexts, both formal and informal, in which the settings are embedded" (Bronfenbrenner, 1977, p. 514). Further, Bronfenbrenner's Definition 2 (D_2) states that the environment is "a nested arrangement of structures, each contained within the next" (p. 514). Figure 2.1 provides a visual representation of ecological systems theory, which includes the microsystem, mesosystem, exosystem, macrosystem, and chronosystem. Although the chronosystem was not a part of Bronfenbrenner's original conceptualization, it has been included in contemporary revisions to the model. Read the vignettes about *Miguel* and *Emily* that are provided below. These fictitious scenarios will highlight the significance of the microsystem, mesosystem, exosystem, macrosystem, and chronosystem for Miguel, Emily, and their families.

> **As you're reading this book, please keep Miguel and Emily in mind. They are referred to in later chapters to help illustrate important concepts.**

The Microsystem

The first level of the ecological system is the **microsystem** and includes **the interactions between an individual and their immediate environment or setting** (e.g., home, school, workplace). A setting is a place with physical features in which individuals with specific

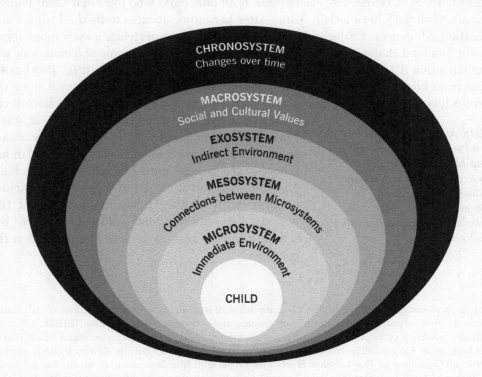

FIGURE 2.1. Bronfenbrenner's ecological systems theory.

roles (e.g., child, sibling, parent, spouse, teacher, employee) engage in specific activities for specified periods of time.

Miguel Hernandez is 15 and is the oldest of four siblings. Though he, his brother, and his two sisters were born in a Virginia suburb near Washington, D.C., his parents, Hector and Maria, are immigrants from El Salvador. Despite initially speaking little English, Mr. and Mrs. Hernandez attended English Learner (EL) classes for adults, earned their high school equivalency degrees, followed by their associate's, bachelor's, and master's degrees through evening and weekend classes. They are currently working as teachers in the same school district that their children attend. Mr. Hernandez has come a long way from working as a day laborer who hoped to find carpentry jobs (e.g., painting houses) to support his family. Similarly, Mrs. Hernandez still thinks about the years that she spent long hours cleaning houses and office buildings, often 6 days per week. Miguel is in 10th grade, and his brother and sisters are in elementary and middle school. Though his parents are earning more money as teachers, Miguel works at a local pizzeria after school and on weekends to help send money and gifts to his aunts, uncles, cousins, and grandparents in El Salvador. The Hernandez family is very active in their community and attends Our Lady of Hope, a Spanish-speaking Catholic church.

Emily Jones, a White, 10-year-old girl, is an only child who lives in a small Pennsylvania town with her mother, Anne. After her father unexpectedly died from a short battle with cancer, Emily and Ms. Jones have been experiencing even more significant financial challenges. Emily's parents grew up in low-income and economic marginalization (LIEM; American Psychological Association [APA], 2019),[1] didn't graduate from high school, and worked in low-wage factory jobs in their town since they were teenagers. To help make ends meet, Emily and Ms. Jones are welfare recipients, and Emily also receives free lunch at school. Because her mother works long hours, Emily is cared for by her grandmother—who also didn't finish high school—after school until her mother comes home, often late in the evening. Emily's peer group includes children with similar backgrounds—most of their parents and grandparents didn't complete high school, and they plan to work in factories when they get older.

THINK ABOUT IT. Based on the information presented about Miguel and Emily, how are their microsystems similar? How are they different? Discuss your answers with your classmates or colleagues.

---

[1] Poverty is more complex than not having adequate financial resources, families' income levels, and students' eligibility for free or reduced-price lunch. Low-income and economic marginalization (LIEM; APA, 2019) expands how poverty is conceptualized to also acknowledge its negative impact on sociocultural factors (Barrett, Kendrick-Dunn, & Proctor, 2019). For more information about LIEM, read Barrett, Kendrick-Dunn, and Proctor (2019) and *Guidelines for Psychological Practice for People with Low-Income and Economic Marginalization* (APA, 2019), which can be accessed at the following link: *http://apacustomout.apa.org/commentPracGuidelines/Practice/LIEM_Guidelines.pdf.*

Based on the description above, Miguel's microsystem includes his family (his parents and siblings), high school, job at a local pizzeria, Our Lady of Hope, and the suburban neighborhood in which he lives. Emily's microsystem, however, is very different and consists of her mother, her grandmother, the small town that she lives in, her school, and her friends who also share a very similar background as she and her mother. See Figures 2.2 and 2.3 for visual representations of Miguel and Emily's microsystems, respectively.

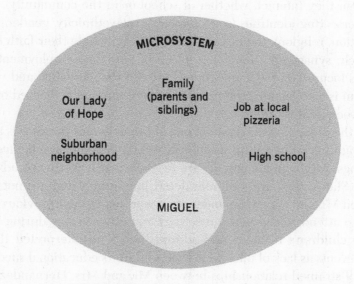

FIGURE 2.2. Miguel's microsystem.

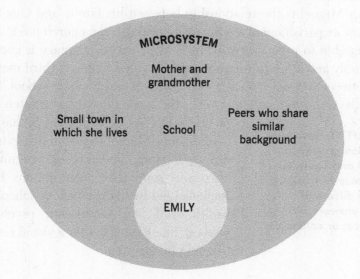

FIGURE 2.3. Emily's microsystem.

The Mesosystem

The second level of the ecological system is the **mesosystem** and includes **the connections between major settings that contain the individual at a particular point in their life.** For example, the mesosystem of a 15-year-old living in the Northeast United States can include the interactions between their family (the persons with whom they are living), school (the place in which they receive their education), and peer group (the persons with whom they interact, whether at school or in the community). Depending on the child's intersecting identities (see Chapter 4; race/ethnicity, gender/gender identity, sexual orientation, religion), the mesosystem can also include their faith institution (e.g., mosque, church, synagogue, temple) or place of part-time employment. Whereas the microsystem is focused on the connections between the individual and various settings, the mesosystem is a collection (system) of microsystems and is focused on the interrelationships between microsystems.

Based on the preceding description, one of Miguel's mesosystems is the relationship between his high school in a Virginia suburb and the home where he lives with his parents and siblings. Although his parents are teachers and have earned advanced degrees in the United States, they are still considered immigrants and are not native English speakers. When Mr. and Mrs. Hernandez were working in their previous jobs, they were often unable to attend school-based meetings and other events during the school day. Because their children's teachers and administrators misinterpreted their absence at meetings and events as lack of interest in their children's educational success, there were several years of strained relationships between Mr. and Mrs. Hernandez and their children's schools. Now that they have more flexibility to request paid leave from work, Mr. and Mrs. Hernandez can participate differently in their children's education. Another mesosystem for Miguel is the relationship between his family and Our Lady of Hope. Because most of its parishioners are Spanish-speaking, the church holds weekly mass in Spanish. Being able to pray and worship in their native language is comforting to the Hernandez family and other immigrants in the United States. A third mesosystem is the connection between Miguel's job at a local pizzeria and his high school. Due to his late hours during the week and long hours over the weekend, Miguel is often tardy to school or sleeps in class. Additionally, he has many missing assignments. Miguel has been disciplined for his tardiness, sleeping, and missing assignments, but creative and supportive interventions have not been implemented by his teachers or school-based mental health staff (e.g., counselor, psychologist, social worker). See Figure 2.4 for a visual representation of Miguel's mesosystem.

THINK ABOUT IT. Based on the information presented about Miguel and Emily, how are their mesosystems similar? How are they different? Discuss your answers with your classmates or colleagues.

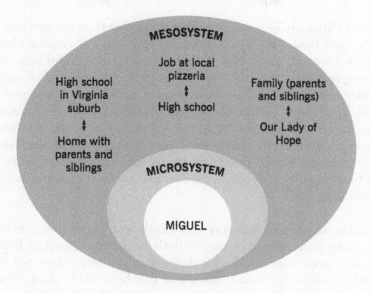

FIGURE 2.4. Miguel's mesosystem.

The Exosystem

The third level of the ecological system is the **exosystem**, which is an extension of the mesosystem. Although the mesosystem includes formal and informal social structures that do not directly contain the individual, **the exosystem encompasses an individual's immediate settings and ultimately influences what happens in these settings**. These structures include significant societal institutions such as neighborhoods; mass media (television); social media; local, state, and national government; the distribution of goods and services; and public transportation facilities.

Miguel and his family live in a very close-knit Latinx community. Most of the families are from Central American countries such as El Salvador, Guatemala, and Honduras. Although the older generations, such as Miguel's parents, his friends' parents, and their aunts, uncles, and grandparents, were born in Central America, Miguel's peers, like Miguel and his siblings, were born in the United States. Because many people in Miguel's community share ties to Central America, in addition to holding mass in Spanish, Our Lady of Hope celebrates many traditional holidays and sponsors cultural events that aren't recognized by his school or American friends. Similarly, most of the families regularly watch television shows in Spanish and read newspapers from their home countries. Despite having many Spanish-speaking peers at school, Miguel, his siblings, and their friends also occasionally feel uncomfortable. Sometimes their teachers make assumptions that aren't true (e.g., sending forms home in Spanish because they don't think that their parents can read or write in English), and they don't like being taken out of their regular classes to attend EL classes with small groups of other Spanish-speaking children. Even at work, despite being teachers, Mr. and Mrs. Hernandez experience microaggressions[2] and other unfair treatment from their coworkers (e.g., only being assigned to teach ELs rather than all students). Although Miguel, his siblings, and their friends were born in Virginia, some of their parents, aunts, and uncles have not obtained legal status as American citizens. From time to time, especially during national election cycles, Miguel's friends are fearful that their family members will be deported based on what they hear in political debates or see on Facebook, Instagram, Twitter, and other social media sites.

Because of the significant stressors that Emily and her family continue to experience, they have a significant history of both mental and physical health problems. Ms. Jones has been diagnosed with depression but often does not have the time or financial resources to attend therapy or purchase medication. Her employer at the factory only covers three counseling sessions, and even with her insurance, the copay for her antidepressant medication is exorbitant. Further, there are very few mental health providers in her area, which leads to being placed on waitlists that are several months long. Lack of access to public transportation makes traveling beyond her small town both difficult and time-consuming. Partially due to Ms. Jones's mental health difficulties and other stressors, she has been abusive to Emily, which has led to numerous calls to Child Protective Services (CPS) and a temporary placement in foster care. Because Emily's grandmother has been more involved in her life, she's been allowed to return home to Ms. Jones. At school, Emily experiences academic difficulties in a variety of classes but rarely receives extra support from specialists or interventionists due to lack of funding from the school board.

It is worth highlighting that the close-knit and supportive neighborhood in which Miguel and his family live is a tremendous source of support and strength for them. Because many families share a similar background, they can relate to one another in ways that are more natural than when they are interacting with their American neighbors, friends, and coworkers. Being able to read about and discuss current events in their native countries or watch television in their native language makes them feel connected to their heritage and loved ones in Central America. On the other hand, the periodic debates about immigration reform, especially during national election cycles, is a significant stressor for some of Miguel's friends and their families.

For Emily, there are two exosystems that are quite significant in her life. First, lack of access to public transportation exacerbates her mother's mental health difficulty due to

---

[2] Brief and commonplace daily verbal, behavioral, and environmental indignities, whether intentional or unintentional, that communicate hostile, derogatory, or negative racial slights and insults toward people from minoritized backgrounds (Sue et al., 2007).

the limited availability of psychotherapy. And because Emily lives in an area with many underfunded and underresourced schools, she rarely receives the academic interventions that are necessary to improve her skills in reading, writing, and math. Like Ms. Jones, most of the families in Emily's neighborhood are often working to provide for their children. As a result, they have less time to advocate for increased school funding and staffing by lobbying their school board members and district officials. See Figures 2.5 and 2.6 for visual representations of Miguel's and Emily's exosystems, respectively.

The Macrosystem: Ecological Systems Theory and the Unequal Opportunity Race

The **macrosystem** is fundamentally different from the microsystem, mesosystem, and exosystem. Rather than representing the specific situations that affect an individual, the macrosystem is the general framework that establishes the pattern for the structures and activities that occur within the microsystem, mesosystem, and exosystem. The fourth level of the ecological system, a macrosystem is **the overarching institutional patterns of the culture or subculture, including the economic, social, educational, legal, and political systems.** Coupled with their structural significance, macrosystems also carry information and ideologies that explicitly (directly) and implicitly (indirectly) give meaning to the lower levels of the ecological system. In other words, microsystems, mesosystems, and exosystems are manifestations of macrosystems. Though written more than

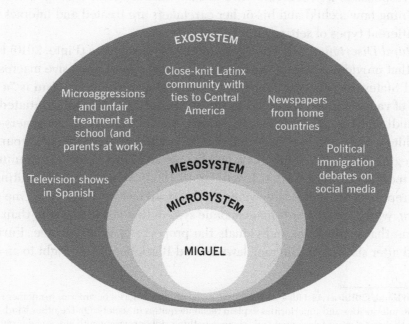

FIGURE 2.5. Miguel's exosystem.

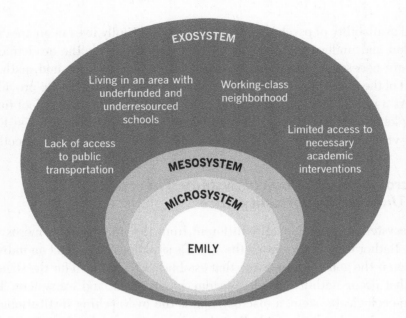

FIGURE 2.6. Emily's exosystem.

four decades ago, these words by Bronfenbrenner (1977) highlight the systems orientation of social justice and its implications for children: "What place or priority children and those responsible for their care have in such macrosystems is of special importance in determining how a child and his or her caretakers are treated and interact with each other in different types of settings" (p. 515).

Structural Discrimination: The Unequal Opportunity Race (Pinto, 2010) is a 4-minute video that provides a helpful summary of one of the most pervasive macrosystems in the United States: racism. Also known as structural or systemic, **racism is "a powerful collection of racist policies that lead to racial inequity and are substantiated by racist ideas"** (Kendi, 2019, p. 20).[3] As a brief synopsis, the video shows four runners—a White male, a White female, and two (male and female) runners from REM backgrounds. When the race begins (1492), the White male and female are allowed to start running, though the REM individuals must wait 472 years (until 1964). While they are waiting, numerous terms representing significant events in American history are shown. One such term was *slavery,* which was not only an economic system that lasted for more than 200 years but also one that made Black individuals the property of White people. Further, both during and after slavery, antiliteracy laws denied Black people the right to an education

---

[3] According to Kendi (2019), a racist idea "suggests one racial group is inferior or superior to another racial group." Further, these inferiorities and superiorities explain racial inequities in society. On the other hand, an antiracist idea suggests that racial groups are equal and "there is nothing right or wrong with any racial group." Antiracist ideas also argue that "racist policies are the cause of racial inequities" (Kendi, 2019, p. 20).

(i.e., learning to read and write), the right to vote (before the Voting Rights Act of 1965), and affected the jobs that they could have and the financial base that they were able to develop compared with White individuals. Another term shown was *Manifest Destiny*: the idea that the United States was destined (entitled) to expand throughout North America. This foreign policy included the belief that American values, American people, and American institutions were superior to individuals and cultures in other parts of the world. Among the significant consequences of Manifest Destiny, Indigenous Americans were displaced from their ancestral homes and endured genocide. Between 1830 and 1850, in a removal known as the Trail of Tears, Indigenous Americans who were members of the Cherokee, Muscogee (Creek), Seminole, Chickasaw, and Choctaw nations, and the Black people who were enslaved to them, were forcibly removed from their lands in the southeastern United States to areas that were west of the Mississippi River and designated as Indian Territory (reservations). These actions were authorized by the Indian Removal Act in 1830, and thousands of Indigenous Americans died from disease and starvation. The relationship between these events and the macrosystem is that these actions were once legal in the United States. These state-sanctioned policies (laws) led to practices that negatively affected generations of people. Slavery, Manifest Destiny, the Trail of Tears, and *Jim Crow segregation* (the separation of public facilities based on race) were not individual instances that happened to some people; they were broad, systems-level realities that affected people based on being Black or Indigenous.

As the video continues, because the White male and female have been running for several hundred years longer than the REM individuals, they have also accumulated wealth and passed this to subsequent runners (i.e., generational wealth). But even after the REM runners were finally allowed to begin their races, they faced significant obstacles that their White counterparts never encountered: discrimination, poor schooling, underachievement, standardized tests, the school-to-prison pipeline, housing segregation, racial profiling, wealth disparities, and a shortened lifespan. At the end, the video shows a conveyor belt being installed in the White male's lane to indicate the privileges that are afforded not only to White people in general but White males in particular (e.g., connections, networks, increased wealth).[4]

Although there are other types of marginalization and discrimination (e.g., ableism, sexism, homophobia, transphobia, xenophobia), because of how pervasive racism is in American society, and as depicted in *The Unequal Opportunity Race*, next I briefly discuss the significance of racism as an example of a macrosystem.

According to Kendi (2019), **"Racism is a marriage of racist policies and racist ideas that produces and normalizes racial inequities"** (p. 18). As mentioned in Chapter 1, racial inequity occurs when two or more racial groups are not standing on approximately

---

[4]Although the video is helpful for showing how systems operate and differentially affect people, it is also an oversimplification. In other words, White individuals, like Emily and Ms. Jones, also experience significant hardships. The video's overall premise, however, shows how racism, in particular, negatively affects REM individuals in virtually every aspect of life.

equal footing, and it assumes that racial difference is not a legitimate explanation for the outcome. Therefore, as it relates to systems and structures, more than individual situations or events, racism, which is the result of racist policies, is embedded within institutions (e.g., both written and unwritten laws, rules, procedures, processes, regulations, and guidelines that affect people) and produces or sustains racial inequities between groups in their respective microsystems, mesosystems, and exosystems. When Black students, for example, are more likely to be suspended or expelled compared with their White peers, discipline policies are inherently racist because they are perpetuating racial inequity. When Latinx students are less likely to be identified for their school's gifted program compared with their White peers, the assessment and identification process is inherently racist because it is reinforcing inequities between groups. And although it's important to hold people accountable for their actions, it is more important to address the policies that allow such actions and ultimately lead to inequitable outcomes.[5]

Although there are other examples and metaphors, *The Unequal Opportunity Race*, which I have shown to numerous educators and graduate students, is a particularly powerful depiction of the systemic nature (macrosystem) of racism. It highlights that the individual (child, student) isn't the only person responsible for their success or difficulty making progress. Whether it portrays the White runners who were allowed to immediately begin their races, ran unencumbered, and enjoyed the benefits of generational wealth and connections or the REM runners who were not only delayed but also experienced significant obstacles throughout the race, the video reinforces the structural significance of social justice and how policies in every societal institution (e.g., housing, education, law enforcement, health care) affect people. From discrimination (e.g., implicit bias) and poor schooling (e.g., attending schools with less qualified teachers, less funding, and less access to resources) to the school-to-prison pipeline (i.e., the likelihood that REM students will prematurely enter the criminal justice system due to zero-tolerance discipline policies that increase suspensions and expulsions), the video gives educators valuable perspective on their students.

Imagine meeting a student as a school psychologist, school counselor, or school social worker. Like Miguel, he is 15 and in the 10th grade. The student is referred to you by his teacher for displaying a variety of problem behaviors: being disengaged from school, skipping classes, and not completing assignments. Though it's appropriate to address the student's presenting behaviors, it's also important to consider his history. In other words, the student's current presentation is only a snapshot in time; but how did he present throughout middle school? How did he behave in elementary school? What did his grades and report card comments reflect over the course of his educational history? As educators, before forming impressions about students based on what we see in the moment, we must take a broader perspective by learning more about their histories. For example, talking to the student may reveal that his current presentation is the result of feeling frustrated,

---

[5] See Chapter 8 for a more detailed discussion of the role of policy in promoting equitable outcomes for students.

defeated, and discouraged. The student might tell you that he tried to work hard in elementary or middle school but received failing grades due to lack of adequate support and interventions from overwhelmed teachers who had limited time and resources. The student might tell you that his older siblings, parents, or aunts and uncles tried to get ahead in life but were repeatedly denied access to meaningful opportunities, perhaps due to racist policies and practices when they were in school. These things taken together reveal that there is a more comprehensive (systems-oriented) explanation for the student who seems disengaged from school and uninterested in his academic success. And when his behavior is viewed through this orientation, which includes examining what is happening around him as much as what's happening within him, more appropriate and effective interventions can be implemented.

The Chronosystem

Like other scientific ideas, ecological systems theory has evolved from its original conceptualization. Specifically, subsequent iterations expanded to give further consideration to factors such as how maturation and the historical moment (time) in which individuals live influence child and adolescent development (Rosa & Tudge, 2013). In other words, **the chronosystem** refers to **the environmental events and transitions that occur throughout a child's life.**

For Miguel, the chronosystem includes his academic growth and social, emotional, and behavioral maturity throughout elementary, middle, and high school. In fact, Miguel remembers how nervous he was when he started kindergarten because he didn't know how to speak English. Miguel's chronosystem also includes the births of his three siblings that led to his added responsibilities as an older brother, especially when his mother and father were working full time and finishing their college degrees. Last, it includes his parents' professional growth from day laboring and cleaning homes and offices to becoming teachers. Miguel remembers not being able to spend much time with them because they were often working; but now he enjoys attending events together at Our Lady of Hope and occasionally sightseeing in Washington, D.C.

For Emily, although she was very young, her chronosystem includes the death of her father. Emily remembers being very sad and often seeing her mother crying in their kitchen. It also includes the short time that she spent in foster care, which she called "the blue house with the nice lady," and being happy when she could return home and see her mother and grandmother every day.

For both Emily and Miguel, their chronosystems include the COVID-19 pandemic, which caused significant disruptions to their lives. Although they were both separated from their friends, they also experienced differing levels of success with virtual or distance learning. Whereas Miguel's transition to distance learning was fairly smooth because his parents were teachers and he had access to technology and adult support, Emily experienced more difficulty. First, developmentally, she is younger than Miguel.

As a 10-year-old, although she was somewhat familiar with computers because she used them at school, she was less independent than Miguel and needed her mother to wake her up for school, make sure that she was ready for the day, and take her to school, where she received free breakfast and lunch. But because Ms. Jones was considered an essential worker, she continued going to her factory job. As a result, Emily was often alone during the school day until her grandmother was able to babysit her in the afternoons. Knowing that Emily and her peers couldn't afford devices or internet (Wi-Fi) access, her school district provided iPads or Chromebooks and hot spots for all of their students. And although this was helpful, Emily often required one-on-one adult support, which wasn't available, to understand her assignments.

The significance of the chronosystem is that its events alter the relationship between the individual and their environment, which leads to further developmental changes (Bronfenbrenner, 1989). Consider these words from Bronfenbrenner (1995): "The individual's own developmental life course is seen as embedded in and powerfully shaped by conditions and events occurring during the historical period through which the person lives" (1995, p. 641). Thinking about Emily and Miguel before, during, and after the COVID-19 pandemic shows how, as with other children, events associated with this significant time in history have influenced their development.

ECOLOGICAL SYSTEMS THEORY AND PUBLIC EDUCATION

As put forth in Bronfenbrenner's (1977) D_1 and D_2, the nested arrangement of the microsystem, mesosystem, exosystem, macrosystem, and chronosystem show the interconnectedness of the ecological system. And in trying to understand the relationship between the individual and their environment, altering one and observing its effect on the other can be informative. Because the interaction between person and place, or student and setting, is dynamic and not static, for every action there is a reaction or response to the action (Bronfenbrenner, 1977). From a systems perspective, it's important to identify not only what affects (influences) behavior but also what is affected by the behavior and development of the individual within the ecological system. Though referring to research, Bronfenbrenner's critique of methodologies that included observing only a single variable in a single setting and within a single person at one point in time is relevant to contemporary school-based practice that is informed by social justice.

For educators (e.g., teachers, administrators, school-based mental health providers), rather than viewing children as being isolated from their environments or their behavior as being unrelated to (separate from) what is happening around them, an ecological approach appreciates the circumstances within their families, schools, communities, and the larger society. Because human behavior is a complex and dynamic interaction among many systems, an ecological approach takes into account as many factors as possible to more comprehensively understand individuals' functioning.

SOCIAL JUSTICE IS . . .

Having reviewed ecological systems theory as the framework for this book, let's shift our attention to another central theme: **social justice.** Although there are many definitions and conceptualizations of social justice, the following will be used for our shared understanding throughout *Social Justice in Schools*. Further, though developed by school psychologists and for school psychologists, this definition is applicable to all educators and stakeholders (e.g., school board members) who serve students, families, schools, and communities:

> **"Social justice is both a process and a goal that requires action. School psychologists work to ensure the protection of the educational rights, opportunities, and well-being of all children, especially those whose voices have been muted, identities obscured, or needs ignored. Social justice requires promoting non-discriminatory practices and the empowerment of families and communities. School psychologists enact social justice through culturally-responsive professional practice and advocacy to create schools, communities, and systems that ensure equity and fairness for all children" (NASP, 2017).**

This chapter and the remaining chapters address several elements of this definition. To begin, let's briefly consider the points below.

Social justice is both a process and a goal that requires action. Social justice is something that educators are actively engaged in and actively working toward. As the title of this book suggests, social justice is the vehicle by which we achieve equitable outcomes. In other words, social justice is how we achieve equitable results. For educators who are committed to socially just practices, and because social justice is a process, there are specific and actionable steps that can be taken to promote positive outcomes for students, families, schools, and communities.

School psychologists [and all educators] work to ensure . . . opportunities. Fundamental to social justice are the concepts of opportunity and access. As noted previously, because socially just practices lead to equitable outcomes, when schools and school systems identify inequities, also known as disproportionality, opportunity and access are often at the root of these results. By increasing opportunity and access, inequities should decrease and equity should increase.

Social Justice Is About Opportunity and Access

Amidst a global pandemic that has claimed the lives of more than 1 million people in the United States (Centers for Disease Control and Prevention, 2022), issues of opportunity and access were accentuated in ways that have likely never been clearer. After many public schools throughout the United States closed their doors to in-person learning in

March 2020 to protect the health and safety of their students, families, staff, and community members, almost immediately the injustices and subsequent inequities that have been built into our systems (including education) were even more evident. Said another way, the COVID-19 pandemic didn't create inequities, but it exacerbated existing inequities.

In the early days of the pandemic, and with schools no longer open for face-to-face instruction, building- and district-level administrators, as well as state and local government officials, were scrambling to provide access to the resources and services that have become deeply connected to schools. For students and families living in LIEM, schools provided free or reduced-priced breakfasts and lunches. Various community outreach programs, often facilitated by schools, provided canned goods and other nonperishable food items so that children and their families were able to eat during weekends and extended school holidays.

To continue students' learning, schools transitioned to virtual or distance learning by providing instruction in both synchronous and asynchronous online formats. This, however, required that students had access to both technology (e.g., Chromebooks, laptops, or iPads) and reliable internet (Wi-Fi). From the end of the 2019–2020 school year and throughout the 2020–2021 school year, significant interruptions to some students' learning had detrimental effects. When discussing some families' decisions to disenroll their children from public schools and hire tutors or teachers to provide small-group or one-on-one support in what became known as *pandemic pods*, consider these words from a 2020 Minnesota *Star Tribune* article: "But the sudden rise of the student groups is raising questions about how the pandemic could widen the achievement gap and contribute to educational inequities between families who can afford more educational support and those who can't" (Klecker, 2020). Discussed in greater detail in Chapter 3, a more socially just framing of these outcomes would be to use the term **opportunity gap** rather than **achievement gap.** Because achievement gaps are often symptomatic of opportunity gaps, before concluding that some students are underachieving (underperforming) in various academic areas, we must first consider the extent to which all students received adequate opportunities and access to meaningful learning experiences (e.g., instruction) throughout the pandemic. Similarly, Dorn, Hancock, Sarakatsannis, and Viruleg (2020) used the term *unfinished learning* when referring to students not having the opportunity to complete all of the instruction (learning) that they would have been exposed to in a typical year.

Whether because of opportunity gaps or unfinished learning, Dorn and colleagues' (2020) preliminary data show significant negative effects for school-age children. For example, using i-Ready, a popular school-based assessment platform, data from more than 1.6 million elementary school children in 40 states who were tested in spring 2021 and compared with similar students before the pandemic began showed that, on average, students were performing 5 months behind in mathematics and 4 months behind in reading. Further, some student groups (REM children and those living in LIEM) were affected more than others. Specifically, children who attended schools with majority Black students ended the year 6 months behind in both math and reading compared with students who attended schools with majority White children, who ended the year 4 months behind in math and 3 months behind in reading. Compared with their peers in high-income rural and suburban schools, students attending schools with large numbers of children living in LIEM and urban settings also lost more learning (Dorn et al., 2020).

Especially those whose voices have been muted. . . . Central to social justice is the significance and intentionality of language. Coupled with its communicative function, words can be a window into how we think and understand the world in which we live (Barrett, 2021a). For example, like me, you've probably heard people say, "I'm here to speak for the voiceless" or "those who don't have a voice." Although I understand the sentiment in these statements, my constructive critique is that there are no voiceless people. There are, however, people "whose voices have been muted" (NASP, 2017). Albeit subtle, this distinction has tremendous implications for how we perceive communities who have been marginalized by systemic factors. Rather than centering themselves, even unintentionally, as the advocates, educators who are committed to social justice and socially just practices center those for whom they are advocating by using language that consistently reflects how structural realities lead to negative outcomes for children, families, schools, and communities.

Social justice requires . . . the empowerment of families and communities. Among other topics, Chapter 7 discusses the importance of educators intentionally empowering families by establishing meaningful home–school collaborative partnerships. It has been said that "knowledge is power." What is equally important, however, is access to knowledge or information. When schools and school systems actively and proactively engage their students' families, they also equip them with the necessary information to make the most informed decisions for their children. Educators establish a school culture that is flexible enough to meet families' needs, including being mindful of when meetings are scheduled, having interpreters present for meetings, and, to the greatest extent possible, providing relevant information to families in their native language. Because knowledge is power, the more parents know about their children's schools and the education system, the more prepared they are to support their social, emotional, behavioral, and academic success. And by sharing power, especially decision-making power, schools do not unfairly influence families by superimposing what they believe is in the best interest of their children.

School psychologists [and all educators] enact social justice through culturally responsive professional practice . . . to create schools, communities, and systems that ensure equity . . . for all children. As I detail in Chapter 3, social justice involves being committed to ongoing professional learning and development. Personally, the more I learn, grow, and develop in my understanding of social justice, the more intentional and conscientious I become about the words I use as an individual and as a school psychologist. For example, I no longer use the word *competent* (i.e., cultural competence) as this suggests that there is an end or endpoint to my growth, learning, and development. As an alternative, I prefer *responsive* (i.e., culturally responsive) to describe my goal as an educator. Because responsive connotes ongoing, dynamic, and active engagement between two or more parties (i.e., being responsive or responding to someone during a reciprocal conversation), as educators learn more about their students and families they can become more responsive to their needs, adjusting their behavior and approaches as necessary to be more effective.

Social Justice Is Embracing Discomfort and Challenging Ourselves

Coupled with the ongoing professional learning and development that is necessary for educators who are committed to social justice is asking difficult questions and being willing to engage in uncomfortable discussions with our colleagues. Albeit unsettling at times, these questions and discussions will likely reveal areas within our schools, school districts, departments, and individual practice that require significant policy changes. For example, is our teaching unintentionally contributing to inequitable outcomes for students? Are our assessment practices unintentionally overidentifying REM students with various educational disabilities? Are our discipline practices unintentionally leading to more REM students (Black, Indigenous, Asian/Pacific Islander, and Latinx) or those with educational disabilities being suspended or expelled from school? In the words of poet, novelist, and essayist James Baldwin, "Not everything that is faced can be changed; but nothing can be changed until it is faced" (Baldwin, 1962, p. 11). Though widely debated in popular culture, social justice is not a fad, buzzword, or the next hot topic in contemporary psychology or education. Similar to the theoretical orientations and philosophical frameworks mentioned earlier in this chapter, social justice is a way of thinking about student functioning and informs how we practice as educators.

Having highlighted key elements of NASP's (2017) definition of social justice, we can make important connections to ecological systems theory. Most notably, Bronfenbrenner's seminal work and NASP's conceptualization of social justice both take a broad, systemic orientation that not only focuses on what is happening within the individual (child) but also appreciates what is happening around them in their families and communities. Consider this: As educators, we have likely come to the realization that sometimes the most effective way to help children is by helping (influencing) the individuals (e.g., parents, families) and systems (e.g., schools, communities) around them. For example, and especially for young children, equipping parents or guardians with behavioral strategies to effectively respond to and manage target behaviors of concern is often as important as providing direct services (e.g., therapy) to the child. And before children can be ready to learn (i.e., be attentive to and actively engaged in instruction), they need to be well rested, well fed, and feel safe in their schools. Therefore, working with families to ensure that they understand the importance of adequate rest by establishing bedtime routines, providing access to free breakfast and lunch for students living in LIEM, and creating physically and emotionally safe and supportive learning environments are essential. In both examples, coupled with focusing on the child, people and circumstances around the child are also intervened with. As discussed in the next section, if educators want to promote equitable outcomes for all students, we must intentionally work toward changing schools, communities, and systems—variables that exist around children—more than the children themselves.

THE PRINCIPLES IN ACTION: ASSESSING CONTEXTUAL VARIABLES

In this, the last section of this chapter, a fictitious study, principles of research design, and a metaphor based on the criminal justice system are used to illustrate the importance of thinking broadly (systemically) to make the most appropriate and informed decisions for students.

A Brief Research Example

Read the fictitious scenario below (Barrett, 2018, pp. 78–79) and think about the importance of assessing contextual variables to rule out alternative explanations for children's performance.

> Mrs. Ramirez teaches algebra at City High School. She is interested in whether a 6-week after-school tutoring program will improve her students' performance on the end-of-year exam in algebra. One day, Mrs. Ramirez allowed her class of 20 students to divide themselves into two equal groups. In addition to attending regularly scheduled algebra classes during the school day, Group A received 30 minutes of after-school tutoring each week for 6 weeks. Group B did not receive extra math support but continued to attend regularly scheduled algebra classes during the school day. At the end of 6 weeks, all students were assessed using the end-of-year exam in algebra. Somewhat surprisingly, the average score of students in Group B was significantly higher than the average score of those in Group A.

If you're reading this book and are a mental health provider, you likely know that this vignette is an example of a very simple (and poorly designed) experiment. If you're reading this book and haven't taken psychology or research methods courses, an experiment is a type of research design. Though it's used casually in our everyday vernacular when referring to trying something (e.g., "I'm going to experiment with moving this student's seat" or "I'm going to experiment with a new instructional strategy"), technically, an experiment is a specific approach to investigating a problem. Importantly, an experiment includes at least two groups. The experimental (treatment) group receives the intervention (e.g., medication, therapy), and the comparison (control) group either doesn't receive anything (i.e., no treatment) or continues their lives as usual (also known as business as usual). In the example above, the treatment group (Group A) received the intervention (6 weeks of after-school math tutoring) and the control group (Group B) continued to attend their regularly scheduled math classes during the school day. See Figure 2.7 for a visual representation of this example's groups or treatment conditions.

As mentioned earlier in this chapter, the research question is critical. Broadly speaking, all research questions can be framed as, "What is the effect of the independent variable (IV; intervention) on the dependent variable (DV; outcome)?" For this example, what is the effect of the 6-week after-school math tutoring program on the end-of-year exam in algebra? But to adequately answer any question that uses an experimental design, there must be strong experimental control.

The Intervention Didn't Work

In thinking about this example, and specifically that Group B (the control group) outperformed Group A (the treatment group), some might conclude that either the intervention did not work or the teacher was ineffective. Although both are plausible explanations, they are also premature based on how poorly the study was designed and conducted.

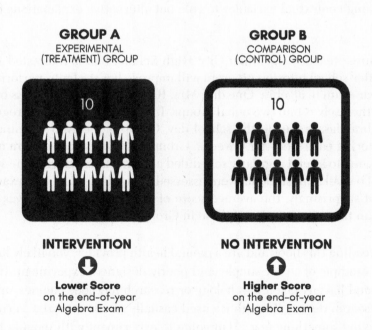

GROUP A
EXPERIMENTAL
(TREATMENT) GROUP

GROUP B
COMPARISON
(CONTROL) GROUP

10   10

INTERVENTION   **NO INTERVENTION**

Lower Score   **Higher Score**
on the end-of-year   on the end-of-year
Algebra Exam   Algebra Exam

FIGURE 2.7. Mrs. Ramirez's algebra intervention at City High School.

Research Study Limitations

Like all studies, this fictitious example has several limitations. In this case, however, its limitations also prevent us from accurately understanding the effect of the intervention on the outcome. Importantly, this example violated a fundamental condition of well-designed experiments: random assignment. When conducting an experiment, the goal of random assignment is to ensure that the groups (i.e., the treatment group and the control group) are as similar as possible before the study begins. If this is achieved, when the treatment group receives the intervention, there is more certainty (confidence) that the outcome is truly attributable to the intervention and not other (extraneous) factors. Because Mrs. Ramirez allowed her students to group themselves (self-select) into two groups, it's also possible that Group A and Group B were meaningfully different *before* the intervention began. Did students who were friends want to be in the same group? If so, did the students in Group A spend more time socializing than paying attention to the tutoring? Did students who enjoyed math more than their peers choose to be in the same group (Group B)? And perhaps Group B, despite not participating in the 6-week intervention, have higher math interest or achievement compared with Group A?

Alternative Explanations

The previously mentioned questions suggest that there are viable alternative explanations to the premature (and perhaps wrong) conclusion that the intervention didn't work or the teacher was ineffective. Ultimately stemming from the absence of random assignment, and the fact that reasonable steps were not taken to ensure that the only difference between Group A and Group B was that one (Group A) received the tutoring intervention, all of these alternative explanations are justifiable reasons to not accept the idea that the intervention or teacher was ineffective.

Internal Validity

In research, internal validity is the extent to which we are confident that the IV (the treatment or intervention) is responsible for the change in the DV (the outcome). For experiments, the absence of random assignment poses a significant threat to internal validity and lessens our confidence in the IV's effect on the DV.

In applying a social justice orientation to school-based practice, particularly identifying students with educational disabilities, internal validity is critically important. When school psychologists, school counselors, school social workers, speech pathologists, educational diagnosticians, teachers, and administrators are making significant decisions that can alter a child's educational trajectory and life, the following question should be asked: Does the child's disabling condition—and not other factors—account for (explain) why they are not accessing or making progress in the general education curriculum? In other words, through thoughtful consideration, we must first rule out (account for) the alternative explanations (other factors) to be confident in our determination that it is truly a within-child deficit (disability) that provides the most accurate and appropriate explanation for their difficulty.

Consistent with an ecological framework, educators recognize that children are products of their interactions with multiple systems. By appreciating the complex interplay among and between these systems, they acknowledge how myriad stressors can influence students and view these as legitimate alternative explanations to within-child deficit orientations that can prematurely and erroneously lead to disability identification. In sum, before concluding that students' social, emotional, behavioral, or academic difficulties lie within themselves, educators investigate, interrogate, and exhaust all other relevant and alternative explanations.

An Analogy from the Justice System

Before offering another metaphor to illustrate the importance of using an ecological perspective in school-based practice, I want to acknowledge that some may find this example problematic. The analogy is based on the criminal justice system, which seems to be far from just for REM individuals. Nevertheless, I am confident that it can highlight the importance of assessing contextual variables to rule out alternative explanations for children's performance.

In the United States, when individuals are accused of crimes, they are presumed innocent until proven guilty. Similarly, in research, the default assumption is the null hypothesis (H_0), which states that there is no difference between groups (the treatment group and the control group). In other words, in the absence of data (evidence), the assumption is that a person who has been accused of a crime is no different from someone who has not been accused of the crime. Further, when an individual has been accused of a crime, is arrested, and placed on trial, the burden of proof rests with the prosecution; the prosecuting attorney, for example, must bring sufficient evidence to demonstrate that the accused person is indeed guilty of the crime for which they are being charged. *To be clear, when school-based teams are considering whether students have educational disabilities, I am not suggesting that they are accusing children of committing crimes or placing them on trial. Nevertheless, similar to trials and their subsequent outcomes having the potential to alter the trajectory of individuals' lives, the evaluation process and its results can also change students' lives in meaningful ways. The analogous connection between the criminal justice system, the null hypothesis, and an ecological systems orientation can be instrumental in understanding the weight of a multidisciplinary team's responsibility for making life-changing decisions for children.*

As the U.S. criminal justice system presumes that individuals are innocent until substantial evidence proves otherwise, and as the principles of research design assert that there is no difference between groups until data show that there is, students, including those who are suspected of an educational disability, deserve the benefit of the same presumption: that they are no different from their peers without disabilities (accepting the null hypothesis). If, however, a comprehensive evaluation provides sufficient evidence that a student's difficulty indeed lies within themselves, there could be a defensible (legitimate) reason to reject the null hypothesis because the child is different from their peers without disabilities. Very importantly, the evidence that is presented (e.g., performance on standardized cognitive ability and academic achievement tests; behavior rating scale data; teacher, family, and student interviews; developmental milestone information; historical accounts) is not always absolute or without discrepancies or inconsistencies. Nevertheless, the team-based decision, to borrow a legal term, should be beyond a reasonable doubt. Ultimately, school-based multidisciplinary teams should consider the degree to which it is reasonable that an educational disability, and not other (i.e., exclusionary) factors (e.g., limited English proficiency; lack of access to appropriate instruction in reading and math; environmental, cultural, or economic disadvantage), is the primary and most appropriate explanation for a child's presentation in school. If so, an educational disability might be warranted. If not, teams should default to accepting the null hypothesis and the child not be identified with an educational disability.

CHAPTER SUMMARY

This chapter introduced a framework for not only understanding children but also embedding a social justice paradigm into school-based practice. Like other theoretical orientations and perspectives, ecological systems theory (Bronfenbrenner, 1977) gives educators a way to think about their students and the factors that are affecting their behavior and performance in school. Because it considers the significance of systems, structures, and policies that exist around children, an ecological approach is highly informative for educators who want to embed socially just practices into their day-to-day roles and responsibilities. The ideas that have been introduced in this chapter—including a definition of social justice that is applicable to all educators and the essential components of that conceptualization—are reinforced and covered in greater detail in the forthcoming chapters. Last, social justice is more than what educators do, but it begins with how they think about their students, families, schools, and communities, in addition to how they can effectively serve in their respective capacities. Therefore, the next chapter encourages educators to challenge themselves and their colleagues when their actions aren't consistent with social justice.

DISCUSSION QUESTIONS

1. Watch *Structural Discrimination: The Unequal Opportunity Race*. After watching the video, think about and write your responses to the following questions:

   a. What are your general comments, questions, thoughts, or reactions to the video?

   _____

   _____

   _____

   b. Who won the race? What is your definition of winning?

   _____

   _____

   c. For those who did not win the race, how do you think they feel?

   _____

   _____

   _____

   d. For those who did not win the race, how might this outcome (event) affect them in future races or other competitive endeavors?

   _____

   _____

   _____

2. At the beginning of *The Unequal Opportunity Race,* the REM individuals weren't allowed to start running until 1964. What event occurred in American history in 1964 and why is it significant to REM individuals beginning to race (compete)?

   _____

   _____

   _____

3. Consider this quote from Bronfenbrenner (1977): "What place or priority children and those responsible for their care have in such macrosystems is of special importance in determining how a child and his or her caretakers are treated and interact with each other in different types of settings" (p. 515).

Based on your role as a graduate student or educator, why is this statement significant?

_____

_____

_____

4. Read the NASP (2017) definition of social justice on page 23. As a graduate student or educator, how can you engage in these activities? If you are an administrator or leading a team, how can you encourage your colleagues and staff to incorporate these ideas into their professional roles and responsibilities?

_____

_____

_____

5. Think about the students in your class, school, or school district. For those who are experiencing academic, social, emotional, or behavioral difficulties that resemble educational disabilities, what are some plausible alternative explanations for their functioning?

_____

_____

_____

6. Based on your response to the preceding question, what are some interventions or accommodations that can be implemented to support students rather than identifying them with educational disabilities?

_____

_____

_____

CHAPTER 3

Social Justice Is About Challenging Ourselves and Others

Challenge the status quo by continually refining our professional practice. When necessary, we challenge the professional practice of our colleagues.

Becoming a social justice–oriented educator is a maturation process that takes time and intentionality.

LEARNING OUTCOMES

After reading this chapter, you should be able to . . .

1. Explain why the word gap, zero-tolerance discipline policies, and multi-tiered system of supports (MTSS) frameworks (e.g., response to intervention [RTI], positive behavioral interventions and supports [PBIS]) that ignore relevant child, family, school, and community identities are harmful to students.

2. Identify socially just alternatives to the word gap, zero-tolerance discipline policies, and poorly implemented RTI and PBIS.

3. Identify guiding principles and language to effectively challenge colleagues when their behavior is harmful to students and not aligned with social justice.

4. Identify terms that are rooted in deficit thinking and reframe them using socially just language.

CHAPTER OVERVIEW

After reviewing theories, policies, and practices that perpetuate educational inequities, socially just alternatives are provided to help schools and school systems promote positive outcomes for students. To show the importance of educators challenging their colleagues when their actions, even unintentionally, are inconsistent with social justice, two real-world examples that contain harmful language and helpful responses are discussed. Additionally, the responses highlight 11 principles that educators can use to have constructive conversations with their colleagues. The chapter ends with a brief review of terms that are commonly used in psychology and education, reframing them to be more consistent with a social justice orientation.

INTRODUCTION

Through what have become known as the twin pandemics, racism and COVID-19 have led many of America's educational institutions to reimagine what PreK–12 schools, colleges, and universities can be for students. Compared with previous years, and as more schools and school districts have committed to being antiracist (see Kendi, 2019), the current climate is pregnant with possibility and opportunities to make meaningful changes that are in the best interest of all students.

As this work unfolds, behavioral principles are relevant. In addition to wanting certain things (e.g., behaviors) to change (stop) because they are not helpful to children, we must also replace them with healthier and more productive practices. Known as replacement behaviors, these must be taught and reinforced to sustain lasting and systemic changes. As an example, it's not enough to tell children to stop running; we must also teach them to walk, or as some elementary school teachers say, "use walking feet." Similarly, it's not enough to tell students to stop being disruptive; we must also teach them what to do instead of talking, distracting their peers, and leaving their seats (e.g., raising their hands and waiting to be called upon). Regardless of your role, as you're interrupting and interrogating, decolonizing (e.g., ensuring that REM voices, perspectives, and authors are represented in your curricula, syllabi, and instructional materials), and disrupting and dismantling ineffective policies, remember to replace them with socially just practices that ultimately lead to positive and equitable outcomes. Let's begin by reviewing a few harmful theories and practices, followed by socially just alternatives.

THE WORD GAP

In *Meaningful Differences in the Everyday Experience of Young American Children* (1995) and their subsequent article, "The Early Catastrophe: The 30 Million Word Gap by Age 3" (2003), Betty Hart and Todd Risley report data about language development in children whose families were classified into high, middle/low, and welfare SES categories. Using a sample of 42 families from the midwestern United States, Hart and Risley recorded 60 minutes' worth of language (e.g., communication, dialogue) in each home, one time per month for more than 2.5 years. Their data showed that, on average, children from professional families (high SES) heard 2,153 words per waking hour; children from working-class families heard 1,251 words per hour; and children from welfare families heard 616 words per hour. Though the study was only conducted for approximately 30 months, the authors projected that, over the span of 4 years, children from professional, working class, and welfare families would acquire (learn) approximately 45, 26, and 13 million words, respectively. These data led to the 30-million-word gap, also known as the **word gap.** Essentially, Hart and Risley put forth the idea that **because children from various SES households were exposed to more (or fewer) words, their rate of vocabulary development and subsequent fund of vocabulary would also be different.** Over time, the word gap phenomenon has been used to help explain the achievement gap.

For decades, Hart and Risley's research and subsequent interpretations have been critiqued for reasons ranging from methodological flaws to racial insensitivity (e.g., almost all of the welfare families were Black). And although they reported significant differences in the amount of words that children from different SES groups acquired, they did not report significant differences in the quality of language that children from high, middle/low, and welfare SES categories used. Highly relevant to school-based practice, critics assert that the word gap and achievement gaps are not the result of children's vocabulary exposure but of the mismatch between American public schools' instructional approaches and the home language practices of their students. Steeped in deficit thinking and blaming families for their children's academic difficulty rather than holding systems (e.g., schools, teaching practices) accountable for not meeting the needs of students, the word gap is one of the most pernicious and problematic educational theories of the 20th century.

A SIMILAR PHENOMENON TO THE WORD GAP AND A SOCIALLY JUST ALTERNATIVE

Though not the word gap, a similar phenomenon in American public education is **cognitive academic language proficiency** (CALP; Cummins, 1979). Essentially, CALP refers to the academic language (academic vocabulary) that students for whom English is not their native language (ELs) need to access and make progress in the curriculum, which is almost always presented in English. In discussing the extent to which Spanish-speaking children's academic success is determined by how much academic language (CALP) they have acquired, Flores (2020) says, "I found it troubling that educators, who were predominantly monolingual and White, did not consider the many linguistic strengths of the Mexican-origin students or consider the many other factors that may be contributing to the academic challenges of their large and growing Mexican-origin population" (p. 23). Further, he contends that "academic language is a raciolinguistic ideology that frames the home language practices of racialized communities as inherently deficient" (p. 24).

Like the word gap, CALP problematizes students and families rather than looking broadly at what systems (schools) can do to be more responsive to their backgrounds. Because the welfare SES group in Hart and Risley's (1995) sample comprised almost exclusively Black families, like CALP, the word gap is a raciolinguistic ideology that exposes White supremacy (e.g., the belief that the number of words White children were exposed to is better than those of other groups) as the root of perceived linguistic deficiencies of racialized (e.g., Black, Latinx) students and families. Rather than fixing the home language practices of REM students and families or viewing children's academic performance as resulting from the number of words that they have (or have not) been exposed to, a more socially just response requires educators to think about how they can effectively meet the instructional needs of their students. For example, Flores (2020) encourages educators to develop new instructional practices that value the complex linguistic knowledge that their students already have as part of their lived experience and center this in their schoolwork. When educators view the language practices of their REM students as legitimate, despite the number or types (e.g., academic language, informal/social language) of words they know, and reject the assumption that they are dichotomous with the language practices of the school environment, they can create an instructional setting and learning experience that encourages students to draw from their home language strengths to access and make progress in the curriculum.

Consider this: Assessment data should not be deterministic. More than using such information to show what students are (or are not) capable of achieving, standardized testing of their cognitive abilities, academic skills, and language proficiency should always inform subsequent decisions (e.g., interventions). Given the inherent weaknesses of CALP, if we are not careful, when students are demonstrating lower levels of CALP, we can erroneously use these data to determine (conclude) what they cannot do. Alternatively, it would be better to leverage their linguistic strengths and make the necessary instructional modifications, so the curriculum is more accessible. Because data are imperfect, they should be informative—not deterministic (Barrett, 2022).

As advocated by Flores (2020), **translanguaging is an instructional approach that allows students to use their native language strengths to make learning both accessible and meaningful by rejecting the idea that English, or any language, is superior** (García, 2009). In some ways, translanguaging is an antiracist intervention because, like racial groups—Black, White, Asian, Indigenous, Latinx—languages (e.g., English, Spanish, Farsi, Urdu, Mandarin) are equal despite their apparent differences (Kendi, 2019). Though typically used with students whose home languages are not English, broadly speaking, translanguaging is a pedagogical practice that encourages educators to value their students' language backgrounds, leveraging their skills to foster engagement with, connection to, and understanding of the curriculum (García, 2009).

For bilingual students such as Miguel, whom we met in Chapter 2, translanguaging can be very effective. Despite being born in the United States, Miguel's first 5 years of life were spent in predominantly Spanish-speaking settings. His parents spoke Spanish, and his home-based babysitter was also a Spanish speaker. Miguel did not begin learning English until he started kindergarten and was consistently in an English-speaking environment with his teachers and peers. Though he quickly grasped many words and phrases, for several years, Miguel only heard English while at school—Monday through Friday between 8:00 and 2:30. In the evenings, on weekends, and during holiday breaks and summer vacations, Miguel returned to a Spanish-speaking world in his tight-knit Central American suburban enclave. As a result, there were times in which he experienced difficulty thinking of the English word to answer teachers' questions or complete written assignments. He, however, often knew the

THINK ABOUT IT. Using translanguaging as a broad instructional approach, even if your students are native English speakers, what are some ways in which their home language backgrounds can help them access the curriculum?

answers in Spanish. For his EL or general education classroom teachers, incorporating Miguel's Spanish skills (e.g., using Spanish vocabulary to explain new or complex concepts or allowing him to respond to questions in Spanish) could have been an effective translanguaging technique to make learning more accessible and meaningful and ultimately facilitate greater understanding and achievement.

I completed my undergraduate studies at St. John's University. A Catholic institution, all students were required to take 21 credits of philosophy and religion. Out of curiosity, I took a course on Hinduism. Struggling to understand much of what was presented, I remember talking to the professor, and she said something to the effect of "You can't approach Hinduism from a monotheistic point of view." Hearing this in the early 2000s, I remembered it while reading Zaretta Hammond's *Culturally Responsive Teaching and the Brain: Promoting Authentic Engagement and Rigor among Culturally and Linguistically Diverse Students* (Hammond, 2014). Although a lot can be said about culturally responsive teaching, I am convinced that how we teach can be more important than what we teach. For me, learning about a different religion was valuable; however, the professor's methods, in my opinion, were lacking. Yes, it was important for me to stretch my thinking, especially coming from a Judeo-Christian perspective; however, a culturally responsive framework would have led the professor to adjust her methods so that I could effectively access the content. Like anything related to socially just practices that lead to equitable outcomes, blaming students for what they're not doing or achieving should never be at the expense of interrogating and critiquing our own systemic practices. Although she gave me a C, I learned a lot—about culturally responsive teaching (Barrett, 2021b).

For Miguel's teachers and my former undergraduate professor, translanguaging could have been an effective instructional strategy. Specifically for Miguel, what if his teachers intentionally highlighted cognates when teaching him English words? In junior high and high school, I took five years of French. And in these classes, I was introduced to the word **cognate.** In its simplest terms, *a cognate shares the same root as a word in a different language.* For example, when Miguel's teachers are teaching him English vocabulary, perhaps previewing terms for an upcoming lesson, they can highlight the similarities between these new words and more familiar ones in Spanish. Table 3.1 has a few examples of Spanish–English cognates that teachers can use to build their students' vocabulary in English by leveraging their familiarity with Spanish.

I've long felt that effective instruction is simply meeting people where they are and helping them to move forward. And whether they are EL, general education, or special education teachers, it is not a prerequisite that educators be fluent speakers of their students' native languages. They do, however, need to understand their students' home languages to ultimately meet them where they are and help them move forward (access the curriculum). Similarly, to help me understand the tenets of Hinduism, my former undergraduate professor could have leveraged my Judeo-Christian background to make connections to the content and ultimately allow me to access a new world and way of thinking.

TABLE 3.1. English–Spanish Cognates

English term	Spanish term
Airport	*Aeropuerto*
Bank	*Banco*
Car	*Carro*
Distance	*Distancia*
Explore	*Explorar*
Island	*Isla*
Map	*Mapa*
Ocean	*Océano*
Office	*Oficina*
Restaurant	*Restaurante*
Accident	*Accidente*
Emergency	*Emergencia*
Medicine	*Medicina*
Dollar	*Dólar*
Excellent	*Excelente*
Family	*Familia*
Interesting	*Interesante*
Music	*Música*
Number	*Número*
Perfect	*Perfecto*
Problem	*Problema*

IMPLEMENTING MULTI-TIERED SYSTEM OF SUPPORTS WITHOUT CONSIDERING STUDENT, FAMILY, SCHOOL, OR COMMUNITY IDENTITIES

In recent years, multi-tiered system of supports (MTSS) has become an increasingly popular and effective school-based problem-solving framework. Whether response to intervention (RTI) to support the academic (e.g., reading, writing, and math) needs of students; positive behavioral interventions and supports (PBIS) to effectively prevent and respond to a variety of target behaviors through proactive strategies such as behavior-specific praise and positive practice of schoolwide expectations (Chafouleas & Iovino, 2021); or social–emotional learning (SEL) that teaches children the skills they need (e.g., self-awareness, perspective taking, recognizing and regulating emotions) to work collaboratively with others, develop healthy relationships, and make responsible decisions, MTSS has the potential to increase positive outcomes in all of these areas. Coupled with a prevention orientation (e.g., providing all students with evidence-based Tier 1 instruction and using data to inform subsequent tiering and intervention decisions), SEL and PBIS are also examples of positive (strengths-based) education initiatives (Chafouleas & Iovino, 2021).

In its simplest form, MTSS is a tiered model of service delivery that provides differentiated levels of support based on students' needs. For example, and as depicted in Figure 3.1, most MTSS models show three distinct levels or types of support: Tier 1, Tier 2, and Tier 3.

At Tier 1, also known as primary prevention or core instruction because it is given to all students, most (80%) children are expected to make progress without any additional support. At Tier 2, in addition to Tier 1, approximately 15% of students require targeted or small-group support to make adequate progress. Such support could include weekly small-group academic remediation, group counseling, a daily report card or home–school note, or Check-In, Check-Out (CICO; Hawken, Crone, Bundock, & Horner, 2021) to strengthen reading, writing, or math skills or minimize target behaviors of concern. Last, at Tier 3, approximately 5% of students require the most intensive or individualized support. For these students, individual counseling with a school-based mental health provider, daily one-on-one academic support with an interventionist, or a functional behavioral assessment (FBA) to understand the setting events, antecedents, and consequences that are contributing to target behaviors might be completed.

More than providing differentiated support across its various tiers, for MTSS to be effective, it must consider students' unique demographic characteristics. Consistent with Bronfenbrenner (1977), MTSS should never be viewed or implemented independently of the students for whom it is meant to serve. As noted by Chafouleas and Iovino (2021), MTSS is a way to center the child in the ecological system: offering interventions that are designed for and intended to support healthy child development and ultimately leading to equitable outcomes in schools.

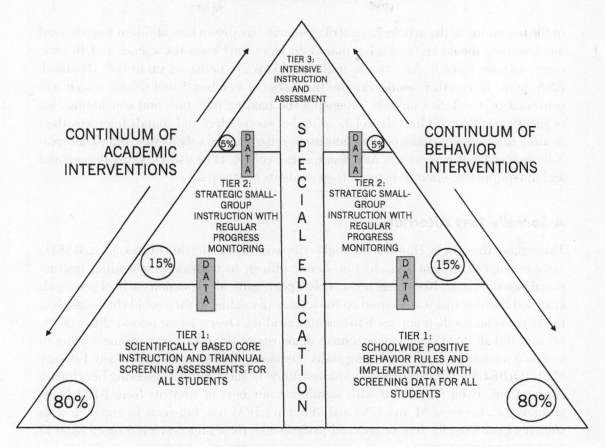

FIGURE 3.1. Multi-tiered system of supports: RTI and PBIS. From Brown-Chidsey and Steege (2010). Copyright © 2010 The Guilford Press. Reprinted by permission.

An Example Using Reading Instruction: Bethlehem Area School District

Written in 2018 by Emily Hanford, a journalist who focuses on equity issues in public education, *Hard Words: Why Aren't Kids Being Taught To Read?* tells the story of how the Bethlehem Area School District (BASD) in Pennsylvania systemically and systematically addressed long-standing challenges with their students' reading achievement. Similar to national trends since the early 1990s, BASD data showed that less than 40% of their fourth and eighth graders were proficient in reading (National Assessment of Educational Progress [NAEP], 1992/1994, as cited in Hanford, 2018). And despite some attempting to use poverty as the reason for BASD's students underperforming in reading, data did not support this explanation, as children in its wealthier schools were also struggling to meet grade-level expectations.

Before outlining the ongoing philosophical debate about reading instruction (i.e., whole language vs. direct instruction in phonics), Hanford makes the following statement in the beginning of the article: "Scientific research has shown how children learn to read and how they should be taught. But many educators don't know the science and, in some cases, actively resist it. As a result, millions of kids are being set up to fail" (Hanford, 2018, para. 1). In other words, despite the National Reading Panel (2000), which was convened by the U.S. Congress, reviewing the reading literature and concluding that explicitly teaching children the relationship between letters and sounds improves their reading achievement, some teacher education programs are vehemently and philosophically opposed to this approach. As a result, entire cohorts of new teachers are ill prepared and ill equipped to effectively teach their students how to read.

A Socially Just Alternative

Throughout the article, Hanford highlights the work and leadership of Jack Silva, BASD's assistant superintendent and chief academic officer, in transforming reading instructional practices in its 16 elementary schools. Specifically, all elementary school principals attended training that was focused on the science of reading so they could challenge their teachers to change their approach to teaching reading. Over a 3-year period (2015–2018), not only did all BASD elementary schools demonstrate significant improvement using an outcome measure related to reading skills (Dynamic Indicators of Basic Early Literacy Skills [DIBELS]), but three schools showed 100% of their students meeting benchmark expectations. Even for schools with significant numbers of students from REM backgrounds (i.e., between 51 and 77%) and living in LIEM (i.e., between 73 and 97% of its students qualifying for free or reduced-price lunch), their improvement ranged from 17 to 51 percentage points.

These data show how schools can effectively meet the Tier 1 (core instruction) needs of their students. If we believe that all students can learn but some are not learning, we must critically examine why this is happening and correct our professional practice (Barrett, 2018). In other words, when schools have inverted RTI triangles because there are more students needing Tier 3 than Tier 1 support, this is fundamentally a systems issue, not a child issue (Harris, personal communication, September 13, 2016). In the case of BASD, like other school systems, their students were not making progress in reading because systemically (across their elementary schools) they were not teaching reading as effectively as possible. But after they looked inward, interrogated their instructional practices, and made the necessary changes by challenging the system and themselves to do better for children, students' reading improved across all of their elementary schools.

In BASD, more than the instructional approach that they implemented being evidence based, it was also appropriately matched to their students' background characteristics. In a school district with a significant number of ELs, using Language Essentials for Teachers of Reading and Spelling (LETRS; Lexia, n.d.), a methodology that shows teachers how to build their students' oral language abilities before the requisite skills of phonemic awareness, phonics, fluency, vocabulary, comprehension, writing, and language, BASD appropriately matched their instructional approach to their students' needs. Though LETRS is used in schools and school districts throughout the United States, more important is its evidence base. Whether or not your school or school system adopts LETRS is secondary to ensuring that students' literacy instruction is aligned with the science of reading. Although BASD and other school districts have accomplished this by incorporating LETRS, there are other empirically supported programs and instructional approaches that can be equally effective for your students. For more information about these programs, see the *Resources for Professional Learning* at the end of this chapter.

An Example Using PBIS: The Case for Culturally Responsive PBIS

According to the U.S. Department of Education Office of Special Education Programs (OSEP), the foundations of PBIS are systems, data, practices, and outcomes (U.S. Department of Education, OSEP, Technical Assistance Center on Positive Behavioral Interventions and Supports, 2015). Similar to the interconnectedness of ecological systems theory (Bronfenbrenner, 1977; see Chapter 2), each element influences the others and allows the framework to be implemented with fidelity (NASP, 2018). As previously stated, when schools and school districts have disproportionate disciplinary outcomes (e.g., suspensions, expulsions), systemic changes in policy and practice are necessary to increase equity.

Culturally responsive PBIS (CR-PBIS) is one way to help schools and school systems reduce disproportionate disciplinary outcomes by influencing the practices of adults, including implementing culturally appropriate interventions, fostering family and community engagement, and developing behavioral expectations that are responsive to the cultures of students and families (NASP, 2018). Rather than assuming a culture-free or culture-blind approach to PBIS, schools are encouraged to intentionally consider culture, broadly speaking, in all aspects of their PBIS framework and programming. Especially in schools that are racially homogeneous (i.e., students are predominantly from a single racial or ethnic background), school-based teams should expand their conceptualization of culture beyond race and ethnicity and examine discipline inequities (disproportionality) in subgroups of students, including gender and gender identity, disability status, SES, and sexual orientation, among other identities. For example, in addition to studies that have focused on the bullying experiences of heterosexual, cisgender students, some data suggest (see Eisenberg, Gower, Rider, McMorris, & Coleman, 2019) that gay, lesbian, bisexual, transgender, and questioning (LGBTQIA+) students are at increased risk for being bullied by their peers.

Schools should also engage families and community members of all backgrounds. Family–school and school–community partnerships can help PBIS teams develop school-wide rules and expectations that are appropriately matched (responsive) to their students' and families' cultural backgrounds. For example, some schools include attendance goals (e.g., being present and on time to school or classes) as part of their schoolwide PBIS expectations. But if a school notices an increase in tardiness or absences that also leads to students from certain backgrounds (e.g., Jewish students, Muslim students) being subjected to negative consequences (e.g., after school or lunch detention) during certain times of the year (e.g., when religious observances require time away from school or run late into the evening), the extent to which the school's expectations should be adjusted to be more accommodating and respectful of students' backgrounds is worth discussing. Having a diverse (broadly defined) coalition that represents the voices and perspectives of as many student groups as possible through parents/families, community partners/liaisons (e.g., faith leaders), and students to serve as an advisory council to the PBIS team, or members of the PBIS team itself, helps to ensure that issues of culture and identity are included in the development and implementation of PBIS.

ZERO-TOLERANCE DISCIPLINE POLICIES

In 2018, *School Psychology Review* published a special issue titled *Closing In on Discipline Disproportionality*. Bottiani, Bradshaw, and Gregory (2018) reported that disproportionate outcomes in exclusionary discipline practices, particularly between Black and White students, has been problematic since the 1970s. Further, and especially related to Black students, schools' excessive exclusion is one of the strongest indicators of opportunity inequality in the education system. Notably, the special issue focused on effective interventions for reducing discipline inequities, including how school psychologists can work collaboratively with their educator colleagues.

From a national perspective, Black students are disciplined more harshly for less severe and more subjective misconduct, such as dress code violations, defiance, and disrespect. White students, however, are more likely to be disciplined for more objective offenses, including vandalism and truancy (Losen & Orfield, 2002; Skiba et al., 2008). Whether cultural differences in assumed expectations and styles of communication or implicit racial, ethnic, cultural, and gender biases (see Gilliam, Maupin, Reyes, Accavitti, & Shic, 2016), these factors contribute to disproportionate exclusionary disciplinary outcomes. Last, Cook and colleagues (2018) noted that disproportionate disciplinary outcomes could be the result of the cultural mismatch between a predominantly White and female workforce who may not be familiar with the interaction patterns of Black males, which leads to misinterpreting their behaviors as disrespectful or inappropriate.

With origins in drug enforcement, since the 1990s, **zero tolerance** has been widely adopted as **"a philosophy that mandates the application of predetermined consequences, most often severe and punitive in nature, that are intended to be applied regardless of the gravity of the behavior, mitigating circumstances, or situational context" (American Psychological Association [APA], 2008).** In practice, zero-tolerance policies include suspending or expelling students for minor behavior infractions (e.g., dress code violations, being late to class). Charged with evaluating the evidence of zero-tolerance policies and making recommendations regarding its use in schools, the APA convened a Zero-Tolerance Task Force. After reviewing the literature, despite its relatively widespread implementation in schools, they concluded that "zero tolerance has not been shown to improve school climate or school safety. Its application in suspension and expulsion has not proven an effective means of improving student behavior. It has not resolved, and indeed may have exacerbated, minority overrepresentation in school punishments" (APA, 2008, p. 860).

Socially Just Alternatives

In addition to its review of the effectiveness of zero tolerance, APA (2008) provided recommendations to serve as alternatives to punitive school discipline approaches. Though not framed as socially just alternatives, their ideas are consistent with practices that will improve equitable outcomes for all students. Additionally, and more recently, Gregory, Skiba, and Mediratta (2017) offer 10 suggestions (principles) for reducing race and gender disparities in school discipline, thereby also increasing equity in schools. Notably, because discipline disproportionality has been such a long-standing problem in American public education, siloed interventions targeting a single aspect are likely ineffective. More appropriately, the authors' principles, which include both prevention and intervention approaches, address all levels of the school ecology (ecological system): intrapersonal (educator beliefs and attitudes), interpersonal (quality of individual and group interactions), instructional (academic rigor, cultural relevance and responsiveness of instruction), and systems levels (access to behavioral supports and paths for collaborative approaches to resolving conflicts).

Implement Preventive Measures That Can Improve School Climate and Improve the Sense of Community and Belongingness

Closely aligned with a PBIS framework, or specifically CR-PBIS, a socially just alternative to zero-tolerance policies is a preventive approach that reinforces students for displaying appropriate, prosocial behaviors rather than punishing them for behaving inappropriately (APA, 2008). Similarly, Gregory and colleagues (2017) encourage schools to *establish supportive relationships,* in which "authentic connections are forged between and among teachers and students" (p. 255). Next, schools should *create bias-aware classrooms and respectful school environments* that are "inclusive" and "positive" and "in which students feel fairly treated" (p. 255). Further, *culturally relevant and responsive teaching* should be provided, which includes instruction that is respectful of the diversity represented in classrooms and schools. Last, schools should *include academic rigor* that holds students to their potential "through high expectations and high-level learning opportunities" (p. 255).

Teachers and Other Professional Staff Who Have Regular Contact with Students Should Be the First Line of Communication with Parents and Caregivers Regarding Disciplinary Incidents

There is a positive correlation between zero-tolerance discipline policies and the school-to-prison pipeline. In other words, schools that use zero tolerance are more likely to prematurely refer students to the juvenile justice system for infractions that could have, and should have, been resolved in the absence of law enforcement (APA, 2008). Not only should teachers and other educators who work closely with students in schools be the ones who contact families concerning disciplinary incidents, but this should also be coupled with sufficient training for educators related to preventing and responding to problem behaviors (Cook et al., 2018), which can also decrease the likelihood of using exclusionary discipline practices.

Increase Training for Teachers in Culturally Responsive Classroom Behavior Management and Instruction

Anecdotally, I've heard principals and assistant principals remark that when students are sent to their office, it's too late. In other words, with students already in the office, the risk of suspension is higher than if the behavioral infraction was effectively redirected in the classroom. If the student is suspended, especially for REM students, administrators could be perpetuating disproportionality. On the other hand, if students are not suspended, teachers can feel unsupported. Therefore, to the greatest extent possible, students' behavioral challenges, especially relatively minor disruptions, should be managed in the classroom by teachers. As noted by Gregory et al. (2017), schools provide *opportunities for learning and correcting behavior* in which "behavior is approached from a non-punitive mindset . . . while providing structured opportunities for behavioral correction within the classroom as necessary" (p. 255). With ongoing professional learning, including using data to identify areas for improvement if it shows preferential (differential) treatment of certain groups (Gregory et al., 2017), teachers remain on the cutting edge of the most effective classroom management techniques that are also responsive to students' cultural backgrounds. For example, training should include explicit instruction in setting classroom expectations, matching instructional content to students' developmental and instructional levels, behavior-specific praise, and planned (purposeful) ignoring to avoid reinforcing inappropriate behaviors. Related to issues of culture and identity, rather than criticizing behaviors that might be valued by students' families or communities, language such as "expected behavior at school" helps children and adolescents understand what they should be doing at school without undermining or demeaning what they've been taught at home. Taken together, the differences in behavioral expectations that students are exposed to at home and school don't make either better or worse.

Carefully Define All Infractions, Whether Major or Minor, and Train All Staff in Appropriate Means of Handling Each Action

One of the most pragmatic recommendations (APA, 2008) is that all schools—elementary, middle, and high schools—should develop clear expectations for staff related to how behavioral incidents are handled. This practice is reinforced by Gregory et al. (2017), who suggest including student and family input related to "policies, procedures, and practices concerning school discipline" (p. 255). As shown in Figure 3.2, a school-based team (e.g., PBIS team), ideally with representation from general and special education teachers, specialists (e.g., art, music, physical education teachers), administrators (e.g., principal, assistant principal, dean), mental health staff (e.g., school psychologist, school counselor, school social worker), students, families, and community partners (e.g., faith leaders) should mutually agree upon which behaviors, for example, are handled by teachers versus the ones that constitute an office referral. A resource such as this not only promotes consistency in staff responses to students (e.g., some students are sent to the office for being late to class while others are not), but it also holds staff accountable for their actions toward students. To practice this principle, see Appendix 3.1 for a shared activity that can be completed with school-based teams.

Replace One-Size-Fits-All Disciplinary Strategies with Graduated Systems of Discipline, wherein Consequences Are Geared to the Seriousness of the Infraction

Similar to the previous recommendation, when schools establish expectations for how behavioral incidents will be managed (e.g., either by teachers in the classroom or by administrators in the office), this naturally leads to a tiered level of consequences based on the significance of the infraction (APA, 2008). Such an approach should also be paired with considering student characteristics, such as the number of prior offenses and other mitigating (contextual) factors surrounding the child. When two students display the same behavior but receive different consequences, it can be confusing for students and staff. This is important for using a broad, ecological perspective in school-based practice. Proponents of zero tolerance argue that it was meant to promote consistency in responses to student behavior. Such consistency, however, does not always mean the same response, which is often at the expense of appreciating relevant contextual variables. Because children within the same classroom or school can live within different ecosystems, and because their behavior is a dynamic interaction between these systems (see Chapter 2), it's also possible that topographically similar behavior (which looks the same) stems from very different causes. As is discussed in Chapter 8, one of the most important principles of socially just practices leading to equitable outcomes is that sameness (i.e., treating all children the same) is often inequitable.

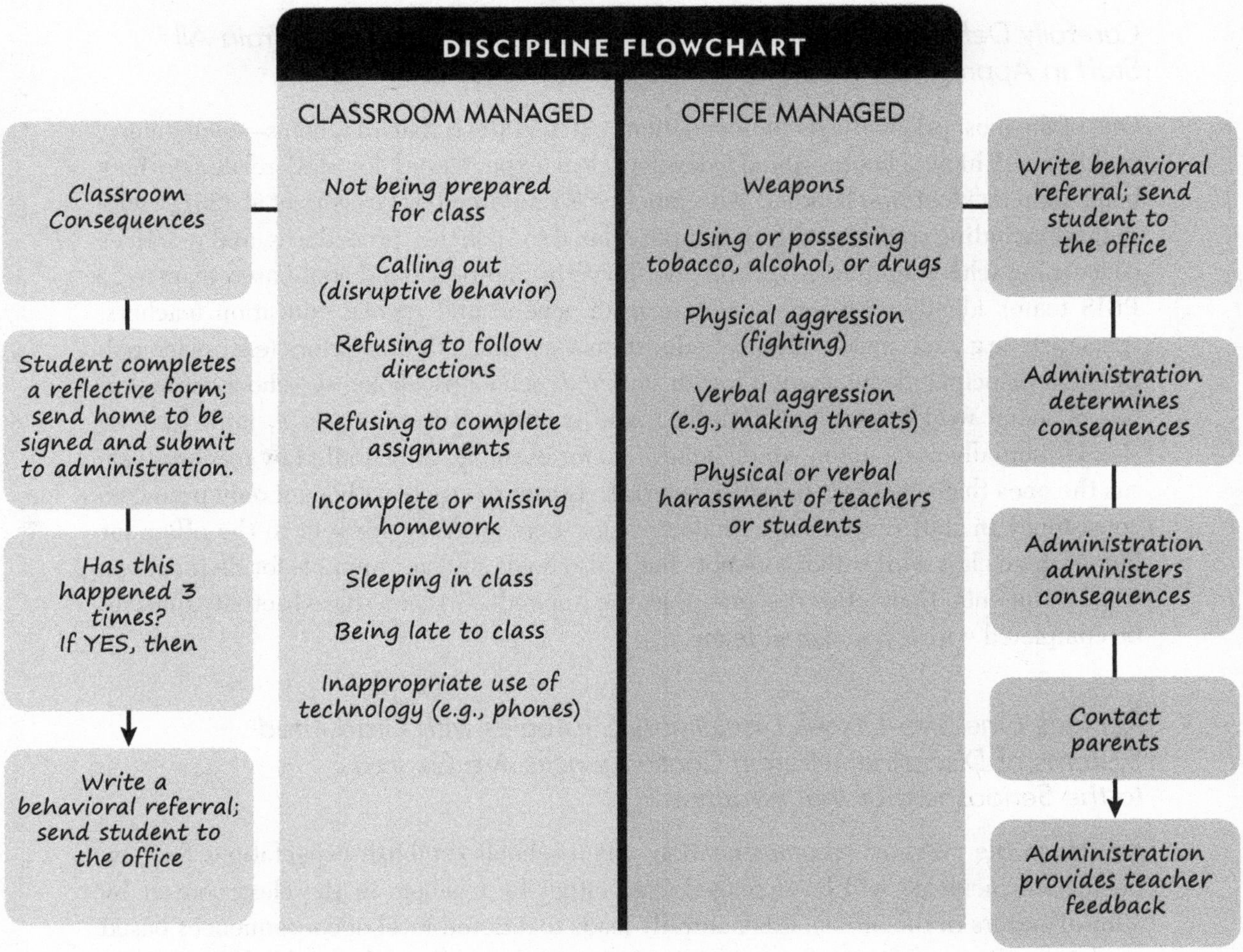

DISCIPLINE FLOWCHART

CLASSROOM MANAGED	OFFICE MANAGED

Classroom Consequences

Student completes a reflective form; send home to be signed and submit to administration.

Has this happened 3 times? If YES, then

Write a behavioral referral; send student to the office

CLASSROOM MANAGED

Not being prepared for class

Calling out (disruptive behavior)

Refusing to follow directions

Refusing to complete assignments

Incomplete or missing homework

Sleeping in class

Being late to class

Inappropriate use of technology (e.g., phones)

OFFICE MANAGED

Weapons

Using or possessing tobacco, alcohol, or drugs

Physical aggression (fighting)

Verbal aggression (e.g., making threats)

Physical or verbal harassment of teachers or students

Write behavioral referral; send student to the office

Administration determines consequences

Administration administers consequences

Contact parents

Administration provides teacher feedback

NOTES

_____

_____

_____

_____

_____

FIGURE 3.2. Sample schoolwide discipline flowchart.

As mentioned in Chapter 1, an FBA is an evaluation that helps staff understand the underlying factors that lead to (antecedents) and maintain (consequences) target behaviors of concern. For example, the function (reason) that one child is displaying disruptive behaviors in the classroom could be to escape (avoid) academic tasks because they are too difficult. Another student, however, could engage in the same behaviors but with the function being to receive attention from peers. Given the different functions for similar target behaviors, the interventions must also be different to effectively teach children appropriate alternatives. For the student whose behavior is maintained by escaping challenging academic tasks, an appropriate intervention could include modifying their assignments to match their instructional level or teaching the child to appropriately ask for a break when overwhelmed. For the student whose behavior is reinforced by peer attention, an appropriate intervention could include teaching their peers to ignore disruptive actions and only providing positive reinforcement when the student engages in socially appropriate behavior. A problem-solving approach to discipline that seeks to uncover the source of behavioral challenges has also been advocated for by Gregory et al. (2017) to address identified needs.

As described in the preceding examples, the response to similar behaviors is different based on knowing more about the specific students and what is leading them to display inappropriate behaviors. For school-based administrators, increasing equity in school discipline is never the result of applying the same consequence to everyone but taking the time to appreciate the unique contextual variables surrounding individual students to be more responsive to their needs.

Reserve Zero-Tolerance Disciplinary Removals for Only the Most Serious and Severe Disruptive Behaviors

In principle, this recommendation (APA, 2008) suggests applying the most severe disciplinary consequences to the most significant behavioral infractions (e.g., weapons or drug violations, situations in which significant physical harm has been caused to another student or staff member). Using the term *zero tolerance*, however, can be misleading because of how it has been applied historically. Although there are instances in which suspension or expulsion can be appropriate, these should be very few, and these decisions should be made as a matter of last resort and absolute necessity, having exhausted all other reasonable alternatives. Like Chafouleas and Iovino (2021), Gregory and colleagues (2017) also advocate for MTSS in which "schools use a tiered framework to match increasing levels of intensity of support to students' differentiated needs" (p. 255). And in the event that it is appropriate to remove students from school, intentional efforts should be made to reintegrate them into the learning community (Gregory et al., 2017).

WHEN EDUCATORS USE HARMFUL LANGUAGE: EXAMPLE 1

Having reviewed school-based policies and practices that are not helpful to children, next we shift our attention to how we can challenge our colleagues when their behavior might be harmful, even unintentionally, to students. Though not comfortable, this is a necessary aspect of socially just practices that lead to equitable outcomes. *Note:* With the exception of very minor edits (e.g., spelling, punctuation), the following text is an email that was sent to the entire staff at a middle school. Additionally, the names of individuals and schools have been changed to ensure anonymity and confidentiality.

> Hi Staff,
>   PLEASE let me know if you see an 8th grade student listed below with a personal item of mine. I used it today to hold down some papers while the fan was blowing and it was missing when they left class. I would like to talk with the student and issue a punishment that will serve as a reminder to not take things that are not theirs. Please keep an eye out for it. THANKS. Here is the list of students that may have it . . .

THINK ABOUT IT. Having read the teacher's email, what are your initial impressions, thoughts, and reactions? What would you do if you received this message? Discuss your answers with your classmates or colleagues.

Using Social Justice Principles to Respond: Example 1

> Good Morning.
>   First, I have thought about sending this message for a few days. After much consideration, I feel strongly that an all-staff reply is necessary given that the original message was sent to all staff. Second, my intent in sharing this message is completely grounded in my concern for children and the manner in which we serve them as professionals. Rather than engaging in a series of reply all messages, feel free to email me if you would like to discuss further.
>   This year marks the beginning of my 5th year at Willowgrove Middle School. However, I have served every school in Willowgrove, with the exception of Jackson Elementary School, over the past 10 years. Having said that, like many of you, I love the children and families of this community. Like some of you, I've seen them grow up: from Head Start, STEP, elementary and middle school, to completing high school.
>   When I read, and re-read the message from Ms. Smith, while I think that I understand her intentions, I was concerned about its subtle message. Importantly, I am NOT accusing Ms. Smith of having any ill feelings toward her students. However, I want to highlight how our actions, mine included, can unintentionally do more harm than good.

While I was not in her classroom, the email seemed to be somewhat accusatory of these young people. Further, providing their names for all staff to see felt like each of them were assumed *suspects* and potentially guilty of stealing. This makes me very uncomfortable for many reasons. Because many of us are parents, how would we feel if our children's names were on such a list for the entire staff to see? Further, how would these students and their parents feel about such a message? And quite importantly, all, or certainly most of these students come from ethnic backgrounds in which others in the larger society already assume more negative things about them than they deserve. Taken together, I was saddened and disappointed to read the message. Coming from someone in their school, it felt like we were reinforcing the systemic challenges and biases that they face beyond the walls of our school every day.

My short note is not meant to judge anyone, but rather to encourage us to carefully consider how our actions, albeit unintended, could be hurtful and harmful to the students and families we serve. In this instance, there could have been a better and more respectful way to communicate the importance of honesty and integrity without unnecessarily exposing an entire group of students to the suspicion of wrongdoing.

I hope that this message is received in the spirit in which it is intended. I enjoy serving you as we serve the students and families of Willowgrove.

Best for the remainder of the weekend.

THINK ABOUT IT. Having read the staff member's response, what are your initial impressions, thoughts, and reactions? Discuss your answers with your classmates or colleagues.

Now that you have read the teacher's email and the staff member's response, the next section highlights five principles that explain why the initial message was harmful to students and important considerations if you are in a similar situation.

Social Justice Principles in Action: Example 1

1. **The level of exposure in your response must be commensurate with the level of exposure in the offensive statement.** Having used this real-world example in workshops and professional learning sessions, I often ask attendees (e.g., school psychology graduate students, school-based mental health providers, teachers, administrators) what they would do if they received a similar email that included the first and last names of 25 students. Almost always, the most common responses are "I would do nothing" (e.g., delete the email) or "I would speak to the teacher privately. . . ." Though I appreciate the participants' honesty, one of the most important principles to highlight is that the level of exposure in the response must match the level of exposure in the offensive statement. In other words, because the teacher sent an email to the entire staff, which also exposed her entire class (25 students), this was a teaching moment for the entire staff. Speaking

privately to the teacher would necessarily, even unintentionally, protect her feelings; but what about the children who were harmed by being exposed in such a manner? If the teacher sent this message to me privately, I would speak to her privately. But because it was sent publicly, it had to be addressed publicly.

2.   **Identify what you're doing, clearly highlighting what was problematic without attacking the individual.** Because challenging our colleagues and holding them accountable isn't particularly easy or comfortable, it's important that we remain focused on the objective: highlighting what was problematic about their behavior (actions) without attacking their character. Though the message was clear and specifically addressed why the teacher's email was harmful to students, it never made accusations or assumptions about her as an individual.

3.   **Clearly articulate what was wrong with the statement and why it was wrong by keeping the focus on children and families.** As mentioned in the response, I was saddened and disappointed after reading the teacher's email. These (my) feelings, however, were not the impetus for responding to the entire staff. This response was solely about the children and their families. The teacher's message was disrespectful, and the children deserved better. Consider this: Even if one student took the teacher's item, which we don't know, the other 24 students who simply went to class were now presumed suspects based on their names being sent to all staff members. And to underscore a previous point, because the children were harmed publicly, they also deserved a public response in their defense. Because of the demographic makeup of the school (mostly Latinx students whose families were living in LIEM), I also wondered whether such a message would have been sent in a school whose students were predominantly White or whose families were more likely to advocate for their children.

4.   **As you are teaching, to the greatest extent possible, use *we statements*.** Coupled with defending the students, my response was a teaching moment for the staff. And because all of us are learning and growing, it was Ms. Smith on that particular day; but it could be me (or you) tomorrow or the following week. Further, *we statements* can soften the overall tone of the message.

5.   **Say what you mean without saying it mean; relationships matter.** In sum, we can say what we mean without saying it in a mean way or behaving in a mean manner. In schools, especially when operating from a social justice orientation, conflict is inevitable; but disagreements and differences of opinion don't have to be devastating or detrimental to our professional practice. Remaining focused on the bigger picture, which is doing what's best for children, is helpful for cultivating relationships with our colleagues.

WHEN EDUCATORS USE HARMFUL LANGUAGE: EXAMPLE 2

Here is another example of educators using harmful language. With the exception of very minor edits (e.g., spelling, punctuation), the following text is a message that was posted on a very popular school psychology forum. Like the previous example, names and details of individuals have been changed to ensure anonymity and confidentiality.

> We have a Mexican student with high functioning autism in 7th grade. He regularly steals candy and tickets for candy from teachers' rooms. We try to keep our doors locked when we are not in the room; however, he finds times and ways to steal candy despite our efforts. He's had specific skill instruction about stealing and he's had his "candy" privileges taken away in the past. We don't have the luxury of 1:1 aide for him, so we are at a loss of what to do. There will be much more serious consequences as an adult if he continues to steal so we have to put a stop to it now! Suggestions? Thanks.

THINK ABOUT IT. Having read the individual's post, what are your initial impressions, thoughts, and reactions? What would you do if you read this message on a public forum? Discuss your answers with your classmates or colleagues.

Using Social Justice Principles to Respond: Example 2

> Hi Mary—
>
> Thanks for your message. Although I may not answer your specific question, I wanted to take this opportunity to highlight a few things, hopefully for your benefit as well as others who may be reading this thread. I also thought about responding to you privately, but felt that it was important to share my response more publicly.
>
> First, I am very concerned that you referenced the child's race/ethnicity. After reading your post twice, I am not sure that being Mexican is relevant to the target behavior of stealing or being a student with High Functioning Autism. I could be overlooking something, but is there a reason why you included this information? For example, I substituted White for Mexican and didn't feel that there was anything lost, or gained, from this information. Relatedly, I couldn't help but wonder if the student was White if his race/ethnicity would have been specifically mentioned.
>
> As professionals, and as a profession, we have to be very careful about perpetuating negative stereotypes of children, especially those from minoritized backgrounds. Although I am not suggesting that this was your intent, the potential impact of your post is nonetheless significant. This, in my opinion, is an example of implicit or unconscious bias at work. Albeit

subtle, the cumulative effect on children and families can be devastating. Towards the end of your post, you also included these words: "There will be much more serious consequences as an adult if he continues to steal so we have to put a stop to it now!" This statement, and the perceived emotion attached to it by ending with an exclamation point, coupled with highlighting his minoritized status in the first sentence of your post, shows how we (as a people/society) can become conditioned to associate minoritized individuals with inappropriate/illegal behavior.

Although I can appreciate your question, I also wanted to highlight the fact that sometimes we (school psychologists) engage in practices/make decisions that are not altogether helpful/beneficial for our students and families. We're all learning and growing and I hope that this note is received in the spirit in which it is intended.

I encourage you, and others, to read and view the resources at the link below. I think that they can be very helpful as we grow as individuals and in our service to children, families, schools, and communities. *www.nasponline. org/resources-and-publications/resources-and-podcasts/diversity/social-justice*

Happy to chat more about this with you (or anyone).

All the best.

Now that you have read the original post and the response, as in the previous example, the next section highlights six principles that explain why the initial message was harmful to students and important considerations if you are in a similar situation.

Social Justice Principles in Action: Example 2

1. **Don't assume that everyone knows as much as you may know about issues of justice and equity. Some of our colleagues are not ill intentioned, but they legitimately don't know.** Similar to Example 1, when these situations arise, we should see them as teachable moments. And when teaching, it's important to assume the most positive intent in our colleagues. In other words, sometimes the mistakes and missteps that adults make are not ill intentioned, but they don't know the impact of their actions on others. When children don't know something, whether academic, social, emotional, or behavioral skills, we teach them. The same approach is appropriate for adults. Instead of assuming a punitive tone or seeking punishment, teaching is also an appropriate response.

2. **Rather than assuming an accusatory tone, ask questions and give the other person a chance to clarify something that you may have overlooked.** When I was practicing as a school psychologist, one of my core beliefs could be summed up in these words: *Maybe it's me* or *Maybe I'm missing something*. In other words, when attending meet-

ings, and teachers and families would share their perspectives about a student, before disagreeing with them, I would ask them to clarify certain things. Why? Because it was quite possible that I didn't fully understand what they were saying, and with additional information perhaps I would no longer disagree. As it relates to this scenario, although I didn't think that mentioning the child's race or ethnicity was necessary, I wanted to ask and give the individual an opportunity to clarify her rationale. Such an approach also shows that we are open to learning and growing.

3. **As you are teaching, to the greatest extent possible, use *we statements* and keep the focus on children and families.** Similar to Example 1, using *we statements* and keeping the focus on children and families are important. Notably, Example 2 is my response on a popular school psychology forum that allows school psychology graduate students, practitioners, and faculty to post questions and comments about various topics in the field. As I mentioned in my response, this example is also important because sometimes we (school psychologists) make mistakes that are harmful to children. And like our educator colleagues, we are not exempt from learning and growing.

4. **Try to point individuals to resources to support their learning, growth, and development.** Because teaching, learning, and ultimately growth is the goal, to the greatest extent possible, share resources with those whom you are challenging to do better. As mentioned earlier in this chapter, rather than simply telling children to "stop running," we also say, "use walking feet." In other words, we teach them an alternative or replacement behavior. When holding our colleagues accountable, more than highlighting what was wrong with their behavior, we should also give them information to support or facilitate their professional growth and development. See Appendix 3.2 for a variety of resources that can be helpful for developing individuals' understanding related to social justice.

5. **Encourage people to grow beyond where they are at the present moment.** In schools, as it is in life, where we are at the present moment isn't necessarily problematic; refusing to grow beyond where we are, however, is concerning. Mistakes are inevitable, but growth is a choice.

6. **Because helping people grow is a process, make yourself available for further discussion.** Similar to #4, coupled with providing a resource to facilitate your colleagues' professional learning, to the greatest extent possible, also make yourself available to assist them in their growth process. Because of how important the currency of relationship is in schools, having critical conversations with those whom we know and trust can be tremendously effective and transformative.

A LITTLE MORE PERSPECTIVE

In live presentations and workshops, I am often asked about Example 1. For example, "Did anyone respond to your email?" or "Did the teacher respond to your message?" The answer to these questions is yes and no. Although the teacher did not respond to me, a few staff members did, including the building principal, and almost all of them were appreciative of the message that I sent. The principal also shared that they—presumably him or the other administrators (e.g., deans, assistant principals)—spoke to the teacher privately. This, however, was one of the most important reasons for how I chose to respond: The staff members who received the email did not benefit (learn) from the administrators' private conversation with the teacher, including why her email was both inappropriate and harmful. And as I mentioned earlier in this chapter, even unintentionally, speaking to the teacher privately protected her feelings, but what about the children who were harmed publicly? Next, I'll provide a little more perspective on when I chose to respond to the teacher's email.

I waited 48 hours before sending the message. The original email was sent on a Thursday morning and I responded on Saturday morning. One reason for my delayed response was that I wanted to think very carefully about what I wanted to say (if anything) and how I wanted to communicate my response. This is important because sometimes it's important to address situations immediately or in the moment. On the other hand, it can also be appropriate to think about what we want to do and the implications of our decisions. Related to this latter point, I sent this message when I was in my 10th year as a school psychologist, my 10th year serving the same community, and my 5th year at Willowgrove Middle School. Therefore, I felt that I had enough relational currency—that people knew who I was and what I believed about children—and that my reputation was strong enough to withstand any potential negative consequences of my decision to respond publicly. Further, this response is not my natural style; but because the email was harmful to children, I felt compelled to act. If you're a graduate student, an early career professional, or perhaps new to your building, I am not suggesting that you don't respond as I did if something similar happens; however, you should also think about the unintended consequences when others don't know you as well as they did me. Ultimately, it was less important that I responded to the situation than it was that someone addressed it. Talking to a professor, supervisor, mentor, or trusted colleague can be prudent based on where you are in your career.

Last, it's also important to acknowledge that the building principal was not my direct supervisor. I was assigned to serve certain schools, and my direct supervisor was a psychologist who was located in the central office. This matters because some support staff (e.g., school counselors, school social workers, school psychologists) are hired by their principals, which could make responding in a similar fashion more complicated.

A SYSTEMS ORIENTATION TO LANGUAGE

Social justice is a way of thinking and practicing that not only requires a systems orientation but also necessitates that we are mindful of the words we use to convey the realities of institutional injustice and structural oppression (Barrett, 2021a). The last section of this chapter briefly addresses a few terms that are commonly used in psychology and education but that are nonetheless highly problematic. Similar to the socially just alternatives that have been modeled throughout the chapter, this section includes ways to reframe language that is rooted in deficit thinking. Last, some of the terms discussed here might be new to you, but new words are necessary to communicate new ways of understanding the profound influence of systems on students, families, schools, and communities (Barrett, 2021a).

Opportunity Gaps versus Achievement Gaps

In recent years, researchers, schools, policymakers, and professional associations have taken strides to reframe the achievement gap as the opportunity gap. More than a semantic difference, the achievement gap focuses on the performance (e.g., underachievement) of student groups (e.g., Black and Latinx students compared with Asian and White students), and opportunity gaps focus on how systems and structures limit access to educational environments and experiences (e.g., qualified teachers, adequate materials and technology, safe and supportive school cultures) that result in differential outcomes. As noted by Kendi (2019), because achievement gaps set up racial hierarchies (i.e., that certain races perform better on standardized tests than others), the concept is also racist. In other words, the achievement gap implies that the deficiency lies within people (e.g., Black or Latinx students) rather than the tests and other systemic flaws. As stated in Chapter 2, achievement gaps are often symptomatic of opportunity gaps and prematurely assume a deficit orientation—that difficulties lie within the child rather than placing the onus on the system, which is where it rightfully belongs (Barrett, 2021a). For a succinct explanation, read "Why We Say 'Opportunity Gap' Instead of 'Achievement Gap'" by Theresa Mooney (2018).

Racially and Ethnically Minoritized versus Minorities

When referring to race and ethnicity, describing non-White individuals as minoritized rather than minorities is one way to use systems-oriented language. Like reframing achievement gaps as opportunity gaps, using *minoritized* versus *minority* intentionally focuses on how federal legislation and policies such as slavery, Jim Crow, and redlining have systematically worked against people of color (i.e., Asian/Pacific Islanders, Black/

African Americans, Indigenous Americans, Latinx; Barrett, 2021a). Further, the term *minority* suggests that some individuals are inherently less than their White counterparts rather than critiquing the systems that have relegated them to inferior positions related to generational wealth and access to other opportunities. Last, statistically speaking, if the term *minority* is used to refer to groups that are smaller in number (percentage), describing REM individuals as such is also factually inaccurate because in many places, and from a national perspective, there are more REM children than White students attending American public schools (Strauss, 2014).

Diverse *and* Diversity

The terms *diverse* and *diversity* can be problematic. Specifically, educators should be careful to not refer to individuals as diverse. When this happens, the assumption is that White is the norm, standard, or expectation, which makes everyone else diverse, different, or even deviant (from White). On the other hand, a group can be diverse if it includes people from various races, ethnicities, ages, faith backgrounds, genders, and a host of other identities. As an example, when teaching, evaluating, or supporting the mental health needs of ELs, educators should not refer to individual students from Honduras, Guatemala, or El Salvador as culturally or linguistically diverse (CLD). Alternatively, it would be best to refer to them as Latinx or their specific nationality (e.g., Guatemalan). On the other hand, if a school's staff includes teachers, counselors, administrators, and mental health providers from different states and countries who speak various languages and have varied experience levels in their respective disciplines, it would be appropriate to describe the group's composition as diverse because it captures the variability of intersecting identities represented.

Speaking for the Voiceless

As I mentioned in Chapter 2, many of us have likely heard colleagues or advocates say that they seek to "speak for the voiceless" or "those who don't have a voice." Though I understand the sentiment, these phrases are also very concerning. First, they reinforce assumptions that people are inherently less than others (i.e., voiceless people compared with those who have a voice) without acknowledging the systems that have tried to strip groups of their ability to advocate for themselves and challenge institutional power. In many cases, those who are described as voiceless include families who are unable to advocate for their children at school board meetings, not because they don't want to or because they care less about their education but because they are working multiple low-wage jobs to provide for their families. Sometimes those who are seen as voiceless are families who might not be as knowledgeable about who to call to hold schools and school districts accountable for decisions that adversely affect their children. So, rather than describing some groups as voiceless, we should critique how systems have tried to mute their voices (NASP, 2017) or ignore what they've had to say.

Additionally, the word *voiceless* is problematic because it unintentionally centers the advocate at the expense of those for whom they are advocating. In other words, the attention is inappropriately placed on what the person is doing for a group that has been marginalized rather than holding the system (and sometimes themselves for being complicit) accountable for marginalizing certain groups. As a socially just alternative, amplifying voices is more appropriate. To borrow a metaphor from sound engineering, the function of an amplifier isn't to produce sound but rather to ensure that whatever sound an instrument is making, including a speaker or vocalist, is clearly heard by the audience. In socially just school-based practice, advocating for students and families doesn't mean that we speak for them but that we facilitate opportunities so they can speak for themselves and be heard by others.

Marginalized versus Vulnerable Populations

Over time, I've thought a lot about the term *vulnerable* and whether it was the most appropriate way to refer to students and families. *Vulnerable*, which is often used by people in loving, committed relationships, describes how open (vulnerable) they choose to be with their spouses or partners. For example, because I love my wife, I choose to be vulnerable with her and share my deepest feelings. Vulnerability, therefore, is a choice and can be an indication of relational trust and intimacy. When referring to students and families who are experiencing difficulty with housing or food insecurity, in almost all cases, they did not choose to be in these positions the way that individuals choose to be open with their spouses or partners in loving relationships. More accurately, systems—whether mental health, criminal justice, housing, or education—have placed people in vulnerable positions.

As a socially just reframing, *marginalized* is a more appropriate term. Whereas *minoritized* refers to issues of racial or ethnic identity, *marginalized* is broader and can refer to multiple identities. For example, as a Black male, I identify as a REM individual. But for a White male who identifies as gay, or a White woman who identifies as lesbian or transgender, as members of the LGBTQIA+ community, though not minoritized, they can experience marginalization due to heteronormativity and other factors. Similar to *minoritized*, *marginalized* appropriately highlights how systemic policies have intentionally placed groups in vulnerable positions, such as LIEM (APA, 2019).

Cultural Competence versus Cultural Responsiveness

Last, the goal of our clinical practice and educational services should not be cultural competence, but cultural responsiveness, which is a by-product of cultural humility—the acknowledgement that we will always have more to learn about our students and families. In referring to the work of Tervalon and Murray-García (1998), Waters and Asbill (2013) highlighted three aspects of cultural humility. First, it requires a "lifelong commitment to self-evaluation and self-critique." In other words, cultural humility is an active process that includes being a lifelong learner—a person who is never satisfied with the knowledge that they have already gained, but perpetually challenges themselves by striving to better understand the students and families they serve. Next, cultural humility seeks to eliminate power imbalances. In schools, for example, despite the advanced degrees and years of training that educators have completed to serve children, professionals who embody cultural humility also acknowledge that they aren't the only ones with valuable information or knowledge. In my own professional practice, I believe in listening to families because they are experts in their own children (Barrett, 2018). Said another way, educators might understand children in general, but families know the idiosyncrasies of their own children. Last, cultural humility involves developing partnerships with those who are advocating for others. More than the individual's commitment to being a lifelong learner and fixing power imbalances, consistent with the theme of this book, cultural humility leads to systemic changes that are only possible by working collaboratively with other individuals and groups. Whereas cultural competence suggests that there is an endpoint to our learning, perhaps after earning our degrees or attending a professional learning session or conference, cultural responsiveness is an ongoing process and commitment to being a lifelong learner. Cultural responsiveness is also the willingness to adjust or modify our behavior if it is not meeting the needs of our students and families.

To review the ideas previously presented, Table 3.2 (on pp. 62–63) includes short scenarios with examples of what educators should not say and what they should say to be more aligned with social justice.

CHAPTER SUMMARY

This chapter focused on the importance of educators interrogating and interrupting systemic practices that perpetuate inequitable outcomes and challenging their colleagues when their actions are harmful to children. Whether it is the word gap, zero-tolerance policies, or MTSS frameworks such as RTI and PBIS that ignore issues of culture and identity, there are socially just alternatives that lead to equitable outcomes for all students. And though uncomfortable, educators can respectfully, yet clearly and directly, respond to their colleagues and hold them accountable for their actions. Last, because words serve more than a descriptive function but are also a window into how educators think and view the world in which they live, the chapter showed how popular terms in psychology and education are laced in deficit ideologies and reiterated the importance of reframing language to center how systems and structures have detrimental effects on the lived experiences of students, families, schools, and communities. Taken together, whether modifying instructional practices, revising PBIS programming, disrupting and dismantling zero-tolerance policies, challenging colleagues, or being mindful of their language when referring to students and families, becoming a social justice–oriented educator is a maturation process that takes time and intentionality. Keep these ideas in mind as we focus on privilege, implicit bias, and intersectionality in the next chapter.

RESOURCES FOR PROFESSIONAL LEARNING

The following resource provides definitions for terms that are related to social justice and seeks to promote shared understanding of what these concepts mean in research and practice. Though presented alphabetically, the terms have also been organized into the following broad categories: gender and sex; history and theoretical concepts; power, prejudice, and oppression; race and racism; allyship and advocacy; culture and religion; disability and size discrimination; and socioeconomic status. Last, because language and terminology, especially related to social justice, evolve over time, the definitions will be updated periodically.

National Association of School Psychologists. (2021a). Social justice definitions. [handout].[1] *www.nasponline.org/resources-and-publications/resources-and-podcasts/diversity-and-social-justice/social-justice/social-justice-definitions*

To learn more about eliminating disparities in school discipline, consider the resources below.

Gregory, A., Skiba, R. J., & Mediratta, K. (2017). Eliminating disparities in school discipline: A framework for intervention. *Review of Research in Education, 47*(1), 253–278.

Welsh, R. O., & Little, S. (2018). The school discipline dilemma: A comprehensive review of disparities and alternative approaches. *Review of Educational Research, 88*, 752–794.

To learn more about MTSS, PBIS, and SEL, check out the resources below:

Center on Positive Behavioral Interventions and Support: *www.pbis.org*

McIntosh, K., & Goodman, S. (2016). *Integrated multi-tiered systems of support: Blending RTI and PBIS*. Guilford Press.

(conttinued on p. 64)

---

[1] Special thanks to the authors who contributed to the social justice definitions: Sherrie Proctor, PhD; Sheila Desai, PhD, NCSP; Jiwon Kim, MA; Celeste Malone, PhD, MS; Thuy Nguyen, BA; Leandra Parris, PhD; Elizabeth Shaver, BS; David Shriberg, PhD; Koryn St. Clair, BA; and Amanda Sullivan, PhD, LP.

TABLE 3.2. Say This, Not That

Term or idea	Not that	Say this
Opportunity gaps versus achievement gaps	"After I completed my class's Fall 2021 benchmark assessments in reading and math, I immediately spoke to the student support team at my school because so many of my students were underachieving. And because I was so concerned about their performance, I wanted to refer them for additional intervention through our Tier 2 Intervention Team."	"After completing my class's Fall 2021 benchmark assessments in reading and math, I noticed that most of my students' scores were lower than the published norms for their grade. This, however, wasn't surprising to me because most of them didn't have the opportunity to consistently participate in instruction. Though we sent work home, including giving them iPads, Chromebooks, and Wi-Fi hotspots, there were so many stressors in their lives that prevented them from either focusing on their work or receiving assistance from their families. These several months of unfinished learning (Dorn, Hancock, Sarakatsannis, & Viruleg, 2020) led to what I think is an opportunity gap for my students, not an achievement gap. In fact, many of them are performing at the level they were when schools closed in March 2020. I'm going to speak with my grade-level teammates and include some of our support staff so we can improve our Tier 1 instruction before referring any of my students for more intensive intervention or remediation."
Racially and ethnically minoritized versus minorities	"As a school psychologist, I serve schools with large numbers of minority students."	"As a school psychologist, most of my students come from racially and ethnically minoritized [REM] backgrounds. Specifically, my students and their families are Black, Latinx, Asian, and Indigenous."
Diverse and diversity	"After reviewing its data in a number of areas, administrators and teacher leaders at Smith Elementary School noticed that its diverse students were less likely to be identified as gifted and more likely to be identified with a variety of educational disabilities."	"After reviewing its data in a number of areas, administrators and teacher leaders at Smith Elementary School noticed that students from REM backgrounds, specifically Black and Latinx, were less likely to be identified as gifted and more likely to be identified with a variety of educational disabilities, including specific learning disability and emotional disability. To address these disparate outcomes, school leaders invited a *diverse group* (e.g., race, ethnicity, professional background) to discuss potential reasons for these results and develop a plan to increase equitable outcomes."
Speaking for the voiceless	To advocate for additional instructional staff to support the needs of its students, several school district employees provided public comments at	To advocate for additional instructional staff to support the needs of its students, several school district employees provided public comments at a school board meeting. A reading specialist offered the following remarks: "As an educator for

	a school board meeting. A reading specialist offered the following remarks: "As an educator for more than 15 years, I am committed to the academic success of my students. I also realize that there are many factors that are standing in the way of their success. Some of the students in our school district have exactly what they need because their parents are here every week making their wishes known to you and the school district's senior leaders. But the parents of my students don't have a voice. As you can see, they're not here. So, here I am with my colleagues; speaking for the voiceless so that our students have what they need to succeed."	more than 15 years, I am committed to the academic success of my students. I also realize that there are many factors that are standing in the way of their success. Some of the students in our school district have exactly what they need because their parents are here every week making their wishes known to you and the school district's senior leaders. But as you can see, the parents of my students aren't here. Do they care about their children? Absolutely. Do they want them to succeed academically? Yes, they certainly do. But unfortunately, many of them are faced with having to work multiple jobs to provide for their families and are unable to attend this meeting. That's why my colleagues and I have collected these statements from 50 families at our schools. As you'll hear from the next 50 speakers, mothers and fathers, aunts and uncles, and grandmothers and grandfathers are sharing in their own words how much they want the school board to provide the necessary funding to meet the staffing needs of their children's schools. It's our pleasure, not to speak for them, but to amplify their voices."
Marginalized versus vulnerable populations	To highlight the efforts of a local food pantry that provides nonperishable items for Smith Elementary School's children and families over weekends and extended vacations, a statement on its website included the following words: "We are grateful for the support of our community partners who have consistently supported us and our vulnerable families who often struggle with having enough food for their children over weekends and extended school vacations."	To highlight the efforts of a local food pantry that provides nonperishable items for Smith Elementary School's children and families over weekends and extended vacations, a statement on its website included the following words: "We are grateful for the support of our community partners who have consistently supported us and our most marginalized families, including those who are living in low income and economic marginalization [LIEM] and who often struggle with having enough food for their children over weekends and extended school vacations."
Cultural competence versus cultural responsiveness	The following statement is included in the syllabus of a course focused on assessing culturally and linguistically diverse students: "By the end of the semester, graduate students will be culturally competent to assess the cognitive abilities and academic skills of culturally and linguistically diverse children."	The following statement is included in the syllabus of a course focused on assessing REM students, specifically ELs: "By the end of the semester, graduate students will develop their ability to be culturally responsive to REM students, including choosing the most appropriate test batteries and methodologies, as they assess their cognitive abilities and academic skills to ultimately make the most informed educational decisions."

Collaborative for Academic, Social, and Emotional Learning (CASEL): *https://casel. org*

Lessons for Social Emotional Learning (SEL): *www.lessonsforSEL.com*

DISCUSSION QUESTIONS

1. Think about the two examples of when educators use harmful language. Based on your professional position (role) and level of experience, what are some reasons that could prevent you from responding in a way that held a colleague accountable and served as a teaching moment for a larger group? Are there other ways to respond that could accomplish the same goals?

   _____

   _____

   _____

2. Based on being a graduate student or your role in a school or school district, identify opportunities for improvement in the following areas—the word gap, zero-tolerance discipline policies, or MTSS—that intentionally consider student and family characteristics. Brainstorm ideas that can be discussed with your classmates or colleagues (e.g., school-based team, department) and a plan for implementing these changes.

   _____

   _____

   _____

3. Think about the words that you use when referring to students, families, schools, and communities. Where are there opportunities to use terms that are more aligned with a systems orientation? How can you hold yourself accountable for shifting your vocabulary to reflect a social justice orientation?

   _____

   _____

   _____

4. What additional words or terms should educators be mindful of when referring to students, families, schools, and communities?

   _____

   _____

   _____

5. In light of what was discussed related to using harmful language, read the following vignette and discuss what you would do with your colleagues or classmates. If it helps, you can refer to Appendix 3.3 and record notes below or in the space provided in the appendix.

> A middle school principal sends an email and voicemail to his school's families. In the message, he says the following: "I have been the principal of Eastern Middle School for 12 years. During this time, the community has changed significantly. As a result, there have been tremendous increases in disciplinary problems with our students. This message is to remind you to please teach your children to behave properly at school, including walking to and from school and riding the bus. Our teachers and administrators work very hard, and I support them whenever they want a student who cannot behave properly removed from their classroom. They are also some of the finest teachers and staff and don't have to work in a school with children who don't care about their education. Thank you for your cooperation so that this school will be a shining example as it was in years past."

_____

_____

_____

_____

_____

_____

Establishing a Schoolwide Discipline Flowchart

As a shared activity with your graduate students or colleagues (e.g., PBIS team), complete the figure below by mutually determining which behaviors should be handled by instructional staff (e.g., classroom teachers) and those that warrant a referral to an administrator (e.g., dean, assistant principal, principal).

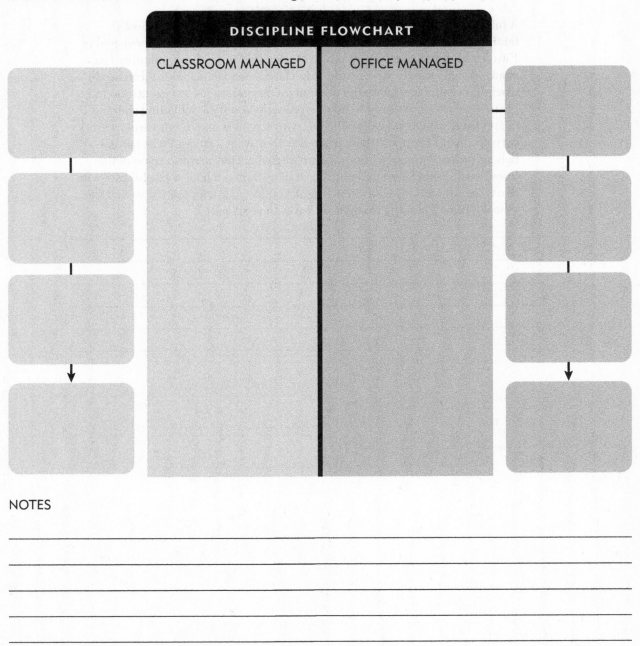

DISCIPLINE FLOWCHART

CLASSROOM MANAGED   OFFICE MANAGED

NOTES

_____

_____

_____

_____

_____

Resources for Understanding Social Justice

The following table includes a variety of resources that can be helpful for developing individuals' understanding related to social justice. The table includes the title of the resource, a link, the type of resource, and the author.

Resource	Link	Type of resource	Author
Implicit Association Test	https://implicit.harvard.edu/implicit	Activity	Project Implicit, Harvard University
"White Privilege: Unpacking the Invisible Knapsack"	https://nationalseedproject.org/about-us/white-privilege	Short essay	Peggy McIntosh
Courageous Conversations about Race: A Field Guide for Achieving Equity in Schools (2nd ed.)	https://courageousconversation.com/about	Book	Glenn E. Singleton
Nice White Parents	https://open.spotify.com/show/7oBSLCZFCgpdCaBjlG8mLV	Podcast	Serial Productions, The New York Times
Learning for Justice: Classroom Resources	www.learningforjustice.org/classroom-resources	Classroom resources	Learning for Justice
Addressing Race and Trauma in the Classroom: A Resource for Educators	www.nctsn.org/sites/default/files/resources//addressing_race_and_trauma_in_the_classroom_educators.pdf	Resource guide	The National Child Traumatic Stress Network
"We Need More White Parents to Talk to Their Kids about Race. Especially Now."	www.washingtonpost.com/lifestyle/2020/05/22/we-need-more-white-parents-talk-their-kids-about-race-especially-now	Article	The Washington Post

Planning Difficult and Uncomfortable Discussions with Colleagues

Because challenging our colleagues can be both difficult and uncomfortable, thoughtful preparation before these interactions can be helpful for removing emotions and remaining focused on what is best for children. The *Planning Difficult and Uncomfortable Discussions with Colleagues* document below is designed to help educators reflect upon the 11 principles that were highlighted in the responses to colleagues and detailed in Chapter 3. The table lists the 11 principles that should be considered and used to the greatest extent possible for the situation. In other words, it might not be necessary to include all of the principles in your response. Instructions for using this resource follow.

1. Think about the situation. What happened? How were the actions of a staff member(s) inappropriate or harmful to students?
2. Think about your response. Why is it necessary to respond to the staff member(s)? What would you like to say?
3. Draft your response. Read each principle and draft a portion of your response (see My Sample Response column) that is consistent with each principle.
4. For more information, refer to Chapter 3 (pp. 50–56).

Number	Principle	My sample response
1	**The level of exposure in your response must be commensurate with the level of exposure in the offensive statement.**	
2	**Identify what you're doing, clearly highlighting what was problematic without attacking the individual.**	
3	**Clearly articulate what was wrong with the statement and why it was wrong by keeping the focus on children and families.**	
4	**As you are teaching, to the greatest extent possible, use *we* statements.**	

(continued)

Number	Principle	My sample response
5	Say what you mean without saying it mean; relationships matter.	
6	Don't assume that everyone knows as much as you may know about issues of justice and equity. Some of our colleagues are not ill intentioned, but they legitimately don't know.	
7	Rather than assuming an accusatory tone, ask questions and give the other person a chance to clarify something that you may have overlooked.	
8	As you are teaching, to the greatest extent possible, use *we statements* and keep the focus on children and families.	
9	Try to point individuals to resources to support their learning, growth, and development.	
10	Encourage people to grow beyond where they are at the present moment.	
11	Because helping people grow is a process, make yourself available for further discussion.	

CHAPTER 4

Social Justice Is About Privilege, Implicit Bias, and Intersectionality

> **Remain aware of our personal biases so that they do not negatively affect students.**
>
> *Although change takes time, if schools and school districts are not taking intentional steps toward changing systems, policies, and practices that are harmful to children, including naming racism, not only will we not increase equitable outcomes for students, but we can no longer hide behind the curtain of implicit bias as the explanation.*

LEARNING OUTCOMES

After reading this chapter, you should be able to . . .

1. Explain how privilege, implicit bias, and intersectionality are related to social justice and achieving equitable outcomes for children.

2. Explain the negative effects of implicit bias on children in educational settings.

3. Explain the importance of educators self-reflecting on their intersecting identities, including their privileges and implicit biases, to continually become more responsive to the needs of their students, families, schools, and communities.

CHAPTER OVERVIEW

For those who might be new to thinking about social justice and its relationship to achieving equitable outcomes in schools, a common question is, "Where do I begin?" Chapter 4 explores three foundational constructs for understanding social justice: privilege, implicit bias, and intersectionality. Additionally, it discusses the importance of individuals engaging in self-reflection to become more aware of how these concepts can negatively affect their professional practice. Although educators are committed to serving children, families, schools, and communities, based on our own intersecting identities and lived experiences, we also have different histories with racism, prejudice, discrimination, inequity, and systems of power and privilege that affect how we view the world (NASP, 2016b). Allowing ourselves the time and space to think critically about, and perhaps wrestle with, these constructs is a necessary first step in promoting equitable outcomes in our respective settings.

INTRODUCTION

The growing prominence of social justice in the fields of education and school psychology is a relatively recent phenomenon. Though significant, actions to elevate social justice in school psychology, including the NASP Social Justice Task Force (2016–2018), the adoption of social justice as a strategic goal (NASP, 2017), operationally defining social justice for the profession (NASP, 2017), and the formation of the Social Justice Committee (2018) have occurred within the last 10 years. If school psychology is similar to other disciplines in education, our colleagues are also likely in the early stages of growing in their awareness, knowledge, and understanding of what social justice is, why it's important, and how it can be infused into their everyday practices. Whether you're a veteran educator or a graduate student, a new teacher or an experienced administrator, Chapter 4 provides foundational knowledge related to privilege, implicit bias, and intersectionality—concepts that are critical to engaging in socially just practices that lead to equitable outcomes.

PRIVILEGE

Of all the concepts that will be discussed in this chapter, privilege is likely the most challenging for some to accept. Especially for individuals who never had to consider their privilege or privileged identities, the term can be offensive and lead to feelings of defensiveness. Before continuing, I have two requests. First, please keep an open mind by considering alternative perspectives to what you have been taught, exposed to, or previously believed. Next, and as discussed in Chapter 1, more than individual people who have been afforded certain privileges or who have privileged identities, think about how systems and structures have led to privilege and maintain, reinforce, or perpetuate who benefits from privilege. Although this can be uncomfortable because it challenges your current worldview, I am also confident that you can learn something that will be beneficial.

First, privilege is applicable to more than a person's race or ethnicity. You've likely heard about White Privilege, and this is discussed later in the chapter. But broadly speaking, **privilege refers to one group having something of value that is denied to others based on their group membership rather than what the group (or individuals in the group) have or have not done to earn it (Johnson, 2006).** In other words, privilege is having unearned advantages. Privilege is the ability to access things or experiences that are highly valued due to identifying with or being born into a certain group (NASP, 2016b). Have you ever stayed at a hotel that you couldn't afford? Purchased an item of clothing that was priced beyond your budget? Maybe you've flown on a *buddy pass* of someone who works for an airline. These things are possible because of a *family and friends* discount or because you are close enough to someone who can give you what you want—and at a (much) lower rate. Here's the lesson: This is how privilege operates. It's a system of unearned advantages that people enjoy by virtue of their association (relationship) with someone else (e.g., a friend or family member). Because of people's positionality (e.g., proximity to wealth and power), they can provide (you) access to what you want for a fraction of the cost. Did you earn it? No. But did you benefit from it? Absolutely (Barrett, 2022).

As an example, privilege can include gender, in which cisgender males enjoy unearned advantages compared with cisgender females. In schools, boys have traditionally been assumed to be more capable or proficient in math (Cvencek, Meltzoff, & Greenwald, 2011). And because of this, they have been given opportunities (e.g., access to advanced classes and other enrichment experiences) to further develop these skills. Another example of privilege is sexual orientation. Though changing over time through state and federal legislation, homophobia and heteronormativity are realities in American society that affect students, families, and schools, including staff. In fact, data suggest that lesbian, gay, bisexual, transgender, and questioning (LGBTQIA+) students are at increased risk for being bullied in schools (see Eisenberg et al., 2019). A third privilege is ability. For those who can move independently in society because they have the full use of their senses and intact cognitive capabilities, this is an unearned advantage considering how many people have congenital conditions that lead to numerous physical or mental disabilities. Last, privilege can also be economic. As mentioned in Chapter 2 and shown in *The Unequal Opportunity Race* (Pinto, 2010), when families have accumulated generational wealth, subsequent generations (e.g., children, grandchildren), by virtue of being born into the family, benefit from the unearned advantage of financial security that provides access to highly valued aspects of life, such as living in safe communities and attending well-funded schools with highly qualified teachers. See Table 4.1 for a short (not comprehensive) list of types of privilege and a brief explanation.

Because of how pervasive racism continues to be in virtually every American institution, including schools, it's important to discuss the reality of privilege based on race, also known as White Privilege. In her 1989 essay, "White Privilege: Unpacking the Invisible Knapsack," Peggy McIntosh wrote, "I realized that I had been taught about racism as

TABLE 4.1. Types of Privilege

Type	Example
Race	White individuals are generally assumed to be law abiding and less likely to be incarcerated for a variety of crimes and offenses (Johnson, 2006).
Gender	Boys have traditionally been assumed to be more capable or proficient in math (Cvencek, Meltzoff, & Greenwald, 2011). As a result, they have been given opportunities (e.g., access to advanced classes and other enrichment experiences) to further develop these skills.
Sexual orientation	Heterosexual individuals are more likely to feel comfortable expressing themselves romantically in public places and to discuss their relationships than homosexual individuals.
Ability	Individuals without visible or invisible disabilities are more likely to experience the world with less stigma or discrimination. For example, for individuals who stutter, because their speech is less fluent, others might perceive them as less articulate or intelligent.
SES	Being born into a higher socioeconomic status (SES) leads to being afforded greater access to beneficial opportunities, including attending well-funded and resourced schools with highly qualified teachers that are located in safe neighborhoods.
Religion	In many ways, American life, including school calendars (e.g., spring break and winter recess), coincide with significant Christian holidays (e.g., Christmas, Easter). Individuals who are not Christian are more likely to request time off from work or are absent from school to celebrate their faith traditions.

something that puts others at a disadvantage, but also had been taught not to see one of its corollary aspects, White privilege, which puts me at an advantage" (p. 1). As noted by Kendi (2019), despite White individuals being more likely than Black or Latinx individuals to sell drugs, and people across races consuming drugs at similar rates, privilege (unearned advantage), among other factors, leads White people to be significantly less likely to be incarcerated for drug-related offenses than Black individuals who experience the other side of privilege: oppression and marginalization, also known as unearned disadvantage (NASP, 2016b). Consider these additional data:

1. The amount of time that nonviolent drug offenders who are Black remain incarcerated is similar to that of violent criminals who are White (Kendi, 2019).
2. As recently as 2016, Black and Latinx individuals were overrepresented in the prison population (56%), which is double their percentage of the United States adult population (Kendi, 2019).
3. Whereas White people are generally assumed to be law abiding (e.g., not being

assumed shoplifters or followed while in stores), REM individuals, particularly those who are Black and Latinx, are routinely assumed to be criminals or potential criminals (Johnson, 2006).

For members of the dominant culture in the United States (i.e., White individuals), learning about and accepting that White Privilege is real can be unsettling. Especially because White or the dominant culture has been considered the norm or standard (see Chapter 3), it's possible that White individuals have never thought about their own privileged status, especially regarding race (NASP, 2016b). Coupled with affecting how we interact with others and our personal judgments, privilege becomes problematic when it blinds us to systemic barriers that create and perpetuate inequities. Whether through race, gender, ability, or SES, individuals and groups who benefit from privilege can either find it difficult to identify or deny that it exists (NASP, 2016b). For example, cisgender males could find it difficult to articulate the unearned advantages that are associated with being male. And for those who are able bodied, having never been faced with thinking about ramps or elevators to access public spaces, it's easy, though not excusable, to overlook the needs of our students, families, and colleagues who have disabilities. Rather than focusing on how policies (systems) have created disparate outcomes for groups based on their privileged identities (e.g., race, gender, ability), being blinded by privilege causes us to attribute inequities to the inherent weaknesses or flaws of individuals or groups (Kendi, 2019). The following brief reflections further illustrate the reality of privilege, particularly the ability to not have to think about privilege and the ability to be seen as an individual.

Privilege Is the Ability to Not Have to Think About Privilege

In the summer of 2020, my wife and I completed a home renovation. And like many others who go through this process, we sought estimates from a few contractors.

One of them, as we walked through the property, seemed rather uninterested. Not wanting to prejudge, we completed the tour, explained to him what we wanted, and said that we looked forward to his estimate. We never heard from him. Could he simply not have been interested in the job? Yes. Could he have lacked the interpersonal skills to earn a customer's business? Yes. But as a Black man living in America, race is always a consideration. Would he have presented as uninterested if we weren't Black? Perhaps. Would he have at least given an estimate if we weren't Black? Possibly. Did he think that we couldn't afford the scope of the work that we were requesting? I don't know. Although using the word that you're trying to define in its definition is not a good idea, it's quite fitting for this situation: Privilege is the ability to not have to think about privilege (Barrett, 2021b). Another example of privilege and home ownership is presented in the following box.

A REFLECTION FROM HGTV

While watching HGTV (e.g., *Love It or List It, Property Brothers, House Hunters*), I often think about the intersection of racism and privilege. These shows, like many others, involve individuals, couples, or families looking for a new home, sometimes while renovating their current home. And although criteria such as, "close to downtown, near walking trails, and access to nightlife" are often mentioned, I wonder about the unspoken, or perhaps unaired, requirements that REM individuals also have. In other words, for minoritized individuals, buying a home isn't as straightforward as it may seem. "What is the racial and ethnic composition of my neighbors? Will my children be the only students of color in their school or classes? Will I be comfortable living in this neighborhood as the only (or one of a few) person/family of color?" These are examples of the real questions that minoritized people often think about. As convenient as it would be to purchase a home simply because it's within their (our) budget and satisfies the requirements that are mentioned, that's not yet true. If you've never thought about these things, it could be the result of privilege: the privilege to not have to think about privilege (Barrett, 2021b).

THINK ABOUT IT. What are your impressions, thoughts, and reactions to the idea that privilege is the ability to not have to think about privilege? What do you think about the scenario used to highlight this concept? Discuss your answers with your classmates or colleagues.

Considered a staple of American culture, *Home Alone* (Columbus, 1990) is one of the most popular holiday movies of all time. Written and produced by John Hughes, and directed by Chris Columbus, there is a 90-second segment in which the McCallister family has landed in France, after realizing on the flight that they have left their son, brother, cousin, and nephew (Kevin) home alone. In the airport, who did Mrs. McCallister, Kevin's mother, call first? The police.

Home Alone was released in 1990, long before America's current reckoning with racism and a host of other systemic injustices, including police violence. But even 31 years ago, it's important to consider: would a Black mother's first call be to the police to check on her son? Though I can't speak for everyone, given the history between law enforcement and Black people, the police wouldn't be my first call. In fact, as a Black male, I don't know that I would call them at all if in a similar situation. The seemingly automatic decision for some individuals, based on their intersecting identities, to call the police—because they are seen as protectors—is yet another manifestation of privilege (Barrett, 2022).

Privilege Is the Ability to Be Seen as an Individual

In thinking about what happened at the United States Capitol on January 6, 2021, a central feature of privilege became clearer to me. A common response, often from White individuals, was "Those people . . ." or even "Those crazy people. . . ." In other words, almost immediately there was separation between those who stormed the Capitol and those who weren't there. Almost immediately, what happened was framed as being directly related to one individual or a few elected officials. And while there is truth to both sentiments, the ability for White people to separate themselves from the larger group and to see themselves as individuals and therefore different is an essential quality of privilege. Other races and ethnicities don't have such luxuries. In fact, as a school psy-

> **THINK ABOUT IT. What are your impressions, thoughts, and reactions? Discuss your answers with your classmates or colleagues.**

chologist, I've heard a fellow White educator say this about a Black individual's performance: "She's not doing her race any favors." When White people behave poorly/badly, they are seen as exceptions—bad apples. But when others (e.g., Black or Muslim individuals) do so, their behavior is projected onto their respective groups and is seen as a flaw (a stain) of the group—not the individual. In the early days following the events at the Capitol, one of my biggest frustrations was the absence of critiquing and rebuking the system (racism, racist policy) at the expense of centering individuality and presumed exceptionality.

IMPLICIT BIAS

> Now you are going to view a series of video clips lasting six minutes. We are interested in learning about how teachers detect challenging behavior in the classroom. Sometimes this involves seeing behavior before it becomes problematic. The video segments you are about to view are of preschoolers engaging in various activities. Some clips may or may not contain challenging behaviors. Your job is to press the enter key on the external keypad every time you see a behavior that could become a potential challenge [experimenter demonstrates]. Press the keypad as often as needed (Gilliam, Maupin, Reyes, Accavitti, & Shic, 2016, p. 6).

Imagine being a teacher or preservice teacher attending a national conference and you're asked to participate in a study. The preceding text is read to you while you're in a booth looking at a computer screen. After listening to the directions, the video begins. There are two girls (one Black, one White) and two boys, also one Black and one White. All of the children are preschool age. The directions above were taken from a study by Gilliam and colleagues (2016). Although they instructed the predominantly White and female participants (approximately 67 and 94%, respectively) to press the enter key every time they saw a behavior that could potentially become problematic, the authors were measuring another response: where the participants looked on the video. In other words, having been primed with *seeing behavior before it becomes problematic,* which student—the Black boy, the White boy, the Black girl, or the White girl—was viewed (looked at) the most by the sample of teachers and preservice teachers who were also representative of educators in United States public schools? Data showed that 43% of participants primarily looked at the Black boy, which was followed by 34% for the White boy, 13% for the White girl, and 10% for the Black girl (Gilliam et al., 2016).

From these data, there are two biases that are relevant to educators. First, not only did 77% of participants look at the boys more than the girls, but the Black boy (or as is discussed later in this chapter, at the intersection of race and gender) was watched more closely than any other child. Notably, the participants didn't intend to look at the boys or the Black boy more than the girls or White children. Nevertheless, their response is an example of implicit or unconscious bias. Though unaware, the participants looked at the children whom they felt required more attention and who they expected to display problematic behavior.

One of the most important details about this study is related to the children's behavior: There was no problem behavior or misbehavior. In other words, despite the children behaving in ways that were developmentally and socially appropriate, 43% of participants looked at the Black boy and 77% looked at boys in general.

Implicit bias is a subconscious process that constantly influences an individual's feelings, thought patterns, actions, and behaviors. Whether applying pejorative beliefs to a specific group of people or seeing one bad action and assuming that it represents everyone in a particular group, implicit bias is usually rooted in prejudice and is often subtle and unintended.

> Biases are inherent attributes that all humans possess and form naturally through the course of everyday interactions and exposure to media. These biases can become very harmful, however, when beliefs about groups lead to unquestioned assumptions about individuals within those groups. . . . When these assumptions lead to important decisions regarding how we choose to educate our youngest citizen learners, or deny educational opportunities through preschool expulsions and suspensions, the potential for lasting harm is great. (Gilliam et al., 2016; p. 16)

In schools, implicit bias can negatively affect outcomes, particularly for REM students. For example, REM children, including preschoolers, are more likely to be suspended and expelled than their White peers (Gilliam, 2005; U.S. Department of Education Office for Civil Rights [OCR], 2014), and they are also more likely to be overrepresented in various special education categories and exclusionary (i.e., self-contained) programs (OCR, 2014). Specifically related to Gilliam et al. (2016), implicit bias contributes to the disproportionate suspension of Black preschoolers who subsequently enter kindergarten less academically and socially prepared than their peers. In effect, even before they are of school age, some children have been placed on a trajectory that leads to poorer educational outcomes. As discussed in Chapter 5, coupled with the role of standardized testing, Black and Latinx students are underidentified as gifted because implicit bias (e.g., being perceived as less intelligent and less academically motivated than their White peers) leads to lower teacher referral rates for gifted consideration (Ford, Harris, Tyson, & Trotman, 2002).

Returning to Gilliam et al. (2016), an important finding was that even the Black participants (22% of the sample) spent more time looking at the Black boy in the video compared with their White counterparts. This is significant because it shows that implicit bias is a fundamentally human phenomenon. Regardless of race, ethnicity, gender, or any other characteristic, everyone, including well-trained and very experienced educators across disciplines, is susceptible to implicit bias. Given that there were no problem behaviors on the video and that implicit bias is universal to the human condition, as discussed in Chapter 5, it can also influence the outcomes of special education evaluations. For example, when teachers and families are asked to complete behavior rating scales for their students or children, how much of what is reported is actually attributable to the child rather than the implicit biases of the adult? Because behavior rating scales are not objective but are heavily influenced by the informants completing them, raters (e.g., teachers, mothers, fathers, guardians) bring their worldviews, including their implicit biases about children's behavior, skills, and functioning, to the assessment process.

As I often tell my undergraduate and graduate students, the definition of *data* is not "facts." Rather, *data* refers to information that must be interpreted in context. Because of implicit bias and other factors, when school-based teams are faced with making life-changing educational decisions about students, data that have been collected by adults should not be assumed to be indisputable fact. As demonstrated by Gilliam et al. (2016), children are subjected to outcomes (e.g., being looked at more often than others) that have a lot less to do with their own behavior—sometimes not at all—than it does with the adults (e.g., the systems) around them.

The Problem with Implicit Bias

Though it is real, I struggle with how much attention is given to implicit bias. From the disproportionate killing of unarmed Black individuals by law enforcement to disparate suspension and expulsion data, whether within or beyond schools, implicit bias is often the first, or one of the first, explanations for these and other inequities. And if implicit bias is believed to account for the ills that plague schools and the larger society, then, as a logical extension, implicit bias training is often the recommendation du jour to place public and private sector institutions on the path to better outcomes.

If implicit bias refers to the judgments or behaviors that result from subtle cognitive processes (e.g., implicit attitudes and implicit stereotypes) that operate at a level below conscious awareness and without intentional control, then, after *intentionally* focusing on implicit bias, how long can schools and school systems continue to use this as the primary explanation for persistent inequities? Although I am not suggesting that implicit bias can be fully eradicated from individuals, I am challenging the idea that it accounts for as much as some say it does. Yes, studies have shown the negative effects of implicit bias in both schools and the larger society. However, if, after professional learning sessions have been offered for multiple years, books have been written, and articles have been published about this phenomenon, disparate outcomes remain, then either these activities are ineffective or we have misplaced our focus. In other words, does implicit bias truly account for (explain) the poor outcomes in schools and the larger society?

What is less popular, especially in schools, are explicit discussions about racism, of which implicit bias is a symptom. Because racism is systemic and exists in every major institution, racist behaviors and racist attitudes lie at the root of implicit bias. In the absence of racism, which is the belief that one group is superior to another, and its subsequent actions that reinforce this idea, implicit bias would not exist. Consider this:

> Author Beverly Tatum talks about how people who live in Los Angeles become smog-breathers. They don't do anything to become smog-breathers, they aren't conscious of being smog-breathers. They just go about their everyday lives as they breathe in the smog. She then added that if we live in America, we are racism-breathers, and it doesn't matter what color we are. We don't try to be, we usually aren't conscious of the racism we have breathed. We just go about our regular lives breathing the smog we live in. (Delpit, 2012, p. 14)

For people who have been raised and conditioned (taught) in a society in which racism exists, bias, or explicit (intentional) bias more directly, is also a real phenomenon and refers to the attitudes or beliefs that a person endorses at a conscious level.

Discussions about implicit bias are healthy and necessary for schools and school systems to have with all staff who are serving students and families; but these conversations are only the beginning. As I mentioned in Chapter 3, effective educators are adept at meeting people where they are and helping them to move forward. To use an analogy from school-based instructional and intervention practices, implicit bias discussions might represent baseline data, that is, where we begin. But over time, we must grow (develop), as individuals and collectively as a staff, department, school, or school district, to talk about more challenging topics such as racism. To use another analogy, for those who might be familiar with Bloom's taxonomy, an instructional model that shows differing levels of complexity, implicit bias might represent the entry point: knowledge. But understanding racism and how it affects children in schools requires the higher level skills of analyzing, synthesizing, and evaluating. Similar to students whose instruction is limited to knowledge (i.e., simply remembering information) without being taught to comprehend, apply, analyze, synthesize, and evaluate data, and who therefore are stunted in their academic gains, when educators only focus on implicit bias they are missing critical elements of what leads to poor outcomes for students, families, schools, and communities.

Though it may be uncomfortable, in the face of stubborn inequities, schools and school systems must consider the extent to which their policies and practices are unfairly and perhaps intentionally targeting students and families from minoritized and marginalized groups. In the absence of such a critique, not only does implicit bias become a comfortable, convenient, and euphemistic excuse for disproportionate outcomes, but it also absolves policymakers who occupy positions of power of their moral and ethical responsibility to promote equity for all students, all families, all schools, and all communities. Although change takes time, if schools and school districts are not taking intentional steps toward changing systems, policies, and practices that are harmful to children, including naming racism, not only will we not increase equitable outcomes for students, but we can no longer hide behind the curtain of implicit bias as the explanation.

INTERSECTIONALITY

The last section of this chapter focuses on intersectionality, a theory that its originator, Kimberlé Crenshaw, describes as being born out of necessity (Crenshaw, 2016). For a visual representation of intersectionality, see Figure 4.1.

Intersectionality is the simultaneous experience of social categories, such as race, gender, SES, and sexual orientation, and the ways these categories interact (intersect) to create systems of oppression, domination, and discrimination. Historically, prior to

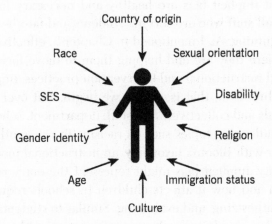

FIGURE 4.1. Intersectionality.

1989, antidiscrimination laws did not protect Black women because they viewed race and gender as mutually exclusive. In recalling the experience of Emma DeGraffenreid, a Black woman who sued her employer (General Motors) in 1976 on the grounds of work-place discrimination and whose case became the impetus for intersectionality as a construct, Cren-shaw (2016) explains that the case was dismissed because Black individuals and women had been hired by the company. Crenshaw, however, highlighted that because the judge considered these identities (race and gender) separately, he did not see how they intersected to create a unique experience for Black women and the multiple ways they experienced dis-crimination (e.g., racism and sexism; Crenshaw, 2016).

> To learn more about intersectionality, watch "The Urgency of Intersectionality," which can be found at *www. youtube.com/watch?v=akOe5-UsQ2o*. After watching the video, discuss your thoughts, feelings, and impressions with your classmates or colleagues.

Crenshaw's work led to a framework for understanding individuals, especially those with multiple marginalized and minoritized identities, by appreciating how various aspects of themselves intersected to influence their experience of the world, including the ones that led to discrimination (Crenshaw, 2016).

When identities intersect, the likelihood of discrimination and oppression increases (Crenshaw, 2016). Further, these experiences are often more intense (magnified) com-pared with those that are related to a single marginalized identity. Though a lot has been written about Black male students' risk for suspension and expulsion, Black female students are also disproportionately (inequitably) represented in school-based discipline practices. They are at higher risk of suspension and expulsion for subjective behav-ioral violations and are subjected to harsher punishment because they are perceived as loud, unruly, or unmanageable and their behavior is in opposition to institutional norms (Crenshaw, Ocen, & Nanda, 2015). As a result, underachievement, school dropout, and involvement with the criminal justice system also become more likely (Crenshaw et al., 2015). Another intersectional example refers to a male student who is also an immigrant, is learning to speak English, and identifies as gay. The intersection of his immigrant sta-tus, limited English proficiency, and sexual orientation can place him at higher risk for discrimination or oppression due to others' (e.g., administrators, teachers, peers) biases about aspects of his identity (Proctor, Williams, Scherr, & Li, 2017). These examples show the importance of educators understanding the complexities of their students and families.

Intersectionality Is for Everyone

Because intersectionality began as a construct for understanding how multiple identi-ties can lead to discrimination and oppression, some people assume that this phenom-enon is only relevant to marginalized or minoritized individuals. But because everyone has intersecting identities, intersectionality has broader implications and applicability. As noted by Kendi (2019), "Intersectional theory now gives all of humanity the ability to understand the intersectional oppression of their identities" (p. 191). An individual's intersecting identities can lead to privilege in some instances and oppression in others. For example, although White students living in LIEM, such as Emily whom we met in Chapter 2, work hard to earn good grades, compared with their REM peers, they are also more likely to benefit from unearned access to resources and social power (privilege) by attending schools where most teachers look and speak like them; to have more quali- fied or experienced teachers; to be instructed in curricula that reflect their culture, his- tory, and background; to have access to more advanced placement (AP) courses, higher quality instructional materials and facilities; and to be exposed to national figures who share their racial background (Holladay, 2000; U.S. Department of Education, 2014). A statewide study in Pennsylvania showed that independent of poverty level, districts with a higher proportion of White students received significantly more funding than districts with REM students (Kendi, 2019). Similarly, results from a national study conducted by EdBuild, a nonprofit organization that researches school funding, showed that because school districts whose students are "non-White" spend an average of $11,682 per student compared with $13,908 per student in school districts serving mostly White students, "nonwhite school districts receive $23 billion less than White districts, despite serving the same number of students" (Gunn, 2019). In sum, a White cisgender female who has physical and cognitive disabilities can simultaneously experience the privilege of having White skin in America and the oppression that is associated with gender (female) and having multiple disabilities.

Implications for Educators

Whether they are teachers or school psychologists (Walcott & Hyson, 2018), it has been well established that most (approximately 80%) educators in American public schools are White and female. These data are contrasted with the students and families attending U.S. public schools, who represent a variety of races, ethnicities, and language back- grounds (National Center for Education Statistics [NCES], 2022). Because it is almost inevitable that educators will serve students from different backgrounds than their own, intersectionality can be helpful for understanding their own identities, as well as those of their students and families.

As such, self-reflection is critical. Whether you're a teacher, school-based mental health provider, graduate student, or administrator, being aware of how your intersect- ing identities lead to both privilege and oppression can be helpful for being sensitive (responsive) to students and families. As a Black, cisgender male who also identifies as heterosexual, although there are some aspects of my identity that are marginalized (i.e., race), I also enjoy certain privileges based on my gender/gender identity and sexual orientation. Having a nuanced understanding of my own intersecting identities helps me to identify with the experiences of REM students and families in schools because I've also experienced racism as a Black man living in America. It allows me to recognize how systems, including schools and school districts, can perpetuate bias, discrimination, and inequities for REM students and families.

In addition to self-reflection, educators are encouraged to learn about their students and how their intersecting identities can place them at greater risk for discrimination and marginalization. Using existing data that have been disaggregated by race, ethnicity, gender, sexual orientation, SES, and other demographic variables, school-based teams are encouraged to critically examine the policies and processes that maintain disparate outcomes for various student groups and engage in efforts to effect changes at the systems (e.g., school building, school district) level.

CHAPTER SUMMARY

As previously stated in Chapters 2 and 3, becoming committed to social justice or socially just practices requires engaging in uncomfortable discussions with our colleagues that allow us to grow into more responsive and effective educators. The topics discussed in this chapter—privilege, implicit bias, and intersectionality—are examples of what schools and school systems must be willing to talk about to achieve equitable outcomes for students and families. Whether for your individual growth and development or facilitating the learning of your graduate students or staff, the *Resources for Professional Learning* section contains a variety of articles, lesson plans, videos, and other activities that can be helpful. And although engaging in these topics can be unsettling for some, sometimes doing what's best for children will be uncomfortable for adults.

RESOURCES FOR PROFESSIONAL LEARNING

Through the efforts of the Social Justice Task Force, the Social Justice Committee, and other volunteer leaders, the National Association of School Psychologists (NASP) has been developing and compiling resources to support the professional learning needs of school psychologists and other educators related to social justice. To learn more about privilege, implicit bias, intersectionality, and a host of other concepts related to social justice, please visit the following website: *www.nasponline.org/social-justice*. The website includes articles, lesson plans, podcasts, and guidance documents on a variety of topics that are relevant not only to school psychologists and school psychology graduate students but also to all educators who are serving students, families, schools, and communities. The list in Appendix 4.1 references specific resources related to privilege, implicit bias, and intersectionality.

DISCUSSION QUESTIONS

1. In Chapter 4, I mentioned that data constitutes information that must be interpreted in context. What does this mean to you? How is this definition of data relevant to implicit bias, privilege, or intersectionality?

   _____

   _____

2. Take a few moments to think about your own intersecting identities. Which aspects are privileged? Which aspects are more likely to experience oppression? How can your awareness of your own intersecting identities inform your service to children, families, schools, and communities?

   _____

   _____

3. Review the *Resources for Professional Learning.* Which materials seem most relevant to your professional growth as an individual? What will you do to continue growing as an educator who is committed to social justice and socially just practices?

   _____

   _____

4. Review the *Resources for Professional Learning.* Which materials seem most relevant to the professional growth of your graduate students, staff, or colleagues? What will you do to facilitate their growth as educators and future educators who are committed to social justice and socially just practices?

   _____

   _____

5. Chapter 3 (see Appendix 3.3) discussed 11 principles to consider when challenging our colleagues when their behavior is harmful to students and families.
   Because discussions about privilege, implicit bias, and intersectionality can be
   difficult and uncomfortable, which of these principles might be helpful when
   facilitating conversations or sessions focused on these topics?

   _____

   _____

   _____

Resources for Understanding Privilege, Implicit Bias, and Intersectionality

The following table includes a variety of resources that can be helpful for developing individuals' understanding related to privilege, implicit bias, and intersectionality. The table includes the title of the resource, a link, the type of resource, and the author.

Resource	Link	Type of resource	Author
Privilege			
The Privilege of Not Understanding Privilege: The Greatest Psychological Privilege Is Not Having to Think about Things	*www.psychologytoday.com/us/blog/feeling-our-way/201702/the-privilege-not-understanding-privilege*	Article	Michael Karson
Why Does Privilege Make People So Angry?	*www.youtube.com/watch?v=qeYpvV3eRhY*	Video	MTV Impact
Understanding Race and Privilege	*https://www.nasponline.org/resources-and-publications/resources-and-podcasts/diversity-and-social-justice/social-justice/understanding-race-and-privilege*	Handout	National Association of School Psychologists
Talking about Race and Privilege: Lesson Plan for Middle and High School Students	*https://www.nasponline.org/resources-and-publications/resources-and-podcasts/diversity-and-social-justice/social-justice/social-justice-lesson-plans/talking-about-race-and-privilege-lesson-plan-for-middle-and-high-school-students*	Handout	National Association of School Psychologists
Understanding Race and Privilege: Lesson Plan and Activity Guide for Professionals		Lesson plan and activity guide	National Association of School Psychologists
Implicit bias			
Your Unconscious Bias Trainings Keep Failing Because You're Not Addressing Systemic Bias	*www.forbes.com/sites/janicegassam/2020/12/29/your-unconscious-bias-trainings-keep-failing-because-youre-not-addressing-systemic-bias/?sh=39bfdea81e9d*	Article	Janice Gassam Asare
Implicit Bias Module Series	*https://kirwaninstitute.osu.edu/implicit-bias-training*	Video	Kirwan Institute for the Study of Race and Ethnicity

(continued)

Resource	Link	Type of resource	Author
Implicit bias *(continued)*			
Studio Sacramento: Unconscious Bias	*www.pbs.org/video/studio-sacramento-unconscious-bias*	Interview	The American Leadership Forum
Implicit Bias: A Foundation for School Psychologists	*https://www.nasponline.org/resources-and-publications/resources-and-podcasts/diversity-and-social-justice/social-justice/implicit-bias-a-foundation-for-school-psychologists*	Handout	National Association of School Psychologists
Implicit Bias, Part 2—Addressing Disproportionality in Discipline: A Prospective Look at Culturally Responsive Positive Behavior Intervention and Supports	*https://www.nasponline.org/resources-and-publications/resources-and-podcasts/diversity-and-social-justice/social-justice/implicit-bias-a-foundation-for-school-psychologists/implicit-bias-part-2*	Handout	National Association of School Psychologists
Intersectionality			
Demarginalizing the Intersection of Race and Sex: A Black Feminist Critique of Antidiscrimination Doctrine, Feminist Theory and Antiracist Politics	*https://chicagounbound.uchicago.edu/cgi/viewcontent.cgi?article=1052&context=uclf*	Article	Kimberlé Crenshaw
Intersectionality and School Psychology: Implications for Practice	*https://www.nasponline.org/resources-and-publications/resources-and-podcasts/diversity-and-social-justice/social-justice/intersectionality-and-school-psychology-implications-for-practice*	Article	Sherrie Proctor, Brittney Williams, Tracey Scherr, and Kathrynne Li
Understanding Intersectionality		Handout	National Association of School Psychologists
The Urgency of Intersectionality	*www.ted.com/talks/kimberle_crenshaw_the_urgency_of_intersectionality#t-1116348*	Video	Kimberlé Crenshaw

Resources for Understanding Privilege, Implicit Bias, and Intersectionality (page 2 of 2)

CHAPTER 5

Social Justice
Is About More Than Numbers

> **Rather than relying on incomplete quantitative data, gather qualitative information from a variety of sources.**
>
> *Intelligence is more than performance on standardized IQ and achievement tests. Children achieve in ways that cannot be captured on tests of basic reading and reading comprehension, spelling and written expression, or math computation and math problem solving. Intelligence is more than report card grades and scores on high-stakes (end-of-year) exams.*

LEARNING OUTCOMES

After reading this chapter, you should be able to . . .

1. Explain the limitations of standardized tests for making educational decisions for children.
2. Describe the components of a multimethod and multisource assessment approach.
3. Explain how a multimethod and multisource assessment paradigm is aligned with socially just practices and leads to equitable outcomes in gifted identification and special education eligibility.

CHAPTER OVERVIEW

To help you accurately understand children's functioning and performance, Chapter 5 focuses on assessment approaches that gather different types of information from a variety of sources. Specific attention is given to evaluating REM students, including ELs and children living in LIEM, for gifted education and Black students for social, emotional, and behavioral difficulties (e.g., ADHD). Implications for developing socially just assessment and identification processes to improve equitable outcomes in schools and school systems are discussed.

INTRODUCTION

Do you remember Miguel from Chapter 2? Although he is currently in high school, the following describes the process his suburban elementary school used when he and other students were being considered for the gifted program.

> As a second grader, Miguel and the other students in his school district were given a group-administered cognitive ability test. This test provided four scores: a nonverbal score, a verbal score, a quantitative score, and an overall composite score. In each area, Miguel's scores were based on a national comparison with other children his age. Though Miguel performed well on the nonverbal and quantitative portions of the test (above average and superior ranges), his verbal abilities were significantly weaker and fell within the below average range. As a result, Miguel's overall composite score fell within the average range. At the time, this instrument played an important role in identifying students for the gifted program. Specifically, Miguel's overall composite score (verbal + nonverbal + quantitative = overall composite) was the only score that his school district used to determine whether he could participate in the enrichment activities that were offered to students in the gifted program. Because Miguel's overall composite fell within the average range, despite his above average and superior scores in the nonverbal and quantitative domains, he was not identified as a student who was gifted or eligible for the gifted program.

Though fictitious, the preceding scenario has been commonplace in American public schools. Whether they use group-administered ability tests (e.g., Cognitive Ability Test [CogAT]) or individually administered IQ tests (e.g., Wechsler Intelligence Scale for Children, Fifth Edition [WISC-5]), the outcome has been the same for decades: Black, Latinx, and students living in LIEM are less likely to be identified as gifted compared with their White, Asian, and wealthier peers (Ford, Grantham, & Whiting, 2008; Ford, 2015). As stated in Chapter 1, because race/ethnicity or SES should not predict a student's eligibility for their school's gifted program, these disparate outcomes (disproportionality, inequities) are the result of policies and practices that have been implemented by schools and school systems.

For Miguel and students who share a similar background, there are several factors that likely affected his performance on the group-administered assessment, especially the verbal domain. First, although Miguel was born in the United States and has only attended English-speaking schools (i.e., he has only been instructed in English), his parents are immigrants from El Salvador, and Spanish is his native language. As mentioned in Chapter 3, for the first 5 years of his life, Miguel was almost exclusively exposed to Spanish and didn't learn English until he began kindergarten and was consistently in an English-speaking environment. As a result, and especially in his third year of formal education (second grade), Miguel's verbal abilities were weaker than his nonverbal or quantitative (e.g., problem solving, reasoning) abilities. Relatedly, and as evidenced through his classroom performance and report card grades, Miguel's math skills were stronger than his reading or writing skills. When Miguel performed significantly better on the nonverbal and quantitative portions of the test, rather than overlooking these scores and only considering the overall composite, Miguel's school district should have taken into account his age, home language background, and other contextual experiences that could have negatively affected his performance in the verbal domain.

As in many schools and school districts across the United States, Miguel's performance on this test was the sole determinant of whether he was eligible to participate in the gifted program. In other words, work samples (e.g., a portfolio) were not collected to demonstrate his creativity and superior problem-solving abilities. Miguel's teachers and parents were also not invited to provide input into the process (e.g., parent and teacher interviews, parent and teacher rating scales) to highlight the ways in which he stood out among his peers and how he would benefit from an educational program that enriched his already well-developed abilities.

In sum, the process that was used by Miguel's school—one in which all students, regardless of their race/ethnicity, language background, or SES, were administered the same assessment—was a process that only considered the overall composite score to inform eligibility decisions, one that didn't include parent and teacher input, and that didn't involve work samples of children's performance over time. It ignored the significance of the ecological system in which students lived and how it affected their scores on standardized cognitive ability tests. Later in this chapter I provide suggestions for socially just assessment practices that are applicable to gifted eligibility. Additionally, to learn more about assessing and identifying students from REM backgrounds and those who are living in LIEM, see Ford (2015); Ford et al. (2008); and Ford et al. (2002).

STANDARDIZED TESTS

Because of their role in the assessment and identification process for both gifted and special education, this section briefly discusses the limitations of standardized tests, especially when used with REM students and those living in LIEM.

As noted in Chapter 3, achievement gaps set up racial hierarchies because they imply that certain races (White, Asian) perform better on standardized tests than others (Black, Latinx; Kendi, 2019). Further, because the numbers (scores) that are derived from standardized tests claim to be an accurate representation of students' intelligence, not only does this suggest that some children's (e.g., Black and Latinx) intellectual capacity is inherently less than that of others, but policies that allow decisions to be based solely on these numbers effectively exclude some children and adolescents from accessing certain spaces, including gifted programs (Kendi, 2019).

In one of my school psychology graduate courses, my students and I read *Enrique's Journey* (Nazario, 2006). A journalist who focuses on social and social justice issues, including immigration and immigrant children from Central America, Sonia Nazario tells the true story of Enrique, a 17-year-old from Honduras, whose bravery leads him on a harrowing journey atop trains, wading in water with strangers, and through small towns and cities to be reunited with his mother, who left him and his sister in pursuit of making a better life for them in America. Though the entire book is worth reading, the following excerpts from pages 99 and 100 are particularly compelling.

> "Blending in is critical. Migrants clip labels off clothes from Central America. Some buy Mexican clothes or ones sporting the name of a Mexican soccer team. Most ditch their backpacks shortly after entering Mexico. . . ."
>
> "He mutes his flat Central American accent and speaks softly and singsongy, like a Oaxacan. He asks for a short crop, military style. He pays with the last of his own money, careful not to call it pisto, as they do back home. That means alcohol up here."
>
> "He is mindful about what else he says. Migra agents trip people up by asking if the Mexican flag has five stars (the Honduran flag has, but the Mexican flag has none) or by demanding the name of the mortar used to make salsa (molcajete, a uniquely Mexican word) or inquiring how much someone weighs. If he replies in pounds, he is from Central America. In Mexico, people use kilograms. . . ."
>
> "Migra agents particularly like to test suspected migrants with words that have the same meaning in Mexico and in Central America and sound similar but are not exactly the same. . . ."

These passages describe what Enrique and others do to survive their life-threatening odyssey from Honduras and other Central American countries through Mexico to the United States. But what is particularly striking is Enrique's sophisticated problem solving, code switching, and adaptability that allows him to blend in with his surroundings and avoid being detected as a migrant. As educators, whether we're directly involved in assessing students' cognitive abilities or academic skills or serving as members of multidisciplinary teams who are responsible for making eligibility decisions, we must guard against having narrow conceptualizations of intelligence or achievement. In other words, intelligence is more than performance on standardized IQ and achievement tests. Children achieve in ways that cannot be captured on tests of basic reading and reading comprehension, spelling and written expression, or math computation and math problem solving. Intelligence is more than report card grades and scores on high-stakes (end-of-year) exams. And students who might not speak English fluently are no less intelligent than their peers who are native speakers. For children who have survived a months-long underground passage, often by themselves, their lower scores on commonly used IQ tests in American public schools do not define their intellectual capacity or capabilities. As reflected in the preceding excerpts, some students have already demonstrated highly developed, on-the-spot problem solving, critical thinking, reasoning, and analytical skills to overcome more than the educators who are making eligibility decisions have experienced.

Using an ecological perspective, consider this question from Kendi (2019): "What if different environments lead to different kinds of achievement rather than different levels of achievement?" (p. 103). In other words, what if students' varied experiences lead them to develop different strengths? What if their unique circumstances foster skills and abilities that are not present in their peers who have not been exposed to such situations? Despite their scores on standardized ability tests, which is only one type of intelligence, children such as Enrique who are cognizant of the words they use or their accents when in different countries are no less able than their peers whose experiences are more aligned to what standardized tests have been designed to measure. When schools and school systems broaden their view (conceptualization) of what it means to be gifted, including how they define and understand intelligence, they will increase access and opportunity to programs and environments that are beneficial to all children.

Directed by Robert Zemeckis and produced by Paramount Pictures, *Forrest Gump* is one of my favorite movies; I have seen it numerous times. There's a scene in which a school official (I'm pretty sure Mr. Haycock is the principal) uses a bell curve to show Mrs. Gump (Forrest's mother) where he scored on an IQ test. And because it was below 80, he would not be allowed to attend a public school in Alabama. Mrs. Gump, not willing to accept this answer, and in the words of Forrest, wanting him to " . . . have the finest education . . ." replied, "He's not going to some special school to learn how to retread tires!" (Barrett, 2020).

As educators, what can we learn from this brief interaction between two fictional characters? First, families (parents) often know their children better than professionals think they do and can be their most effective advocates. Next, IQ tests never tell the complete story of who children are—especially who they are capable of becoming and what they are capable of accomplishing. Third, and as one of my former Howard University school psychology graduate students has said, "Not all IQ tests are created equal" (Artis, personal communication, September 10, 2019). As you'll see later in this chapter, perhaps the school psychologist administered the wrong or a less valid test to a young Forrest.

As the movie unfolds, although Forrest may have performed below normative expectations on an IQ test, he was gifted in other ways. Albeit a cliche, every child is gifted. As educators and parents/guardians, our job is to help them identify their gifts. For Forrest, it was running. His speed could not be taught or developed through practice alone. And as he began to use his gift, it opened numerous opportunities for him that changed his life—and the course of history (Barrett, 2020).

Standardized Tests: A Lesson in Harm

In a 1971 California class action lawsuit, *Larry P. v. Riles*, Black students and their families challenged the use of IQ tests. To protect his privacy, *Larry P.* was the pseudonym given to the main plaintiff: one of six Black students who was labeled educable mentally retarded (EMR) by the San Francisco Unified School District and subsequently placed in special education. As I have been echoing throughout this book, more than 50 years ago, disproportionality existed in American public education. Specifically related to *Larry P.*, in 1968, nearly 60,000 students were eligible for special education services in the EMR category. And despite Black students making up less than 10% of the student body statewide, they were more than 25% of the students identified as EMR. Eventually, Black parents became upset that their children were "being called retarded when they didn't believe their children were retarded" (Baba, 2020).

Because disproportionality is an outcome (see Chapter 1), the higher rates of Black students being identified with EMR was the result of policies and practices in California public schools. Specifically, the identification of Black students as EMR and their placement in special education was due, at least in part, to the fact that they performed poorly on IQ tests compared with other student groups. In a landmark decision that continues to influence school-based practices today, the judge ruled that IQ tests were biased toward knowledge that Black students hadn't acquired. In other words, and as noted by Naglieri (personal communication, January 11, 2019), the knowledge (i.e., information) required to answer the verbal questions gets in the way of measuring the child's ability to think, which is the essence of intelligence. Like the instrument that was used with Larry P., traditional IQ tests tend to embed a great deal of culturally loaded and context-specific items such as defining words, describing how words are similar, and answering *where do you find* and *what do you do with* questions. And if children haven't been exposed to these vocabulary terms or had the opportunity to access experiences that give them the requisite background knowledge to answer the questions, they are placed at a significant disadvantage for responding correctly. For students such as Miguel when he was in second grade; for ELs who are in the early stages of acquiring English; or even for Emily (see Chapter 2), a White child who is living in LIEM, it is not surprising that their performance on verbal subtests negatively affects their overall score.

The tragedy of *Larry P.* extends beyond a child being misidentified with an educational disability. Having revealed his identity after the trial, Darryl Lester, the real Larry P., has spoken about his pain-filled life as a student and an adult. Mr. Lester, now in his 60s, recalls that he was "very good in math," but not reading. In fact, his difficulty with reading was quite specific and would likely lead to a determination of SLD, not EMR, by current evaluation and eligibility standards. It is an indictment of public education that Mr. Lester never received the help that he needed, which led to very poor reading skills even as an adult. To learn more about *Larry P.*, and to hear Mr. Lester as he describes his life and experiences, please listen to "The Miseducation of Larry P.," a podcast produced by RadioLab (Romney, Cusick, & Walters, 2019; see the *Resources for Professional Learning* section at the end of this chapter).

SOCIALLY JUST ASSESSMENT PRACTICES ARE MULTIMETHOD AND MULTISOURCE: IMPLICATIONS FOR GIFTED EVALUATIONS

Socially just assessment practices for gifted education are multimodal and multisource. They incorporate different types of information (e.g., standardized testing, interviews, rating scales) from a variety of sources, including the people who know children best (families, teachers, and, when appropriate, the students themselves), to ultimately make the most informed decisions. As it relates to Miguel, what would a socially just assessment approach entail? Based on Ford (2015), the following recommendations can help schools and school districts modify their policies and practices to achieve more equitable outcomes for students.

Consider Differences in Students and Their Backgrounds

Importantly, to consider differences in students and their backgrounds, educators must first acknowledge that these differences exist. Though a popular phrase, educators should not be *color blind*. While I was practicing as a school psychologist, most of the students in my schools or school district did not look like me. One day, after testing a first grader whose complexion was similar to mine, at least one of her classmates asked, "Is he your father?" Having overheard this question many times over the years, on this particular day it led me to consider the following: If children can admit to seeing color, why don't we (Barrett, 2020)? As educators, saying "I don't see color" isn't helpful, especially to the students and families who are negatively affected because of their color (race). And as noted by Kendi (2019), when individuals proudly proclaim that they are color blind, they also fail to see race and racism and cannot actively work against policies and practices that reinforce racial inequities.

One of the most significant practice-based implications of *Larry P.* was that Black students were no longer allowed to be assessed using IQ (cognitive ability) tests in California. In recent years, however, the California Association of School Psychologists (CASP) has advocated for lifting this ban, particularly because issues of disproportionality remain despite these instruments not being used with Black students. Though not perfect, cognitive ability tests have improved significantly since *Larry P.* For example, there are more reliable and valid nonverbal tools that allow clinicians to calculate the most appropriate IQ score based on the child's background characteristics. When compared across races, data from some of the commercially available tests have shown that individuals (children) perform in similar ways, which suggests less cultural bias in current instrumentation compared with what was available more than 50 years ago.

Given the technological advancements in assessment tools, considering differences in student backgrounds also means allowing practitioners (e.g., school psychologists) the professional flexibility and clinical judgment to use the most appropriate instrument, including those that yield nonverbal scores, to assess students' cognitive abilities. Albeit narrow, if a school or school district has determined that a child's IQ is the best indication of giftedness, the child should be evaluated using an instrument that is most likely to demonstrate their true functioning. Though cognitive ability tests are not inherently good or bad, they are better or worse for certain students. Whereas reliability refers to consistency over time and is a "yes/no" question, validity is a more nuanced question that's best answered as *valid for whom.* For example, if an IQ test demonstrates adequate test–retest reliability, when it's given to the same student within a few weeks, the scores should be similar. But despite being reliable (consistent), an IQ test that has significant cultural and language demands is likely to be less valid for a student who is new to the culture (e.g., Western culture) and in the early stages of learning the language (e.g., vocabulary), both of which are necessary for understanding and responding correctly to test items. As is discussed in Chapter 8 and has already been mentioned in Chapter 3 related to zero tolerance, when schools overemphasize using the same practices for all students, this is often inconsistent with social justice and does not lead to equitable outcomes.

Teachers Provide Input into the Assessment Process, but Are Not the Only Referral Sources

Like Miguel, many children spend their earliest years with differing levels of access to language (e.g., English), literacy, high-quality preschool, and educational experiences that influence their performance on academic (school-based) tasks. As a result, some students (e.g., Black and Latinx) and those from LIEM backgrounds are less likely than their White, Asian, and higher income peers to be referred for gifted consideration by their teachers. In response to fewer Black and Latinx students being referred for gifted consideration, and subsequently not being eligible for gifted programs, schools can increase access and opportunity to these programs by universally screening all students (e.g., in first or second grade) and also encouraging (empowering) families (e.g., parents, guardians) to refer their children for gifted consideration rather than relying on teachers to initiate the assessment and identification process.

RATING SCALES AND SOCIAL, EMOTIONAL, AND BEHAVIOR ASSESSMENT

Though standardized cognitive ability and achievement tests have their limitations, they are not the only tools that can negatively affect outcomes for REM students. This section focuses on the role of behavior rating scales in the assessment of ADHD, one of the most common childhood behavior conditions. Whether you're a graduate student preparing to serve children in schools or a teacher, administrator, or school-based mental health provider, you will or have already met a student with ADHD.

A Quick Overview of the Research: Rater Ethnicity, SES, Acculturation, and Direct Observations

Because behavior rating scales have been developed using large normative samples, provide national comparison data for children of similar age and gender, are convenient for respondents to complete quickly, and generally have strong psychometric properties (i.e., acceptable levels of reliability and validity), they are often used in the assessment process, especially in school-based evaluations for children who are suspected of having ADHD (Barkley, 2015). Numerous studies, however, have shown that there is a significant interaction between the race of the child and the race of the rater. For example, because teachers in U.S. public schools are predominantly White (and female), clinicians (e.g., school psychologists) should consider the degree to which rating scale data are a reflection of the rater (e.g., teacher) and not child characteristics.

Next, several studies have shown that SES can impact behavior ratings. When vignettes were used to describe children from various SES backgrounds, children from lower SES backgrounds (i.e., living in LIEM) typically received higher ratings of problem behaviors (Stevens, 1981).

Acculturation—the extent to and the process through which ethnic minorities (REM individuals) participate in the cultural traditions, values, beliefs, assumptions, and practices of the dominant society (Landrine & Klonoff, 1996)—can also help explain between-group differences as a function of culture rather than race or ethnicity. When they studied it in Hispanic (Latinx) teachers, de Ramirez and Shapiro (2005) found that acculturation accounted for group differences between Latinx children who received higher ADHD ratings and their White peers.

Last, although rating scale data have shown that Black children frequently received higher ratings (more indicative of problem behaviors) than their White peers, in the absence of direct observations, it is difficult to determine the extent to which Black children are indeed displaying more problem behaviors. Including direct observations of children in their natural settings (e.g., classroom) provides more information about the consistency between rating scale and observation data. Several studies have shown inconsistent results between rating scale and direct observation data. For example, Puig et al. (1999) reported that although Black children living in the United States received higher ratings than their Caribbean peers, Caribbean children were observed to display more problem behaviors. And although Asian and English children were rated to be equally hyperactive, Asian children were observed to be less hyperactive (Sonuga-Barke, Minocha, Taylor, & Sandberg, 1993).

In graduate school, my research was focused on the assessment practices that have historically led to the misidentification of Black boys with ADHD (Barrett & DuPaul, 2018). Based on the trends mentioned above, and using a sample of 123 Black and White mothers, we investigated the extent to which race, SES, and acculturation influenced their ratings of Black and White boys. Using a 2 × 2 factorial design (see Figure 5.1) that led to four possible combinations, Black and White mothers watched a 13-minute video of either a Black or White boy displaying behaviors that were indicative of ADHD. Because the videos were essentially identical (i.e., the target child was displaying more behaviors that were indicative of ADHD compared with the other children in the video), if their ratings on the ADHD Rating Scale (ARS-4, Home Version; DuPaul, Power, Anastopoulos, & Reid, 1998) were different, then race, SES, and/or acculturation were possible contributing factors to these outcomes.

In both areas (hyperactivity–impulsivity and inattention), and when rated by Black and White mothers, the Black boy was rated as displaying more of these behaviors than the White child. When rated by White mothers, the Black boy was perceived as less hyperactive–impulsive than the White boy. Additionally, parent race (i.e., being a Black or White mother) was the most significant predictor of child behavior ratings.

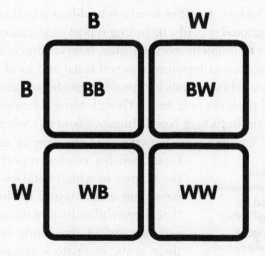

FIGURE 5.1. 2 × 2 factorial design (Barrett & DuPaul, 2018).

SOCIALLY JUST ASSESSMENT PRACTICES ARE MULTIMETHOD AND MULTISOURCE: IMPLICATIONS FOR SOCIAL, EMOTIONAL, AND BEHAVIOR DISORDERS AND SPECIAL EDUCATION EVALUATIONS

Whether in schools, clinics, or private practice settings, there is a range of assessment approaches used to evaluate students for ADHD and other social, emotional, and behavior conditions. Similar to the implications for gifted assessment, and as advocated by Barkley (2015), a multimethod and multisource paradigm provides teams with the necessary data to make the most informed decisions for children suspected of having these disorders. Specifically in schools, what does this evaluation approach include? Consistent with the RIOT (record review, interview, observation, testing) framework (Hosp, 2006), school psychologists and other school-based clinicians are encouraged to incorporate record reviews, interviews, observations, and standardized testing in the comprehensive assessment of social, emotional, and behavior disorders (e.g., ADHD). The following sections provide more information about these evaluation components and how they help school-based multidisciplinary teams make informed decisions for students. For a summary of each component and its unique contribution to comprehensive evaluations, see Appendix 5.1.

File Review

When discussing the video *The Unequal Opportunity Race* (Pinto, 2010) in Chapter 2, I noted that although children are displaying certain target behaviors that lead to referrals for additional support, these behaviors should not be viewed in isolation of their academic or educational history. In other words, school-based evaluators are encouraged to review students' educational records, including report card grades and comments, discipline history, referrals to problem-solving teams, intervention effectiveness, and performance on state (end-of-year criterion-referenced tests) and local assessments. A careful examination of report card comments can provide greater insight into children's day-to-day performance and progress over time. Though some schools might assign grades of Satisfactory (S), Outstanding (O), or Needs Improvement (N), what did teachers say (comment) about students' conduct over the course of the year or grading periods? Albeit

> **THINK ABOUT IT.** Think back to Chapter 4. How could implicit bias be related to report card comments? What are some ways to mitigate the potential consequences of implicit bias?

time-intensive, reading report card comments shows the degree to which children's behaviors have been consistent across years. In the absence of a pattern that shows difficulty sustaining attention, completing assignments, or frequently being off-task or out of their seats, evaluators are encouraged to consider how much a teacher's comments might reflect their expectations for a student's behavior, which might be unrealistic and developmentally inappropriate, rather than the child being evaluated. In sum, when report card comments for a student are significantly different from year to year, though it's possible that the child's behavior has changed, it's also worth considering the extent to which the teacher, their perceptions of the child, and what constitutes problem behavior have also changed.

Teacher, Family, and Student Interviews

As helpful as behavior rating scales, standardized tests, and report card grades are, children can never be fully captured by quantitative data (numbers). When the individuals who know children best are invited to meaningfully participate in the evaluation process by providing qualitative input about children's day-to-day functioning, including their strengths and weaknesses across settings, what is learned through these face-to-face interactions is invaluable. For students in elementary school, teacher interviews likely involve one teacher. But for children and adolescents in secondary school, asking multiple teachers, including those who teach their core (English, math, science, history) and elective (e.g., art, music, physical education) subjects to comment on their performance, yields insightful information about their functioning. See Appendix 5.2 for sample questions that can be used to facilitate teacher and family interviews.

As reported in Barrett and DuPaul (2018), parent race was the most significant predictor of child behavior ratings. For this reason, input from families is critical in developing a comprehensive understanding of children's functioning. Especially when teacher and family rating scale data are inconsistent, engaging both (all) parties in a collaborative process that allows them to explain or qualify their ratings is ultimately beneficial to the student. Rating scales include response choices such as *never, sometimes, often,* or *always*; but these qualifiers can also be interpreted differently by different raters. Further, what a family considers typical behavior based on their other children or family members could be different from a teacher's comparison with other students either in their class or whom they've taught throughout their career. In the absence of data that suggests rating scale information should be interpreted with caution, school-based clinicians are encouraged to assume that ratings of children's behavior are honest appraisals of the rater's perceptions. Especially when the evaluator and family don't share the same cultural background, interviews can be an effective way to learn about families' values, beliefs, cultural dynamics (i.e., the child's ecological system), and expectations related to child behavior that can assist with case formulation.

Whenever possible, interviewing students can also be helpful. Allowing students to share how they feel about their academic skills and social, emotional, and behavioral functioning provides useful data to inform not only eligibility decisions but also interventions. For students whose difficulties are internalizing in nature (e.g., anxiety, depression) and might not be as apparent to their families or teachers, interviews can be especially informative.

Classroom Observations

When evaluators work directly with children through one-on-one cognitive ability or academic achievement testing, they are seeing the child at one point in time and in an optimal learning environment (i.e., having individualized adult attention in a highly structured and distraction-free setting). Classroom observations, in addition to being required for special education evaluations (Individuals with Disabilities Education Act [IDEA], 2004), allow evaluators to see the child in comparison with their typically developing peers and assess the extent to which their social, emotional, or behavioral functioning could be affecting their ability to access the general education curriculum. A school social worker could collect frequency data on the number of times a student needed to be redirected or prompted after being off-task. A school counselor might record how often a student was out of their seat during a lesson or independent work activities. A school psychologist could compare a target student's behavior with that of a peer to determine the degree to which they were on- or off-task. Observation data could also be used to corroborate rating scale information, teacher and family interviews, and historical information gained through report card grades and comments. Even during synchronous distance-learning sessions, school psychologists and other evaluators can complete virtual classroom observations. Though not without their limitations, classroom observations allow educators to see students in their learning environment and the extent to which they are actively engaged in instruction and other academic activities.

Cognitive Ability
and Academic Achievement Assessments

Because it's important to rule out alternative explanations for children's performance (see Chapter 2), to the greatest extent possible, cognitive ability and academic achievement evaluations should also be included when students have been referred for social, emotional, or behavioral concerns. These data, for example, can show whether a child's inattentive or hyperactive–impulsive presentation is related to ADHD or is better explained by underlying academic (reading, writing, or math) difficulties. When school-based teams refer students for special education evaluations, as the process unfolds and data are collected, additional concerns and hypotheses can emerge. A student, for example, who is experiencing significant difficulty maintaining appropriate levels of attention during whole-group instruction or when completing independent assignments could show signs of a reading disability (e.g., dyslexia), which leads to being frustrated when presented with academic tasks. Though their behavior resembles ADHD, a more appropriate conclusion could be dyslexia; and if the child's reading weaknesses are intervened with, it's possible that their behavioral difficulties will dissipate.

CHAPTER SUMMARY

After many schools and school districts transitioned to distance learning in the spring of 2020, special education eligibility evaluations also changed. Though some school psychologists, educational diagnosticians, and speech pathologists completed standardized assessments in a virtual setting, this wasn't always possible for a variety of reasons, including students' access to adequate technology (e.g., devices) and Wi-Fi. But despite the inconveniences and frustrations of the pandemic, it also taught us valuable lessons. Across disciplines, educators creatively responded to the needs of their students and fulfilled their job responsibilities in ways they likely never contemplated. Specifically, school-based evaluators expanded their practice to use other types of data when students were unavailable for standardized assessments.

This chapter provided practical suggestions for thinking broadly about students. From the limited scope of standardized cognitive ability and achievement tests to the multiple factors that contribute to behavior rating scale outcomes, quantitative (numbers) data are incomplete and insufficient for making decisions that affect the educational trajectories of children. Alternatively, the most effective way to understand students is to implement multimethod and multisource assessment paradigms that gather different types of data (including qualitative information) and allow school-based evaluators to tell complete and accurate stories about children. And though some educators and clinicians already operate in this manner, from a systems perspective, all students will benefit when these approaches are written into policy expectations.

RESOURCES FOR PROFESSIONAL LEARNING

For more information about assessing and identifying students from REM backgrounds and those who are living in LIEM, please read the following publications:

Ford, D. Y., Harris, J. J., III, Tyson, C. A., & Trotman, M. F. (2002). Beyond deficit thinking: Providing access for gifted African American students. *Roeper Review*, 24(2), 52–58.

Ford, D. Y., Grantham, T. C., & Whiting, G. W. (2008). Culturally and linguistically diverse students in gifted education: Recruitment and retention issues. *Exceptional Children*, 74(3), 289–306.

Ford, D. Y. (2015). Multicultural issues: Recruiting and retaining Black and Hispanic students in gifted education: Equality versus equity schools. *Gifted Child Today, 38*(3), 187–191.

To learn more about *Larry P.*:

Romney, L., Cusick, R., & Walters, P. (Producers & Hosts). (2019, June 7). G: The miseducation of Larry P. [Audio podcast episode]. *Radiolab.* WNYC Studios. *https://radiolab.org/episodes/g-miseducation-larry-p.*

DISCUSSION QUESTIONS

1. In your respective role as a graduate student or educator, and based on Chapters 1 through 5, how can schools and school systems improve their practices to avoid what happened to Larry P.? Brainstorm possible solutions in the space below and share them with your classmates, colleagues, and respective leaders (e.g., principals, supervisors, directors).

   _____

   _____

   _____

2. Think about your school's or school system's approach to identifying students as being eligible to participate in the gifted program or other selective courses (e.g., honors, advanced placement, international baccalaureate). First, if your school or school system has a gifted program, how is giftedness defined? Next, what do your data indicate about students who are eligible to participate in the gifted program by race/ethnicity, limited English proficiency (i.e., ELs) and those who are living in LIEM? Last, after reading Chapter 5, what do you see as opportunities to improve processes and practices in this area? Brainstorm possible solutions in the space below and share them with your classmates, colleagues, and leaders (e.g., principals, supervisors, directors).

   _____

   _____

   _____

3. As a school-based evaluator, think about your approach to assessing students for gifted education and/or special education, including social, emotional, and behavioral conditions. What do your data indicate about students who are eligible for various special education categories by race/ethnicity or limited English proficiency (i.e., ELs) and those who are living in LIEM? After read-

ing Chapter 5, what do you think are the opportunities to improve processes and practices in these areas? Brainstorm possible solutions in the space below and share them with your classmates, colleagues, and leaders (e.g., principals, supervisors, directors).

_____

_____

_____

4. In your respective role as a graduate student or educator, and based on Chapters 1 through 5, how can schools and school systems improve their practices to avoid overlooking the strengths and abilities of children like Enrique?

_____

_____

_____

RIOT: Considerations and Contributions

The table below summarizes the benefits of using a multimethod and multisource assessment paradigm. As discussed earlier in the chapter, the RIOT (record review, interview, observation, testing) framework (Hosp, 2006) allows evaluators to contribute a variety of data to multidisciplinary teams that ultimately informs the most appropriate decisions for students' educational programming. In your practice, think about how you can incorporate each of these elements into your evaluations of students.

Evaluation component	Important considerations	Participants	Contribution to the evaluation
Record review	Evaluators should seek information about students, especially qualitative data (e.g., report card comments), that allows them to develop a more complete understanding of students over time.	Evaluator	Students' historical performance (e.g., report card grades and comments, performance on end-of-year standardized assessments, benchmark data, prior evaluations) informs the extent to which their presentation might be due to temporary circumstances (e.g., unfinished learning or opportunity gaps due to the COVID-19 pandemic) or long-standing academic difficulties that have been reported by multiple sources.
Interviews	Identify the individuals who know students well and can provide helpful information to inform educational decisions. For example, for elementary students suspected of a reading disability, it would be important to speak to their reading teacher. Additionally, it would be important to speak to those who teach the student other subjects to uncover potential similarities or differences in their behavior. Set aside sufficient time to speak to multiple individuals, including parents/guardians, teachers, and the students themselves.	Parents/guardians Current teachers Students	Interviews allow the individuals who know students the best and in different settings to provide valuable qualitative information about their day-to-day functioning over time. Additionally, they allow evaluators to learn important information about students that might not be observed in naturalistic observations.

(continued)

Evaluation component	Important considerations	Participants	Contribution to the evaluation
Observations	Identify settings (e.g., classes, task demands/assignments, times of day) in which the target behavior that led to a referral (e.g., inattention, aggression, frustration) is likely to occur. Additionally, it could be helpful to identify settings in which the target behavior is not likely to occur, which can inform intervention recommendations.	Students Teachers	When evaluators complete standardized assessments of students, given the artificial testing environment (e.g., a one-on-one setting completing highly structured tasks), the student's behavior might not resemble their typical functioning throughout the school day. Naturalistic observations allow evaluators to develop a more complete understanding of students, which is valuable for their overall impressions.
Testing	Evaluators, including central office administrators who make decisions about which instruments to purchase for their staff, should choose assessment tools that provide the best (most valid) data for the construct that is being measured (e.g., cognitive ability, academic achievement).	Students Evaluators	Valid data allow multidisciplinary teams to make the most informed decisions for students' educational programming.

Semistructured Family and Teacher Interview Form

Particularly suited for school psychologists, school counselors, and school social workers, the questions below can be used to gather qualitative information from teachers and families about their students and children. Consider asking these questions as part of comprehensive special education evaluations or during multidisciplinary problem-solving team meetings. Based on the responses, educators can ask follow-up questions to gather additional information, develop hypotheses, determine next steps in the intervention or evaluation process, or inform case formulation and conceptualization.

Questions about Student Behavior

1. Do you have any concerns about [student's] behavior? If so, please explain.

2. Over the course of the year, has [student's] behavior improved? If so, when? How?

3. Over the course of the year, has [student's] behavior become worse? If so, when? How?

4. Please describe [student's] typical behavior at home or in the classroom.

5. Do you think [student's] behavior explains their academic difficulties? For example, does [student's] misbehavior in the classroom prevent them from benefiting from academic instruction?

6. Do you think [student's] academic difficulties explain their behavior? For example, are [student's] behavioral difficulties a function of frustration with academic assignments?

7. How does [student] interact with other children and adults?

(continued)

Semistructured Family and Teacher Interview Form *(page 2 of 2)*

Questions about Academic Functioning

1. Do you have any concerns about [student's] academic performance and/or academic skills?

2. Over the course of the year, has [student's] academics become worse? If so, when? How?

3. Please report on [student's] homework (e.g., completion, accuracy).

4. Please report on [student's] classwork (e.g., completion, accuracy).

5. Does [student] try to complete their work? Do they put forth sufficient effort?

6. Does [student] participate in class?

7. Please report [student's] grades.

Subject	Quarter 1	Quarter 2	Quarter 3	Quarter 4
Math				
Reading				
Science				
Social Science				
Other academic subject				
Other academic subject				

General Questions

1. What are [student's] strengths?

2. What are the areas in which they need the most improvement?

3. Please provide any additional comments about [student].

CHAPTER 6

Social Justice Is About the Children, Families, Schools, and Communities We Serve

> **Seek to understand those whom we serve—their respective histories and current cultural, social, political, and economic realities.**
>
> *Social justice is being as concerned with what is happening around children as what is happening within them.*

LEARNING OUTCOMES

After reading this chapter, you should be able to . . .

1. Explain the importance of understanding students and families, including their respective histories, for achieving equitable outcomes for children in schools.
2. Explain what it means to make political statements on behalf of students and families.
3. Explain the significance of Black Lives Matter.[1]

CHAPTER OVERVIEW

Chapter 6 discusses the importance of educators understanding the students, families, and communities they serve. Using contemporary history (i.e., the polarizing 2016 presi-

---

[1] To learn more about Black Lives Matter, visit their website: *www.blacklivesmatter.com*.

dential election, the COVID-19 pandemic, and the murders of several African Americans throughout 2020) and an interdisciplinary example from a pediatrician who studies the relationship between police violence, equity, and child health outcomes, the chapter shows how children's behavior can be functionally related to, and sometimes better explained by, events that are happening around them (e.g., exposure to national crises or chronic community violence). Additionally, because Black Lives Matter and making political statements on behalf of children are frequently misunderstood and conflated with other ideas, the chapter includes a brief discussion of what these terms mean and how they are related to promoting equitable outcomes for students, families, schools, and communities.

INTRODUCTION

If you haven't already, as an educator you will meet families who seem resistant to your ideas and suggestions related to their children. For school psychologists, a family might disagree with your data about their child's disruptive behavior. For teachers, families might question your comments about their children's performance in reading. For school counselors and social workers, a conference with a student's family almost immediately becomes more about your training, experience, and credentials than about the emotional regulation skills that you are helping them develop. Having been in situations in which families not only had different opinions than I did about their children but also seemed defensive about what I was saying, over time I began to ask myself two questions. First, could their response have nothing to do with me and my skills as a school psychologist? Next, what if their response also has a lot less to do with their child than it does their own experiences in elementary, middle, or high school?

Very early in my career, I learned that schools are some of the most emotionally charged places anywhere. Whether you're a preschool teacher in the suburbs, a school psychologist serving an urban elementary school, a principal leading a rural middle school, or a school social worker supporting students at a large high school, what holds true across all of these levels and settings is that children and adolescents are at the epicenter. And not only are teachers passionate about their students and protective about what happens in their classrooms, but families are equally passionate and protective, too. Because all families want what's best for their children, it can be difficult for them to hear (and accept) things about their child that are less than what they dreamed or expected. When the reality of what's happening with students clashes with families' aspirations, at best disagreements are inevitable and at worst conflicts become contentious. Though not what educators look forward to, most also understand that people will occasionally disagree. But as I alluded to in the previous paragraph, sometimes the disagreements between schools and families have a lot less to do with the child than it does the adults (e.g., their parents, guardians).

UNDERSTANDING FAMILIES

Returning briefly to *The Unequal Opportunity Race* video (Pinto, 2010) that was discussed in Chapter 2, do you remember what was said about a high school student (e.g., a 10th grader) who was referred to the school psychologist, school counselor, dean, assistant principal, or principal based on repeatedly skipping classes and seeming uninterested in school? You can refer to pages 20–21, but I'll also remind you: The child could have shared additional information that helped staff members have a broader (more complete) understanding of the ecological system in which they were raised and its effect on their current behavior. The same holds true for families: Their presenting behavior, namely defensiveness and seemingly rejecting what educators have to say about their child, could be a function of their own experiences growing up and attending public schools in the United States.

Using Indigenous Americans as an example, the Indian Boarding School Era, which lasted from 1879 until 1978, was a period in which children were separated from their families and not allowed to speak their native languages or practice their culture. Known as *epistemicide*, or the removal of Indigenous Americans' knowledge of their culture and replacing it with forced assimilation into the mainstream culture, many Indigenous Americans were not allowed to engage in their traditional ceremonial practices until the Religious Freedom Act of 1978. Further, *deculturalization* was the educational process of destroying a people's culture and replacing it with a new (dominant) culture.

Why is this information important? What Indigenous Americans experienced throughout their history, including the recent past, likely affects how they engage with American public schools, including its educators. In light of the Indian Boarding School Era, which ended less than 50 years ago, as well as epistemicide and deculturalization, it is not surprising that Indigenous families might be skeptical of what the system (i.e., American public education) and those who represent it have to say about their children. For educators, rather than assuming that families' disagreement is synonymous with being dismissive of what you have to offer, an equally plausible alternative interpretation is that interacting with public schools can be traumatizing and retraumatizing based on their personal experience and collective history with American public schools.

Imagine attending a multidisciplinary team meeting with the parents of a child who has been experiencing significant academic difficulties for several years. After reviewing multiple data points, including progress monitoring information in reading and math, performance on end-of-year exams, and national benchmark assessments (e.g., Measures of Academic Progress), the team recommends the student for a comprehensive evaluation to determine whether they have an educational disability that warrants special education services. The school psychologist begins explaining the types of assessments that will be completed, and the meeting quickly becomes contentious. As the discussion unfolds, the parents say that although they were not involved in the *Larry P. v. Riles* class action lawsuit (see Chapter 4), one of the plaintiffs was a close family friend and they have read a lot about the potential limitations of standardized tests with Black children. Additionally, the mother shared that she experienced academic difficulties as a child, including being retained in elementary school. Although they understood the data that were presented and didn't necessarily disagree with the recommendation to have their child evaluated, based on what they'd heard about special education and IQ tests, they were not only nervous but uncertain whether this was the best decision for their child. Albeit for different reasons, like Indigenous Americans, Black families' responses to educators might have less to do with their children than with their own painful histories in school or those of their loved ones.

Do you remember *Enrique's Journey* (Nazario, 2006), mentioned in Chapter 5? Among other topics, the book shows the significance of systems in the lives of children and families who have emigrated to the United States. For example, while trying to get her "papers," Enrique's mother was taken advantage of several times, including paying people thousands of dollars only to be scammed on multiple occasions. And for Enrique and his fellow migrants, the police often took their money as bribes so they could continue on their journey to America. Why is this important? When families finally arrive in the United States and are sitting in our schools and attending our meetings, their skepticism about what we're offering is valid and informed by their previous experiences. In other words, schools and school-based professionals represent systems and authority figures—similar to the ones that previously took advantage of them. Though all families want what's best for their children, it's also possible that they don't trust what we're saying. Perhaps they're thinking, "Why should I trust this person who is saying that they're going to help me and my child? I've heard that before and it wasn't true." In light of this, not only should educators be patient with families by being mindful of what they have experienced, but they should also remember that more than being individual teachers, principals, or school psychologists, they also represent systems that haven't been fair to children and families (Barrett, 2022).

A POLARIZING 2016 PRESIDENTIAL CAMPAIGN

Consistent with an ecological perspective that's been reinforced throughout this book, this and the next sections offer examples of significant events in contemporary American history that could have differential effects on children and families.

Regardless of your preferences for the Democratic candidate, the Republican candidate, or neither candidate, the 2016 presidential election cycle was a polarizing event in American history. Though all elections can be challenging as contenders use advertisements and debates to make their case for why they should be elected, for a variety of reasons that are beyond the scope of this book, the days, weeks, and months leading up to the nomination and election of the 45th President of the United States were filled with angst and a range of other emotions. And because children live in an ecological system that extends beyond their families and schools, not only were they aware of these issues, but some were affected in more negative ways than others.

In the wake of the election, I was serving a high school with a significant number of students from REM backgrounds, particularly Central American adolescents. One of my students, whom I'd known since she was in third grade, asked to talk about how she and some of her classmates were feeling. Given the outcome of the election, a common theme that resonated among the students, especially those from REM backgrounds, was fear. Because immigration and immigration policies were intensely debated throughout the election cycle, in their minds they were no longer welcome in America. Like Miguel's friends (see Chapter 2), some even felt that they would be forced to leave their homes and return to their native countries. Whether they were right or wrong is less important than how they felt. And because these feelings were real for them, they became real for me as their school psychologist.

As emerging adults, this was likely their first time reckoning and wrestling with issues of racism and inclusion. Through a series of informal meetings, I listened to what was on their minds and validated their feelings of frustration, fear, disappointment, and perhaps hurt and anger. I shared with them some of the social justice resources that had been developed and compiled by NASP (see the *Resources for Professional Learning* section in Chapter 4) and supported them when they met with some of their teachers, assistant principals, and principal. As educators, and perhaps school-based mental health providers, our passion for children and commitment to serving them can lead us to thinking that we must solve (fix) whatever challenge they're facing. But when it comes to long-standing and complex issues related to justice and equity, quick fixes are both unreasonable and impossible. My professional experiences with the young ladies I mentioned above have led me to believe that they aren't looking for their teachers, principals, or anyone in their school to fix what is happening around them. More importantly, they want to be heard and understood.

THE CHALLENGE OF DIVERSITY

As much as schools and school districts highlight their diversity to attract highly qualified candidates to fill various positions, it is also true that serving students, families, and staff who represent a variety of races, ethnicities, and language backgrounds can also be challenging. Though slogans such as "Diversity is our strength" or "Join our team of educators who serve a diverse student body" make schools sound like great places to work (and they are), educators, especially school leaders, must also be willing to commit to doing the work that's necessary to truly make their schools safe, affirming, and welcoming environments for everyone. A natural consequence of increased diversity are the myriad issues facing children, families, and schools in their respective communities. For the REM students in my high school, the election was significant. And though this might not have been your experience, the ending of a decades-long war in Afghanistan could have been on the minds of the students and families in various parts of the country. After fleeing regions of the world that were highly volatile and embroiled in civil unrest, often with only the clothes on their backs and minimal financial resources, some students have arrived in U.S. public schools as refugees and asylum seekers who have also been exposed to unthinkable trauma. Whatever it may be for you and your students, as educators who are committed to social justice, it's imperative that we're actively curious about young people and their histories to understand them and more effectively meet their needs.

A TUMULTUOUS 2020

Regardless of racial, ethnic, or language background, most would agree that 2020 was a year that ranged from unexpected and inconvenient to frustrating and devastating. On one front was COVID-19—a pandemic that has claimed the lives of more than 1 million people in the United States (Centers for Disease Control and Prevention, 2022), upended the American public education system, including the mental health needs of students, families, and staff, and overwhelmed physicians, nurses, and other medical professionals. But intersecting with COVID-19 was the ongoing tragedy of racism, including a rise in hate crimes against Asian American and Pacific Islander (AAPI) individuals (NASP, 2021b).

The United States' ongoing struggle with racism led to the highly publicized murders of three unarmed Black individuals: Ahmaud Arbery in February 2020, Breonna Taylor in March 2020, and George Floyd in May 2020. Whether jogging in a Brunswick, Georgia, neighborhood, sleeping at home in Louisville, Kentucky, or handcuffed and lying face down in Minneapolis, Minnesota, the circumstances surrounding the deaths of two Black men and one Black woman were aired on local and national news outlets and shared widely across social media platforms. Though the murders—two of which were at the hands of police officers—were tragic enough, the timing of these events and potential impact on children were even more significant given where many of them were beginning in the spring of 2020 and through the remainder of the year: home. Because many schools were closed and children were engaged in virtual or distance learning activities, they were more likely to be exposed to the details of these incidents, including what wasn't developmentally appropriate. From incessantly watching the news or scrolling Facebook, Instagram, and Twitter themselves to overhearing what their older siblings, parents, aunts and uncles, grandparents, and other family members were discussing, children were aware of what was happening around them and could have been affected by these events.

Toward the end of the 2019–2020 school year, and for many students at various points during the 2020–2021 school year, virtual or distance learning quite literally meant that home was school and school was home. Consequently, the overlapping of these settings presented new challenges and opportunities for educators. Some teachers, for example, literally saw into the lives of their students in ways that they had never thought possible. Seeing their home environments and living conditions, including the number of people in their homes and the lack of privacy or a dedicated space for learning, gave them a profound appreciation for what children had been contending with to achieve and succeed in school and life.

A PEDIATRICIAN'S RESEARCH: POLICE, EQUITY, AND CHILD HEALTH

Related to the events that were just described, this section briefly reviews the work of Rhea Boyd, a Stanford University pediatrician who researches the effects of police violence on equity and child health outcomes.

Boyd, Ellison, and Horn (2016) discuss how exposure to differing levels of police violence can lead to different behavioral symptoms in children. One level involves children being exposed to racial profiling (e.g., young men who report frequent encounters with police), which leads to symptoms of anxiety and trauma. As mentioned in Chapter 4, when individuals from REM backgrounds, or those who have certain intersecting identities, are repeatedly assumed to be suspicious and subsequently questioned or searched by police, even if they aren't arrested, not only is stress a likely result of these encounters, but the cumulative impact can also lead to adverse adult health outcomes. On another level, children who witness or are directly exposed to police violence can experience symptoms of posttraumatic stress disorder (PTSD), substance abuse, depression, poor self-rated health, attentional impairment, poor school performance, and school suspensions and expulsions. Last, when children are vicariously exposed to police encounters through their caregivers (e.g., parents, guardians, or family members are incarcerated, injured, or killed as a result of a police encounter), not only is this traumatic to witness, but also families and communities are forced to function in the absence of their loved one's social and financial support (Boyd et al., 2016).

Understanding the students, families, schools, and communities that educators serve includes taking a broad perspective on what is happening around children as potential explanations for their behavior. What are children watching on television? What are they consuming on social media? What are they overhearing their families discuss? To use language from Chapter 2, perhaps the child's microsystem was disrupted because a family member died from complications associated with COVID-19. Maybe the child's microsystem was significantly altered because they witnessed a family member being detained and eventually arrested by law enforcement. Especially at a time (chronosystem) in which America was reckoning with issues of race and racism in ways that children have potentially never experienced, their aggressive, irritable, or hyperactive behaviors may resemble various educational disabilities (e.g., other health impairment, emotional disability), but a social justice orientation challenges educators to consider whether identifying them as needing special education services is the most appropriate decision given what was happening around them. In other words, social justice is being as concerned with what is happening around children as what is happening within them.

POLITICAL AND PARTISAN

Using a social justice orientation, this section clarifies what is meant by making political statements on behalf of children and families, followed by a brief discussion of Black Lives Matter.

When presenting to various audiences, in addition to the learner objectives for a particular session, I always have two purposes. The first is to encourage people. Whether graduate students, school psychologists or other school-based mental health providers, teachers and principals, or central office administrators, I never want to be overly critical of anyone's practices because everyone is learning and growing, including me. Rather, I want to encourage educators in their service to children, families, schools, and communities. Specifically related to social justice, my second purpose is to equip people with information and inspire (motivate) them to challenge systems. What is meant by challenging systems? It is a word that can evoke feelings and images of being confrontational, but challenging systems isn't necessarily about being combative. By using data to inform your position, challenging systems could begin with asking questions and engaging in an open dialogue with leaders and policymakers. For example, when speaking to a building principal, you might say something like, "Based on the data that were shared at our last few PBIS meetings, we seem to be suspending students with disabilities more than other groups. I have some thoughts about this, but I would like to know what you think could be leading to these outcomes." Or perhaps you're meeting with a school board member about the school system's proposed redistricting plan. You might say, for example, "Ms. Greene, I've been following the plans to modify the school zone boundaries in the eastern area of the district. I also realized that the plan you put forth will place significantly more English learners and students who qualify for free- or reduced-price lunches in a single school. I have some ideas, but I'm curious about your thoughts on the matter. Do you think that this is beneficial to the students who would be attending this school?" Though challenging systems can involve asking questions, it also can include more direct actions, including writing op-eds for local news outlets or offering public comments at school board and local government meetings.

Challenging systems also includes making political statements that target inequitable outcomes on behalf of children and families. At a time in which our local and national discourses are polarized and people are more likely to only engage with those who share their beliefs and values, it's important that we have a common understanding of what is meant by making political statements on behalf of children and families. Most importantly, political statements about inequities that affect our students and families are not synonymous with partisan politics or partisan affiliation. Making political statements does not depend on being a registered Democrat, voting for a Republican candidate, or being an Independent or Libertarian. In virtually every school, school district, department, or graduate program, there are people who subscribe to different partisan positions ranging from very liberal to extremely conservative. Though we might not always agree, we can work together as professionals who are committed to what's in the best interest of children. Moreover, a single party doesn't have all of the answers to the crises facing American public education. As a result, more than focusing on who is occupying school board seats; more than who's leading our town, city, or county governments; more than who controls the state legislature; and more than who is sitting in the Executive, Legislative, or Judicial branches, our focus must be on the policies that politicians and other policymakers put forth. Specifically, are they consistent with socially just principles to achieve equitable outcomes for students, families, schools, and communities? How are they increasing access and opportunity? What are the implications for school funding? Is more attention being given to placing law enforcement in schools at the expense of hiring mental health providers? As is discussed further in Chapter 8, making political statements that challenge inequitable outcomes for children and families is more about policy than it is about politicians. Making political statements that challenge inequitable outcomes for children and families is more about checks and balances on power and privilege than it is the people we are challenging. Making political statements that challenge inequitable outcomes for children and families is about systems and structures, which is the essence of social justice.

Though not always easy, challenging systems and making political statements on behalf of children are not only necessary actions to shift the systems and structures that lead to disparate outcomes for students and families, but they also represent our moral and ethical responsibility as educators who are committed to social justice. Although we can't control what people, including politicians and policymakers, do, we can (must) tell them when their actions and proposals are harmful. When exposing ineffective policies and practices that reinforce inequities, people in positions of power don't always change what they're doing—at least not immediately. What should we do? Tell them anyway. What if they ignore us? Tell them anyway. What if it seems to not be working? Tell them anyway. Though change is the goal, as educators, our job is to uncover what's inherently wrong in and with our systems. And after these things have been revealed, we hold people accountable for what they can no longer say they did not know (Barrett, 2021b). Whether you're working with your school or school district to rewrite policies that have led to inequities, partnering with community organizations to hold schools accountable for how their practices affect children and families, or are actively involved in your state or national professional associations by advocating for more socially just legislation, these are some of the necessary and important ways that educators challenge systems and make political statements on behalf of children and families.

BLACK LIVES MATTER

In response to the acquittal of George Zimmerman for the February 2012 murder of Trayvon Martin, an unarmed Black teenager in Sanford, Florida, Alicia Garza, Patrisse Cullors, and Opal Tometi founded Black Lives Matter, "a Black-centered political will and movement building project" (Black Lives Matter, n.d., para. 1). As a movement, Black Lives Matter protests, marches, and demonstrations bring attention to long-standing racism and injustice that requires the attention of lawmakers and policymakers. Depending on what you've heard about Black Lives Matter, you might have strong opinions about the organization and its policy positions. Because my purpose isn't to defend Black Lives Matter as an entity, I encourage you to learn more about them by reading their materials at *www. blacklivesmatter.com* and watching a short video that features its founders at the following link: *https://www.ted.com/talks/alicia_garza_patrisse_cullors_and_opal_tometi_ an_interview_with_the_founders_of_black_lives_matter?referrer=playlist-talks_to_ help_you_understand_r.* I do, however, want you to read the following short story.

Black Lives Matter and All Lives Matter through the Lens of Happy Birthday

While driving on I-95 on August 6, 2016, these thoughts occurred to me: Everyone has a birthday. And because each person's birthday is special, it should be celebrated. But consider this: How would you feel if it was your birthday but a party was thrown for everyone at your school, church, place of employment, or even in your family? How would you feel if everyone received presents on your birthday? This is the difficulty with pitting All Lives Matter against Black Lives Matter. Black Lives Matter was never intended to reduce the significance of all lives. As everyone's birthday is special, significant, meaningful, and deserves to be celebrated exclusively, it is also fitting to only acknowledge the person whose birthday it actually is. For example, "Today is John's birthday and we will celebrate him with a song and gifts." Or, "Today is Jane's birthday and we will celebrate her with dinner and gifts." Rather than saying, "Happy Birthday to everyone!" when in fact it's only John's or Jane's birthday today, we will only honor John or Jane because they matter most for this moment. When it's your birthday, we'll be sure to only highlight and honor you.

Though I recognize that a simple analogy such as this one doesn't fully capture the complexity and significance of Black Lives Matter and what it represents, I wanted to introduce educators to the idea that Black lives are worthy of value and specific attention because of what is and has been happening to Black people, including children. In other words, Black Lives Matter does not mean, and has never meant, that all lives don't matter. Black Lives Matter does not mean, and has never meant, that Black lives are more important than others' lives or all lives. And although birthdays are joyous occasions that should be celebrated, the point still stands: They are meant to focus on the person who matters most for that moment. When it's your best friend's, husband's, wife's, partner's, or child's birthday, does it mean that they are more important than you? No. It simply means that they are worthy of special, even singular acknowledgment because it's their birthday. Because of how Black people in America have been treated, including being denied meaningful access and opportunity to achieve their dreams, Black Lives Matter is an attempt to highlight, on a systems level, that they are worthy of the same value, rights, protection, access, and opportunity that has been afforded to others' lives.

Though 45 years before Black Lives Matter began, the following excerpt is taken from a 1967 interview with Martin Luther King, Jr., and underscores the importance of focusing on Black lives. Essentially, when asked by a reporter why Negroes (as Black people were referred to at the time) haven't been able to make the same progress as other immigrants, this was Dr. King's response:

> White America must see that no other ethnic group has been a slave on American soil. That is one thing that other immigrant groups haven't had to face. The other thing is that the color became a stigma. American society made the Negro's color a stigma. America freed the slaves in 1863 through the Emancipation Proclamation of Abraham Lincoln; but gave the slaves no land or nothing in reality . . . to get started on. At the same time, America was giving away millions of acres of land in the West and the Midwest, which meant that there was a willingness to give the White peasants from Europe an economic base. And yet it refused to give its Black peasants from Africa, who came here involuntarily, in chains, and had worked free for 244 years any kind of economic base. And so, emancipation for the Negro, was really freedom to hunger. It was freedom to the winds and rains of heaven. It was freedom without food to eat or land to cultivate; and therefore, it was freedom and famine at the same time. And when White Americans tell the Negro to lift himself by his own bootstraps, they don't look over the legacy of slavery and segregation. I believe we ought to do all we can and seek to lift ourselves by our own bootstraps; but it's a cruel jest to say to a bootless man that he ought to lift himself by his own bootstraps. And many Negros, by the thousands and millions, have been left bootless as a result of all of these years of oppression and as a result of a society that deliberately made his color a stigma and something worthless and degrading. (Hallmark Media 254, 2018, 00:15–2:04)

CHAPTER SUMMARY

As I often share with my graduate students and early career professionals, relationships are foundational to our success and effectiveness as educators. And developing relationships begins with getting to know the students and families we serve. Though national events or international crises might not have a particular impact based on your own intersecting identities (see Chapter 4), if they are significant to your students and families, they should become a priority. The relationships that we develop with students and families should also sensitize us to what they have experienced in their respective histories. Such perspective, including what children have been exposed to, is invaluable to culturally responsive practices and making the most appropriate educational decisions for children. Coupled with clarifying the difference between political and partisan affiliation and what Black Lives Matter means in principle, this chapter encouraged educators to make political statements that target inequities on behalf of children and families. As an extension of the content in Chapter 6, the next chapter discusses the importance of educators intentionally empowering families to be their children's most informed and effective advocates, including specific examples for school-based practice.

DISCUSSION QUESTIONS

1. As a graduate student or educator, what are some ways that you can grow in your understanding of the students and families you serve?

2. Thinking of the students and families attending your school(s), what are some current or historical events that have likely affected them negatively? In your respective role, how can you advocate for services and supports that are responsive to their needs?

3. Although challenging systems and making political statements that challenge inequitable outcomes for students and families isn't easy, what is one action that you can take in this area to advance socially just practices in schools and school systems?

4. Read the section Black Lives Matter and All Lives Matter through the Lens of Happy Birthday. What are your thoughts and impressions about this analogy?

What questions do you have about Black Lives Matter? Discuss your ideas and questions with a classmate or colleague.

_____

_____

_____

5. Read the excerpt from a 1967 interview with Dr. King. What are your thoughts and impressions? Discuss your ideas with a classmate or colleague.

_____

_____

_____

CHAPTER 7

Social Justice Is About Empowering Families

Intentionally empower families by establishing meaningful home–school collaborative relationships.

Knowledge is power, but access to information is key.

LEARNING OUTCOMES

After reading this chapter, you should be able to . . .

1. Explain the importance of educators empowering families to achieve equitable outcomes for students in schools.
2. Identify specific ways that educators can intentionally empower families by providing access to information and creating inclusive school environments.
3. Explain the differences between diversity, inclusion, and equity.
4. Explain how diversity, inclusion, and equity are related to socially just practices that lead to equitable outcomes for children and families.

CHAPTER OVERVIEW

Central to social justice, including NASP's (2017) definition, is empowering families to be their children's most informed and effective advocates. Chapter 6 focused on educators knowing the students and families they serve, and this chapter discusses the importance of educators intentionally creating environments that are genuinely inclusive for families. Anecdotes to explain the differences between diversity, inclusion, and equity are included.

INTRODUCTION

Several years ago, my wife and I attended Back-to-School Night for my stepson. At the time, he was in high school, and there was a session in the school's career center. After a staff member explained the different diplomas that students could earn (e.g., standard, advanced studies), a father asked a clarifying question. Essentially, he wanted to know the requirements for his child to receive a certain diploma. And though the question might not have been asked in the clearest or most succinct manner, I was disappointed in the staff member's response. I felt that she dismissed the father's question and didn't answer it, which left him feeling even more confused. Because I had been a school psychologist in a neighboring school division for close to a decade, I understood what the father was asking, and the staff member should have, too. Not having children of my own, this was the first time that I experienced what schools can feel like for those who are unfamiliar with our terminology, policies, and practices. In a very real way, watching this unfold, quite literally before my eyes, taught me a lot about what schools can and should do for families.

KNOWLEDGE AND ACCESS

Many of us have likely heard the phrase *knowledge is power*. And although this is true, through the lens of social justice, something essential precedes knowledge. In other words, what leads to knowledge? As stated in Chapter 2, central to social justice are issues of access and opportunity. Therefore, it could be said that *knowledge is power, but access to information is key*. Although knowledge (information) is important, being able to access knowledge (having the key that makes it available) opens the door to information.

As educators, we have read numerous articles and books or seen firsthand the benefits of meaningful family engagement. When schools and families work together as partners in young people's education, children succeed. As it relates to knowledge being power, the more information that families have—the more they know about their children's schools and understand the educational system—the more equipped and prepared they will be to support their children's academic, social, emotional, and behavioral success.

Returning to my stepson's Back-to-School Night, what did I learn as I watched a father's question go unanswered? First, schools can be unnecessarily complicated and confusing. The language and terms that we use, though familiar to us, are often foreign to noneducators. It is easy to get lost in the alphabet soup of jargon that is almost second nature to school-based professionals: IEPs (individualized education programs), BIPs (behavior intervention plans), and FBAs; IDEA (Individuals with Disabilities Education Act), 504 (Section 504 plans based on the Americans with Disabilities Act), SLD (specific learning disability), OHI (other health impairment), and ED (emotional disability); CST (Child Study Team), SST (Student Support Team), or MDR (Manifestation Determination Review) meetings. Next, understanding the complexity of schools, including special education terminology and processes, can be difficult. In fact, this could be one reason that families hire advocates—someone who understands the language of the education system and can support (come alongside) them as they're navigating uncertain territory on behalf of their children. I have even seen families who have advanced degrees and are high-performing professionals in their respective industries struggle to understand the nuances of what schools are proposing for their children. Because of these complexities, what can schools do to be more inclusive and responsive to families?

SCHOOLS AND POWER

Inherent in American public education is power. If knowledge (information) is power, then schools have a great deal of both information and power. From the staff who have been empowered to propose or make decisions for children to the systems and policies that govern schools, both are powerful entities. Whether teachers, principals, or school-based mental health providers, staff members often know more about the education system, which not only makes them more powerful but also places families at an unfair disadvantage. Further, schools are powerful because their decisions can alter the educational path and life trajectories of students (see Chapter 5 for a discussion of *Larry P. v. Riles*). But though they are powerful, schools and educators who are committed to social justice empower families by partnering with them and sharing their power. Quite simply, they intentionally and preemptively, consciously and proactively, equip families with information so that they can be their children's most informed and effective advocates.

If you are reading this book as a parent, you likely know that children don't come with instructions or a user's manual. Since the beginning of time, mothers and fathers, aunts and uncles, grandmothers and grandfathers, adoptive and foster parents, cousins, older siblings, and anyone fortunate enough to nurture a child have done the best they could to make decisions that are in the best interest of their health, happiness, and safety. Whereas some read books, others seek advice from pediatricians. Some talk to faith leaders and others consult close friends and loved ones. But despite attending parenting classes, watching YouTube videos featuring parenting and child development experts, or having degrees in psychology and education, to some extent, trial and error is a part of everyone's parenting journey.

Because of these things, when schools share power, though never easy, navigating the education system becomes easier for families. Think about Mr. and Mrs. Hernandez, whom we met in Chapter 2. As immigrants from El Salvador, not only were they unfamiliar with English, but they were even more intimidated by many American customs, including its public school system. Although they had been living in Virginia for 6 years, how might they have felt when Miguel, their first child, was entering kindergarten? Did they know about the healthy habits, structures, and routines to facilitate his success in school? Because they weren't teachers yet, how would they learn about the curriculum and other activities that could prepare him for school before he started school? Like other families living in LIEM, Mr. and Mrs. Hernandez couldn't afford to enroll Miguel in a high-quality preschool, which meant that he wasn't exposed to some of the kindergarten readiness skills (e.g., letters, numbers, colors, shapes) and activities (e.g., circle time, playing games that required sharing and taking turns) as his peers.

As mentioned in Chapter 6, when schools invest time getting to know their families, they can also meet their needs more effectively. The following ideas are suggestions for how schools can intentionally provide access to information. And though some schools and educators are already engaged in these activities, it's important that we remind ourselves of creative ways to empower families.

Invite

Schools can intentionally invite the families who are living in their neighborhoods and attendance zones to a series of informational sessions to educate them about the school. Whether they are new parents, as Mr. and Mrs. Hernandez once were, or returning families, because of the complexities of schools and their ever-changing practices, these annual events can be beneficial. From meeting the principal and other administrators, teachers, and support staff (e.g., school nurses, secretaries, and mental health providers) to explaining how they can access the services that are available to them and their children (e.g., free or reduced-price lunch, after-school programs, homework assistance), schools can proactively empower their families by giving them access to information.

Partner

In addition to inviting families, schools should partner with community and faith-based organizations—institutions that have significant relational currency and cultural capital with families. In fact, using a social justice orientation, partnering with families is likely more effective than inviting them. Because social justice is fundamentally about systems, it's important that schools and school districts take responsibility for engaging in outreach efforts by meeting families where they are rather than always expecting families to meet them in unfamiliar and potentially oppressive or traumatizing spaces (see Chapter 6). Whether it involves sponsoring back-to-school fairs and other events at churches, mosques, and temples or periodically visiting these and other organizations to share resources about school, families are more likely to access information when it is accessible. Making information accessible includes avoiding words and terms that are not meaningful or understandable to the family, but it also includes making information available. When schools think about the places that their families frequent (e.g., faith-based organizations, community centers, grocery stores, sports facilities, parks, recreation centers, barber shops, nail salons) and develop creative ways to make resources available in these settings, families can access information.

Especially for families whose native language isn't English or whose cultures have different values than American or Western belief systems, it's important to partner with cultural brokers (e.g., faith leaders, parent or family liaisons) and community organizations. As mentioned in Chapter 3, culturally responsive practice is an ongoing and dynamic process that involves schools modifying and adjusting their behaviors (approaches) as they continually learn about their students and families. Investing time and resources to listen to and learn from people who know and understand your students and families will be time well spent to inform your programming and ensure a welcoming and inclusive environment. Though not comprehensive, the following questions can be important for schools to ask and reflect upon so they are better prepared to meet the needs of their students and families:

1. Which holidays are celebrated by your students and families?
2. How is their education system similar to, or different from, the American public school system?
3. For students who have recently emigrated to the United States, when did their school year begin? When did it end? How long was their school day? Did they attend school daily?
4. What are families' perspectives on education and authority figures? How likely are they to disagree with what schools and educators recommend concerning their children?
5. Are there dietary needs (e.g., kosher, halal) that schools should be aware of to help students feel more comfortable?

Share Decision-Making Power

After children are enrolled in school, schools share decision-making power by not unfairly influencing families to do what the schools feel is best for their children. As a school psychologist, I have participated in numerous multidisciplinary and problem-solving team meetings in which educators and families discussed options for a child. And because of the nature of schools and laws governing education, in almost all scenarios, the family's consent was required before moving forward. For example, a multidisciplinary team might recommend referring a student for a special education evaluation because it suspects the child has an educational disability. But before the various assessments begin, the parent (guardian) must provide their written (signed) consent. And though this is not always specified, it is best practice to assume that consent also needs to be *informed consent*. A term that is commonly used in research settings, informed consent means that a researcher has explained all of the risks and benefits associated with a particular study, including the details surrounding a potential participant's involvement, before they agree to participate (sign consent).

In schools, the same approach should be followed for decisions related to special education, including evaluations, eligibility, IEP services, and placement in more restrictive settings. First, school-based teams should explain the process to families in terms they can understand (using accessible language), including having interpreters present when necessary. Informed consent also involves educators being transparent about the purpose of the evaluations: to determine whether a student has an educational disability. Rather than framing the evaluation process using euphemistic phrases such as "Your child might receive extra help" or "Your child might be allowed to get additional support," it's important for school-based professionals to be honest with families by telling them the potential outcome: "Your child might have an educational disability." Receiving extra help or additional support is both secondary to and contingent upon the student qualifying for a disability. And if it is known at the time of the referral, these discussions should also include naming the area(s) of suspected disability (e.g., autism, intellectual disability, emotional disability). If schools don't tell families the purpose of the evaluations, this might not be consistent with the spirit of informed consent. If schools share, or don't share, information to influence a family's thinking and ultimately their decision, this might also be inconsistent with the intent of informed consent. After giving families information, including the implications of their choices, schools allow them to make the decisions that they feel are in the best interest of their child. And if they disagree with our recommendations, not only is this OK, but it shows that they have listened to our perspective and are exercising their parental rights to choose another option.

Be Flexible

When sharing power with families, educators also establish school communities and cultures that are flexible enough to meet their needs. For example, when are meetings scheduled? Are families able to attend meetings that are held earlier or later in the school day? To ensure informed consent, are interpreters present for these meetings? To the greatest extent possible, is relevant information provided to families in their native language? And although this is not always considered, who speaks first in meetings? How much time are families given to share their perspectives about their children? I've attended many meetings in which educators (e.g., teachers, school-based mental health providers, administrators) share a lot of information, sometimes to the point of overwhelming the family, before they are given an opportunity to contribute. In a meeting that might be scheduled for 60 minutes, it feels like the school spends at least the first 30 minutes telling the family about their concerns and the student's weaknesses before asking, "Do you have anything that you would like to share with us? How are things going at home?" Though unintentional, this meeting format can communicate to the family that what they have to share is less important or less valued by the school. It could feel like the school already knows what they want to do for the child and isn't genuinely interested in hearing families' thoughts, ideas, and perspectives on their learning or social, emotional, and behavioral functioning.

As an alternative, I observed a school psychologist who is also a bilingual Spanish speaker. She is an experienced and outstanding practitioner for many reasons, including her clinical skills in assessment and interpreting evaluation data, but I have been most impressed with her ability to connect to students and families. During an eligibility meeting, this psychologist did something that was subtle yet exceptional. When summarizing the results of her evaluation, she spoke in Spanish first. She intentionally spoke to the mother before speaking to the school-based team. A relatively minor adjustment in practice, this decision spoke volumes of her respect for the family and was likely deeply appreciated by the mother. In telling me more about this aspect of her practice, the psychologist said that families feel empowered to comment on the assessment results or provide examples that are usually helpful for the team. After asking their permission, she includes the family's input when reporting her results in English. Rather than speaking to the team in English, followed by Spanish, and asking if they have any additional input, speaking to the family first, and in their native language, is likely to elicit more feedback and active engagement.

Involve

Using an ecological perspective (see Chapter 2), families and schools represent a mesosystem (the combination of two microsystems) that influences children's growth and development. And because families and schools are likely two of the most significant microsystems (settings) in children's lives, strong collaborative partnerships that reflect shared responsibility for their success are essential (Blandin, 2017). In some ways, equipping families with information (knowledge) so they are more informed (empowered) to be their children's most effective advocates is a moral and ethical imperative. Schools, however, are also required to engage in these practices in accordance with federal policies, whether through the IDEA (2004), No Child Left Behind (2001), or the United States Congress's reauthorization of the Elementary and Secondary Education Act, also known as the Every Student Succeeds Act (ESSA; 2015), which compels schools to provide families with opportunities to be involved in their child's education. For more than two decades, family involvement has been reflected in the laws governing American public education.

Before Mr. and Mrs. Hernandez, described in Chapter 2, earned their undergraduate and graduate degrees, their jobs prevented them from attending meetings and activities at Miguel's school during the school day. As a result, some of their children's teachers assumed that they were uninterested in their educational success. Similarly, Ms. Jones, Emily's mother (see Chapter 2), worked in a factory and couldn't afford to leave for school-based meetings between 8:00 A.M. and 3:00 P.M. In Chapter 3, we discussed the word gap (Hart & Risley, 1995) and CALP (Cummins, 1979) as examples of deficit orientations to children's home language practices. When these ideologies exist in schools, not only are they detrimental to students, but they also impede collaborative interactions with families (Blandin, 2017). Especially when educators and families don't share similar racial, ethnic, SES, or language backgrounds, consistent with becoming culturally responsive, educators must continually develop their skills to effectively engage (invite) and partner with families so these differences don't become barriers to beneficial outcomes for students.

When schools intentionally engage families as partners in their children's education, families' self-efficacy (the belief that they can successfully accomplish a task) increases, which leads to further participation. For example, when educators incorporate translanguaging (García, 2009) and other culturally responsive instructional approaches, families are respected, encouraged, and empowered because their cultural backgrounds are valued and seen as assets that are beneficial to children's success. Notably, more than demographic factors such as race, ethnicity, SES, or language background, how schools engage families is more predictive and effective for promoting family involvement (Eccles & Harold, 1993; Overstreet, Devine, Bevans, & Efreon, 2005). Relatedly, the mesosystem, or the quality of the relationship between families and schools, is a better prediction of students' academic success than any single demographic factor (Blandin, 2017).

DIVERSITY, INCLUSION, AND EQUITY

Whether in psychology, education, or other fields, contemporary discourse has a lot to say about diversity, inclusion, and equity. Many organizations, including schools, use the acronym DEI. This book, however, discusses diversity, followed by inclusion, and then equity because the concepts build on one another. When schools are committed to empowering families, they must be cognizant of issues related to diversity, inclusion, and equity. The last section of the chapter explores how these terms are relevant to socially just practices in schools.

Diversity

As mentioned in Chapter 3, diversity is representation. For example, people from different races and ethnicities compose a group. Inclusion, however, indicates that beyond their representation, everyone in a diverse group (not diverse people; see Chapter 3) is empowered to meaningfully participate in an organization or activity. As it relates to diversity and inclusion, consider this: We can quantify how many people represent various groups (e.g., race, ethnicity, gender, languages spoken, ages), but we can't simply quantify people's experiences in our respective organizations (e.g., schools, school systems, graduate programs; Barrett, 2021b). Instead, we must ask the degree to which (how much) they feel meaningfully included—not just represented—in our cultures, activities, organizations, policies, and practices. And when we ask them, we must listen to what they say and make the necessary changes if some don't feel included. Whereas diversity is quantitative, inclusion is qualitative (Barrett, 2021b).

> **THINK ABOUT IT. What are your impressions, thoughts, and reactions to this description of diversity? Discuss your answers with your classmates or colleagues.**

Inclusion

A Lesson from a Mosque

A few years ago, I attended a funeral for a friend's mother. My friend and her family are Muslim. Because it was my first time in a mosque and attending a Muslim service, I didn't know what to do or what to expect. Shortly after I arrived, I saw another friend, and he made sure that I was included. How? He sat with me. He explained what was happening. He prepared me for what was coming next. Although the environment and traditions were very different from my Protestant upbringing, his sensitivity and attentiveness helped me to feel genuinely welcomed and comfortable. Yes, there were many Black people present, but I was different. And because I was different, my friend made sure that I wasn't left alone or made to feel out of place. On that Friday morning, I went to support my friend but experienced so much more: authentic inclusion through meaningful participation. And this is what I learned: Regardless of the setting, especially schools with students, families, and staff from a variety of cultural and linguistic backgrounds, everyone from a certain race is not the same. And perhaps most importantly, inclusion must be intentional (Barrett, 2021b).

> **THINK ABOUT IT. What are your impressions, thoughts, and reactions to this short story about inclusion? Discuss your answers with your classmates or colleagues.**

If inclusion is the extent to which a person or group of people can meaningfully participate in an organization or activity, it is also one way to measure how much we value others or are valued by others. In other words, when we don't feel that we're a part of something or that our absence would be inconsequential, we question the degree to which we are appreciated (Barrett, 2021b). Though exclusion (the opposite of inclusion) is a logical word choice to describe how people feel when they aren't included, in the words of Bellen Woodard,[1] the world's first Crayon Activist, *disincluded* might be more appropriate. In other words, it could feel like rejection, which leads to disengagement. When people show up but feel unseen, they stop showing up. Who wants to be present, yet ignored? To avoid the disappointment and discomfort of being repeatedly overlooked, they stop participating. As mentioned earlier in this chapter, whether in relationships, leading people and organizations, or serving children and families, inclusion must be intentional. We won't stumble upon it; we must actively pursue it. Especially for administrators, are there people in your school, on your staff, or in your department who don't participate as much as others? If so, don't just ask yourself, but ask them why. It's possible they don't feel that they can contribute in a meaningful way. Last, those whom we fail to include ultimately disengage. And although diversity is necessary, it is not sufficient to fully achieve inclusive environments. Nevertheless, a diverse (broadly defined) team can help highlight a variety of issues (i.e., blind spots) that must be addressed to create and maintain school and organizational cultures that are more than multicultural in their makeup but truly inclusive in their practices (Barrett, 2021b).

A Metaphor from Special Education

As previously stated, inclusion must be intentional. We won't stumble upon it but must actively pursue it. When, for example, schools adopt an inclusive framework to allow students with disabilities to be a part of the same activities and have the same experiences as their peers without disabilities, a great deal of planning and preparation is required. General education teachers receive students' IEPs that delineate their unique needs and the interventions and accommodations that are necessary for them to access the learning environment. Sometimes additional staff members are secured to support students with specific tasks and classroom teachers with effectively differentiating instruction. In the same manner that we intentionally create systems, structures, policies, and practices to meet the needs of students with differing abilities, we should also ensure that children and families who represent minoritized backgrounds receive the same commitment of time and resources—fiscal and otherwise—so that they can meaningfully participate—are genuinely included—in every aspect of the school community (Barrett, 2021b).

> **THINK ABOUT IT. What are your impressions, thoughts, and reactions to this metaphor about inclusion? Discuss your answers with your classmates or colleagues.**

---

[1] To learn more about Bellen Woodard and her More Than Peach Project, visit *www.morethanpeach.com*.

Equity

Throughout this book, I've been referring to equity as an outcome or result of socially just practices. Equity, therefore, could be described as the absence of inequity or disproportionality. Although this is true, equity also relates to power and, more specifically, shared power. In other words, individuals representing the broad spectrum of races, ethnicities, genders/gender identities, sexual orientations, language backgrounds, faith orientations, and numerous other characteristics are not only present or represented (diversity) but are also invited (have access and opportunity) to participate in meaningful ways (inclusion). Moreover, they contribute to decisions (have shared power) that affect systems through significant changes in policy and practice, including the redistribution of financial and human resources. Said another way, it is possible for schools and school districts to achieve diversity goals by simply hiring staff representing a variety of identities, but they may fall short of being inclusive if everyone cannot participate in a meaningful way or doesn't feel welcomed in their respective environment. Further, it is possible for schools and school systems to be diverse and inclusive, yet to have power, particularly decision-making power, concentrated in the hands of a few. Consider the following example:

> The executive committee of Willowgrove Elementary School's Parent–Teacher Association (PTA) is made up of White women from middle- or upper-middle-class backgrounds. Because 70% of Willowgrove's students and families are from Central America, and 50% are eligible to receive free or reduced-priced lunches, the PTA's leadership does not reflect the full diversity of the school or community. Though there is fairly consistent attendance and participation from families representing a variety of backgrounds at monthly PTA meetings, especially since holding them virtually, decision-making power rests in the hands of a few.

This example shows that despite achieving a degree of diversity (who attends) and inclusion (who participates) at its PTA meetings, equity is lacking because decision-making power rests in the hands of a few whose identities don't fully represent the school's students and families. In Chapter 8 I discuss the systems and policy changes that are necessary to prevent diversity being viewed as an alternative to socially just practices that necessitate inclusion and ultimately lead to equity.

CHAPTER SUMMARY

An extension of Chapter 6, this chapter focuses on how schools can empower families to be their child's most informed and effective advocates. By inviting families, partnering with them, sharing decision-making power, being flexible, and involving them in the educational process, schools and school districts demonstrate their commitment to creating welcoming and inclusive environments that are conducive to meaningful family engagement. Last, the chapter describes the differences between diversity, inclusion, and equity—concepts that require intentionality from schools and their educators. Having discussed partnering with families and the importance of diversity, inclusion, and equity, Appendix 7.1 and Appendix 7.2 contain activities that have been designed for educators to plan how they will put their ideas into practice. In sum, more than what is important (e.g., being flexible, inclusion), the appendices are meant to help educators with actual implementation: how they translate theory into practice. Importantly, Chapter 8 continues to explore these ideas.

RESOURCES FOR PROFESSIONAL LEARNING

Please see Appendix 7.1 and Appendix 7.2 for activities that can be completed individually or in small groups with your colleagues. Both activities have been designed to reinforce important concepts from Chapter 7.

DISCUSSION QUESTIONS

1. Think about your school or school district. In your respective role, how can you be more intentional about empowering families to be their child's most informed and effective advocates? Brainstorm ideas and discuss them with a classmate or colleague.

   _____

   _____

   _____

2. In your role as an educator, what thoughts or feelings come to mind when you hear the word *advocate* (i.e., a person whom a family hires to support them through an educational process)? What has influenced your thoughts or feelings about this word?

   _____

   _____

   _____

3. Think about the terms *diversity*, *inclusion*, and *equity*. In your respective role in a school, how would you describe these ideas in terms of your students

and families? Where are you doing well? Where are there opportunities for growth?

_____

_____

_____

4. Think about the terms *diversity*, *inclusion*, and *equity*. In your respective role in a school, how would you describe these ideas in terms of your colleagues or staff? Where are you doing well? Where are there opportunities for growth?

_____

_____

_____

Brainstorming and Planning Document
for Schools Intentionally Partnering with Families

To review how schools can invite, partner, share decision-making power, and be more flexible so families are empowered to be their children's most informed and effective advocates, use the following table to brainstorm ways that you and your colleagues can engage in various activities that are aligned with these broad concepts. For each concept, there is a column for potential activities and a space to document accountability measures to ensure that plans are actually implemented. Refer to the sample idea for inspiration and motivation.

Concept	Potential activities	Accountability measures
Invite	School-based staff (e.g., mental health staff, teachers, administrators) will call the families of rising kindergartners during the summer and invite them to a special Open House.	This activity will be included in the School Improvement Plan (SIP), which is available for review by all school staff and central office administrators (e.g., supervisors and directors).
Partner		
Share decision-making power		
Be flexible		
Involve		

Brainstorming and Planning Document
for Schools Intentionally Pursuing Diversity, Inclusion, and Equity

To reinforce the importance of schools, departments, or school systems intentionally focusing on diversity, inclusion, and equity, use the table below to brainstorm ways to increase these characteristics for students, families, or staff. For each concept, there is a column for potential activities and a space to document accountability measures to ensure that plans are actually implemented. Refer to the sample idea for inspiration and motivation.

Concept	Potential ideas	Target audience	Accountability measures
Diversity	The school district will increase the number of racially and ethnically minoritized (REM) individuals who are hired into licensed positions by 10% within the upcoming school year.	Staff	This activity will be included in the school district's strategic plan, which is available to the public. Additionally, the school district will provide at least semiannual progress to a variety of stakeholder groups (e.g., community-based and parent advocacy groups) that have a vested interest in increasing REM individuals in licensed positions.
Inclusion			
Equity			

CHAPTER 8

A Challenge to Educators

*Whenever there is inequity, there is always an underlying justice
implication. When schools identify the underlying reason(s), often systemic
in nature, that contribute to inequities, they are better positioned to address
them and promote more positive and equitable outcomes for all students.*

LEARNING OUTCOMES

After reading this chapter, you should be able to . . .

1. Explain how the NASP Exposure Project is a model initiative for school psychology and related disciplines (e.g., general and special education, school counseling, school social work) to remedy workforce shortages and increase diversity by recruiting high school students and undergraduates into various education and school-based mental health fields.

2. Describe specific actions that schools and school districts can take to improve equitable outcomes for students.

3. Explain the relationship between policy, social justice, and promoting equitable outcomes for students.

CHAPTER OVERVIEW

As we're near the end of the book, Chapter 8 includes a challenge to all readers. With an explicit focus on advocacy, policy, and systems change, the NASP Exposure Project[1]—a

---

[1] The NASP Exposure Project is the result of the collective efforts of the following school psychologists: Elizabeth A'Vant, Tiara Bland, Sarah Cooke, Krista Edwards, Ashley Gee, Connesia Handford, Erin Harper, Kamonta Heidelburg, Keisha Hill, Erica Hobbs, Niekema Hudson, LaMetrice Lane, Jasmyn Ledford, Sappho Luter, Celeste Malone, Byron McClure, Shalia Moore-Hayes, Janice Nicholson, Tulani Tiah, and Mechelle Williams.

multiyear, national initiative designed to address critical workforce shortages in school psychology and increase the number of REM individuals in the field—is highlighted as an effective strategy to promote diversity, which is necessary but not sufficient for inclusion or equity, in all school-based mental health and education disciplines. While cautioning against prescriptive approaches to addressing educational inequities, the chapter also offers practical suggestions for how individuals can advance systems change in schools and school districts (i.e., making data-based decisions, human resources and staffing changes, mandatory professional learning, developing capacity, strategic planning, and policy led by district leadership and school board members).

INTRODUCTION

As I was preparing to evaluate a student, a 5-year-old Black child pointed at me and exclaimed, "He's Black!" Notably, I wasn't in one of my schools but in a portion of the county that is considerably less diverse. When this happened, I couldn't help but wonder if this student had ever seen a Black male in a professional position. Would he ever have the experience of having a Black male teacher? While the surprise and excitement from his voice made my day, it also renewed my commitment to diversifying the field of school psychology. I shouldn't be an anomaly (Barrett, 2020, p. 16).

THE NEED FOR DIVERSITY: THE NASP EXPOSURE PROJECT AS A MODEL INITIATIVE FOR ALL DISCIPLINES

Aligned with two of NASP's strategic goals (social justice and workforce shortages; NASP, 2017), the NASP Exposure Project (NASP-EP) is a multiyear initiative to increase the number of REM individuals in the profession (Barrett, Harper, Hudson, & Malone, 2020). As the nation has become more heterogeneous, to the greatest extent possible, school psychologists and all educators (e.g., teachers, school counselors, school social workers) should reflect the racial, ethnic, and linguistic background of the students, families, schools, and communities they serve. Data collected through the most recent NASP membership survey showed that only 14% of school psychologists are members of REM groups and only 14% speak a language other than English (Goforth et al., 2021). Similarly, the most recent data (2017–2018 school year) from the National Center for Education Statistics (NCES) showed that 79% of United States public school teachers identified as White, with only 7% identifying as Black, 9% identifying as Hispanic, 2% identifying as Asian American, and less than 2% identifying as either American Indian or Alaska Native, Pacific Islander, or of two or more races (NCES, 2022). In comparison, almost half of the school-age population is from REM groups (Vespa, Armstrong, & Medina, 2018). And though approximately 75% of students speak Spanish at home, more than 400 languages are spoken in the United States (NCES, 2022). Taken together, the fields of psychology and education have a lot to do to increase their racial, ethnic, and linguistic representation.

In school psychology, persistent workforce shortages and the lack of racial, ethnic, and linguistic diversity are long-standing and multifaceted issues (Barrett et al., 2020). One reason is that there are not enough school psychologists entering the profession to replace those who retire or leave the field for a variety of reasons (Castillo, Curtis, & Tan, 2014). Additionally, there are shortages of qualified faculty in graduate education programs, limited access to NASP-approved graduate programs in certain parts of the country, limited numbers of qualified applicants to enroll in some training programs while others have more prospective students than they can accept, shortages of approved internships and qualified internship supervisors, difficulty attracting graduates to areas that have persistent vacancies, and difficulty retaining qualified school psychologists (NASP, 2016a).

> **THINK ABOUT IT.** What factors are contributing to workforce shortages in your respective discipline? How are they similar to or different from the ones that are contributing to workforce shortages in school psychology?

Overview of the NASP-EP

As noted by Barrett and colleagues (2020), using ideas articulated in the literature, the NASP-EP is a practical method to both remedy workforce shortages and increase diversity in school psychology. First, its PowerPoint presentation provides important information about the field to high school students and undergraduates who are actively thinking about their academic future and potential career paths. Specifically, it includes an overview of who school psychologists are, what they do, the settings in which they work, education requirements, and average salary by U.S. region. Next, although the presentation is appropriate for all high school students and undergraduates, most presenters have targeted those who are presumably interested in psychology or education (e.g., enrolled in advanced placement psychology, psychology electives, human development, or education courses; Barrett, Heidelburg, & Malone, 2019). Last, although the NASP-EP is presented to all students, it specifically highlights the need for more REM individuals to consider school psychology by contrasting the current demographic composition of the profession in terms of race/ethnicity, gender, and languages spoken with school-age students (Barrett et al., 2020).

Due to the need for more school psychologists from REM backgrounds, REM school psychology faculty, practitioners, and graduate students are encouraged to introduce young people to the profession (Barrett, Heidelburg, & Malone, 2019). Though important for all students, the opportunity for REM students to see themselves reflected in the field is inspiring and increases the likelihood of them becoming school psychologists. As noted by Lott and Rogers (2011), such representation fosters a greater sense of connectedness to the field. Last, exposing undergraduates who attend Historically Black Colleges and Universities (HBCUs) and other Minority-Serving Institutions (MSIs) not only helps to remedy the shortage of school psychologists, but it can also be instrumental in building a pool of REM graduate students to enter the profession (Bocanegra, Newell, & Gubi, 2016; Castillo et al., 2014; Rogers & Molina, 2006).

Data

Table 8.1 summarizes the number of high school students and undergraduates who have been exposed to school psychology through the various phases of the NASP-EP. And although an international focus was not intentionally considered when the NASP-EP was conceptualized, it has reached students in Canada, China (Taiwan), Haiti, and India.

Next Steps: What Happens after Exposure?

Albeit important, exposure is just the first step to addressing workforce shortages and diversifying the field. After students have been introduced to the profession and are interested in pursuing school psychology or related fields in school-based mental health or education, an infrastructure that supports them through this process is also necessary. As part of the NASP-EP, undergraduates who receive the presentation are given a link or QR code and asked to complete a short survey, provide their email address, year in school, and

TABLE 8.1. Number of High School Students and Undergraduates Exposed to School Psychology through the NASP Exposure Project: Spring 2018 through Fall 2022

Phase	Semester	Year	Number of high school students and undergraduates
Pilot	Spring	2018	860
One	Fall	2018	6,569
Two	Spring	2019	3,221
Three	Fall	2019	4,915
Four	Spring	2020	1,930
Five	Fall	2020	1,584
Six	Spring	2021	1,215
Seven	Fall	2021	4,176
Eight	Spring	2022	2,717
Nine	Fall	2022	4,284
Total			31,471

whether they are interested in learning more about school psychology. This information is used to provide further information about the field and support them through the graduate school application process (i.e., helping students to have meaningful experiences that make them competitive applicants, as well as identifying training programs and funding opportunities). Especially for REM students, such intentional follow-up reinforces school psychology's commitment to increasing its diversity (Zhou et al., 2004). Moreover, after students, particularly those from REM backgrounds, are accepted into school psychology programs, it is imperative that they are effectively supported and mentored to ensure their successful completion (Barrett, Heidelburg, & Malone, 2019).

What's Working and Why: Implications for Practice

Since 2018, feedback from presenters suggests that the NASP-EP's success is the result of two practical, yet critically important factors: material preparation and organization and presentation flexibility. They are offered as recommendations to assist other disciplines in developing and executing strategic initiatives to address workforce shortages and increase diversity in their respective areas.

Material Preparation and Organization

All materials for the NASP-EP were developed and placed in a Dropbox folder that was shared electronically through NASP communities and social media platforms (i.e., Facebook, Instagram, Twitter, and LinkedIn). These materials included a PowerPoint presentation (approximately 35 minutes) and letters that explained the project's purpose to high school principals, college and university professors, and district-level school psychology administrators (e.g., coordinators, supervisors, and directors) in case practitioners needed to request their support before participating. A checklist offered step-by-step guidance for completing the project, and a link to a Google form allowed the collection of data (i.e., high school, college, or university in which presentations took place and the number of students in attendance) to monitor success. Because time is a precious commodity, having high-quality materials prepared in advance and easily accessible maximized the degree to which potential presenters would participate. For sample NASP-EP resources, see Appendix 8.1 through Appendix 8.3 at the end of the chapter.

Presentation Flexibility

Presentation materials were adaptable. For example, presenters were allowed to tell their personal stories about why they became school psychologists, what they love most about the field, and the most challenging aspect of being a school psychologist. By sharing experiences about their journey into the profession, as well as their day-to-day impressions of school psychology, presenters made authentic connections to students. Additionally, although most presentations occurred during regularly scheduled classes, others took place during extracurricular meetings (e.g., psychology clubs) that were more conducive to student and school schedules.

SYSTEMS CHANGE

Having more individuals in school-based mental health and instructional positions is important. Recruiting more well-trained psychologists, counselors, social workers, and teachers, however, is not the only challenge facing American public education. In fact, as we've been discussing throughout this book, more than the amount of people who are employed, the systems in which they are working require significant attention. Even if all schools were fully staffed with the optimal number of mental health providers, teachers, and administrators who also represented the racial, ethnic, and linguistic backgrounds of their students and families, people create systems and policies, and ultimately systems and policies affect the lives of students, families, schools, and communities. The final section of this chapter offers practical suggestions for implementing systems change in schools and school districts. Though the information shouldn't be viewed as being prescriptive (e.g., a checklist of things to do), it can be helpful for embedding socially just practices into the day-to-day roles and responsibilities of educators and informing broader policy decisions.

Data-Based Decision Making

In Chapter 1, I introduced the idea of disproportionality (inequity), and throughout the book I've discussed how disparate outcomes are the result of specific actions that schools and school systems have or have not taken to ensure what is best for children. As an extension of this principle, whenever there is inequity, there is always an underlying justice implication. When schools identify the underlying reason(s), often systemic in nature, that contribute to inequities, they are better positioned to address them and promote more positive and equitable outcomes for all students.

At the core of remedying disproportionality is using data to inform decisions. Because schools have access to a wealth of information, data should always be used as a mirror to continually refine school and districtwide policies and practices. When applicable to various outcomes in schools, including discipline (e.g., suspension and expulsion), special education eligibility, gifted identification, enrollment in honors and advanced placement courses, and graduation rates, and after calculating **risk ratios,** multidisciplinary problem-solving and leadership teams (e.g., PBIS) should disaggregate their data and regularly ask the following questions:

1. Are outcomes equitable by race or ethnicity?
2. Are outcomes equitable by gender or gender identity?
3. Are outcomes equitable by SES?
4. Are outcomes equitable by disability status?
5. Are outcomes equitable by sexual orientation?

A risk ratio is the ratio of the probability of an event (e.g., being suspended) occurring in one group to the probability of the event occurring in a comparison group. This metric can be used to determine the risk related to a variety of factors (e.g., race/ethnicity, gender, SES, disability status) and allows schools and school districts to examine the degree to which outcomes are equitable across groups. For an example of calculating a risk ratio, please read the following scenario.

At East Elementary School, 10 out of 21 Black students were suspended during the 2021–2022 school year. Dividing the number of Black students who were suspended (10) by the total number of Black students at East Elementary School (21), 48% of Black students were suspended at East Elementary School. Also at East Elementary School, 75 out of 315 White students were suspended during the 2021–2022 school year. Dividing the number of White students who were suspended (75) by the total number of White students at East Elementary School (315), 24% of White students were suspended at East Elementary School. Last, by dividing the risk for Black students (target group) being suspended by the risk for White students (comparison group) being suspended, Black students at East Elementary School were twice as likely to be suspended as White students (48/24 =2).

Importantly, whereas risk ratios show that disproportionality exists, they do not reveal the underlying factors that contribute to these outcomes. These data, however, should lead educators to ask questions about their policies and practices that could be contributing to negative results for students. When schools and school districts commit to changing what they do (i.e., how they practice), they will also improve outcomes for students.

Human Resources and Staffing

In addition to making data-based decisions, it is also important for schools and school systems to be mindful of whom they place in positions related to equity and social justice. Especially since the country's most recent awakening concerning issues of racism during the COVID-19 pandemic, schools and school districts have been making even more significant strides to address inequities that have long existed in their systems. As part of their approach, senior staff positions (e.g., directors/senior directors, assistant superintendents, chief equity officers) related to equity, social justice, and culturally responsive instruction have become more common. And though these positions can be instrumental in developing frameworks and building capacity to improve outcomes for students, there are a few important considerations to keep in mind.

First, what are the intersecting identities of the individuals who are being hired into these leadership positions? Although some would argue that individuals from REM and other marginalized backgrounds are ideal candidates for these roles, this can also lead to unintended consequences. Whether at the school or district level, these are critical positions to help advance equity initiatives. Hiring committees should weigh the skill set of applicants and consider their intersecting identities (e.g., race/ethnicity, gender/gender identity, sexual orientation) to make the most informed decisions based on who has the requisite experiences to advance socially just practices in schools and school districts.

Human Resources and Staffing in Black and White

Many highly qualified Black individuals have been hired into prominent positions related to equity. But despite their skills, professional experiences, and sometimes personal lived experiences, one unintended consequence is that they are perceived as the ones who are responsible for achieving a school's or school system's equity goals. And if these goals aren't met, they can also bear the burden of blame for such outcomes. Additionally, the public-facing role that often accompanies these positions can place Black and other REM individuals in precarious positions, as they can be perceived as defending an institution (e.g., school district) that has perpetuated harm to REM and other marginalized students and families. Further, community members and organizations might perceive them as being unfairly tasked with "fixing" inequities that they or others like them (e.g., other Black people) did not create.

On the other hand, there are many White people who are also highly qualified to serve in significant leadership roles related to equity. But similar to Black or other REM individuals in these positions, there can be unintended consequences for someone whose background is the dominant (White) culture. One such consequence could be centering themselves or White, middle-class feelings and values at the expense of the experiences that are salient to marginalized groups. As described in Chapter 3, if they aren't careful, these individuals can also assume the role of *speaking for the voiceless* rather than amplifying voices that have been silenced by systems.

The examples presented here show that staffing decisions are complicated and should not be made in the absence of thoughtful consideration of multiple factors (e.g., racial or ethnic background, gender or gender identity, sexual orientation, languages spoken, as well as personal and professional experiences). Having thought a lot about hiring practices and served on various hiring panels, I've heard the following statement (or something similar): "We want someone who can jump right in and get started right away." Though the latter clause suggests the urgency associated with filling the position, the entire sentence has greater significance. In other words, could it be that those who are making hiring decisions are more committed (even unintentionally) to maintaining the status quo? Could it be that they are more interested in hiring someone who fits the mold of who they are rather than who they can (should) become? This is what I know: Diversifying professions, especially in senior leadership positions, will likely involve intentionally hiring those who have not (yet) had the opportunity to serve in these capacities but are no less qualified or capable. And as a result, though they might not be able to "jump right in" or "get started right away," what they bring to the organization can be what they didn't know they needed because they were blinded by what they thought they wanted (Barrett, 2022).

But despite which person is ultimately hired for the position, schools and school districts must build teaming structures to support these individuals. In other words, it is important that diversity characteristics, broadly defined, are considered to the greatest extent possible and that teams reflect the breadth and depth of diversity represented among their students, families, schools, and larger community. For example, if the chief equity officer is a Black woman, ideally, the directors, supervisors, and support staff in this department should not be primarily Black men and women. Similarly, if the senior director who is responsible for equity initiatives is a White man, the team overseeing various aspects of equity projects and activities should include people who are Black, Asian, Latinx, Indigenous, and a host of other intersecting identities. When teams are diverse and representative of their staff, students, families, and larger community, schools and school districts can more effectively communicate that equity work is truly a shared commitment by everyone. Though consideration of them is well intentioned, REM individuals should not necessarily be given priority consideration for positions that are specifically dedicated to equity and social justice because of their race/ethnicity. Alternatively, after identifying the needs of the school or school district, including its short- and long-term goals, hiring panels should select the candidate who possesses the skills and experiences to advance equity goals, whether they represent a REM background or not. Relatedly, it is more important for schools and school systems to think deeply about how they can shift the culture to not only reflect diversity, inclusion, and equity in their mission, vision, and other statements but also in their actions, processes, practices, and structures. Because achieving equitable outcomes is shared responsibility, REM individuals, for example, belong in building leadership roles as principals as well as district office and senior positions related to curriculum and instruction, special education, human resources, student services, budget and finance, and every other department that affects the lives of students and families.

Budgetary Commitments

Coupled with staffing and personnel changes, schools and school districts should make significant financial and other resource investments to advance equity goals. When leaders are placed in roles without the resources to affect change, it undermines their credibility and communicates to students, families, staff, and community members that schools or school districts (systems) are not committed to making tangible and long-lasting changes.

In the summer of 2020 I saw an image (see Figure 8.1) in which there were two people, one from a REM background and one who was White, climbing a hill. At the bottom of the hill was the following sign: RECOGNIZING RACISM IN AMERICA. The other sign, which is on the lower part of the hill says, DOING SOMETHING ABOUT IT. The two individuals are between the signs, and the REM person is pointing toward the second sign while the White individual seems tired and is slightly bent over and holding their knees. The image included the following caption: "Actually, we're just getting started," and seems to be attributed to the REM person. In light of the image and text, consider this:

> Although I appreciate that everyone is wrestling with what they can do to actively support racial justice, especially for Black people, I wanted to highlight a few things. First, disrupting and interrupting systemic racism that's been perpetuated and reinforced for 400+ years in America requires work. More importantly, this work is not easy. In many ways the books, articles, podcasts, websites, movies, and other resources that are being compiled; the protests and demonstrations that are occurring; and painting Black Lives Matter on the streets of numerous cities is just the beginning. And while necessary, these actions are not sufficient. Systemic racism will only be eradicated from the structures and processes in which it has been allowed to fester and prosper when individuals in positions of power and privilege engage in the everyday, uncomfortable, and uneasy work to dismantle it. Consistently calling attention to racist behaviors, comments, policies, and practices is the only way to hold individuals and systems accountable for eradicating racial injustice. To those who are engaged in this difficult work, keep fighting the good fight that's worth fighting. Let's not get distracted with the flashing lights of what looks like progress at the expense of real justice and equity. (Barrett, 2020)

FIGURE 8.1. Racism in America. Victor Varnado/*The New Yorker* Collection/The Cartoon Bank.

In the wake of the deaths of Breonna Taylor, Ahmaud Arbery, and George Floyd—unarmed Black individuals who were killed by White people between February and May 2020—there seemed to be an awakening in America about the reality of racism that felt qualitatively different from previous times. Whether through media coverage or trending topics and viral posts on social media, the attention was more consistent and lasted longer than other similar tragedies in America's recent history. As a Black male, psychologist, and educator, I watched professional associations and school districts make statements condemning racism and committing to being antiracist. Multi-billion-dollar corporations and colleges and universities released similar statements. On a personal level, I read the Facebook, Twitter, and Instagram posts of many individuals who openly professed to be antiracist. And although these statements are appropriate and appreciated, to some degree, they also left me feeling that they were more performative than substantive. In other words, after one professional association, corporation, school district, or institution of higher learning releases a statement, it almost becomes the expectation that others follow suit to remain relevant to their members, students, families, staff, and customers. Though these statements were likely sincere, what's more important is what has or has not happened since they were made. How have policies in these respective organizations changed? How have day-to-day practices changed in schools and school districts? Have significant investments been made to ensure equitable outcomes? In the absence of long-term budgetary allocations for professional learning, staffing, and other resources, these statements are little more than perfunctory displays rather than seriously challenging systems and structures that create and perpetuate inequities.

Professional Learning

One of the most appropriate behaviors that educators can model for students is being a lifelong learner. As it relates to promoting equitable outcomes, schools and school districts must incorporate a strategic and differentiated professional learning plan that is applicable to all licensed (e.g., teachers, administrators, school-based mental health providers) and professional (e.g., teacher assistants, custodians, secretaries, bus drivers) staff. As was discussed in Chapter 4, such professional learning, at minimum, should teach all staff about how privilege, implicit bias, and intersectionality are relevant to their respective job roles. For staff who are responsible for screening and interviewing candidates and making hiring decisions, the implications for implicit bias are likely different than for a classroom teacher who isn't involved in these decisions. For assistant principals and principals who are involved in making disciplinary decisions for students, professional learning that highlights how implicit bias intersects with students' identities and can influence their thought processes would be beneficial. And for staff who represent the dominant culture (White) yet who serve students from REM backgrounds, understanding how privilege can affect their worldview would be important.

As a matter of policy, such professional learning should be the expectation and not optional for staff. Developing common vocabulary and shared understanding about these concepts so that they are infused into the cultures of schools and departments across school districts shows that socially just practices that lead to equitable outcomes is the essence of educators' work rather than something that is attached to their other roles and responsibilities.

Developing Capacity

As mentioned earlier in this chapter, working toward equitable outcomes is a shared responsibility. Because a single person or policy did not create the inequities that exist and persist in schools and school districts, everyone and every department has a role to play in their disrupting and dismantling. Depending on the size of your school district, it might be appropriate to have this work centralized (e.g., an office of equity or something similar). But even when these offices or departments exist, one of the primary responsibilities of its leader is to ensure that equity work lives in all schools, offices, and departments.

In teaching school psychology graduate students and practitioners about assessing children whose native languages aren't English, I often tell them that everyone needs the skills to do this work well. Even if they aren't bilingual or do not speak the home languages of their students and families, there are principles that allow them (monolingual English-speaking school psychologists) to think critically about their work and how they can make more informed educational decisions. I typically share something to the effect of "Saying that you are going to refer bilingual students or ELs to the bilingual school psychologist is like saying that you're a school psychologist but you don't work with children who have autism or ADHD. As a school psychologist, you must be prepared to meet the needs of all children." Similarly, if you're a teacher in an elementary, middle, or high school, working toward equitable outcomes is your responsibility. If you're a school counselor, school social worker, or school psychologist, promoting equitable outcomes is a part of your role. As a principal, assistant principal, or dean, ensuring access and opportunity for your students is central to promoting equitable outcomes. If you're a central office administrator overseeing entire departments, it is appropriate to empower the school-based practitioners that you supervise and support to think about the social justice implications of their work. Even for employees who work in human resources, business and financial services, or technology departments, whether thinking about hiring practices, budgetary priorities, or who has access to devices and reliable Wi-Fi, social justice is relevant to every aspect of school and school district operations. Through differentiated professional learning, staff members are afforded the opportunity to grow in their understanding of what socially just practices are, why they're important, and how they can be embedded into their day-to-day roles and responsibilities.

Strategic Planning

A fairly common practice in both public and private sector organizations, strategic planning is critical to long-term effectiveness. With input from a variety of stakeholders (e.g., members of professional associations; students, faculty, and staff of colleges and universities; students, staff, families, and community partners of school districts), a strategic plan prioritizes what the organization wants to accomplish over the next several years. For example, Barrett, Heidelburg, and Malone (2019) noted that five strategic goals inform the priorities, policies, and programming of NASP: (1) advancing the NASP practice model, (2) leadership development, (3) promoting school psychologists as mental and behavioral health providers, (4) social justice, and (5) remedying workforce shortages (NASP, 2017). And, as detailed earlier in this chapter, the NASP-EP is focused on two of these goals: remedying workforce shortages and social justice. More importantly, all of the activities of the association are related to the strategic plan and supporting at least one of its strategic goals.

For schools and school districts, is promoting equitable outcomes in your strategic plan? In using data to inform decisions, where are there opportunities to improve or increase equitable outcomes for students? Do licensed staff (e.g., teachers, administrators, school-based mental health providers) reflect the racial and ethnic diversity of your students and families? For whatever inequities that exist in your school or school district, this is an entry point to form strategic actions (i.e., school improvement plans) that include goal statements (i.e., objectives) and accountability metrics to monitor progress.

Policy

In Chapter 3 we discussed several policies and practices that should be interrogated, interrupted, disrupted, and dismantled because they aren't helpful and perpetuate harm to children and inequities in schools and school districts. Here's one more: not holding policymakers accountable for simply talking about social justice without demonstrating their commitment to social justice. Often led by senior leadership in school districts (e.g., superintendents, assistant superintendents, and directors) as well as elected officials (e.g., school board members), policy is critical to advancing socially just practices that lead to equitable outcomes. As mentioned in Chapter 1, if social justice is the vehicle (e.g., the car) that leads schools and school districts to equitable outcomes for students, then policy is the fuel that powers socially just practices.

Focus on the Fence

Whether teachers and their instructional practices, principals and their discipline policies, or school psychologists and their assessment approaches, educators often boast about being student centered. But as was discussed in Chapter 2, sometimes keeping the child at the center of what we're doing has a lot less to do with the individual child than it does with other factors. While speaking to a group of administrators, I showed the popular images that contrast equity and equality (see Figure 8.2). For those who might be unfamiliar with these, there are several versions available on the internet; but essentially one image shows three people of differing heights trying to look over a wooden fence to watch a baseball game. Whereas one image shows each person standing on one box, the other image shows them, depending on their height, standing on zero, one, or two boxes. Meant to contrast equity—giving each person what they need (e.g., the shortest person standing on two boxes vs. the tallest person not standing on any boxes)—and equality—giving each person the same level of support (e.g., everyone standing on one box)—during our discussion, someone said that we need to fix the fence. In other words, more than the differentiated (tailored to the individual) support (e.g., the boxes) that we provide students and families, fundamentally the fence (i.e., the system) is the problem. And if we truly want what's best for children, we must shift our attention to the systemic policies and practices that deny meaningful access and opportunity to everyone. Yes, it's appropriate to give individuals what they need; but we must also focus on the fence.

Focusing on the fence is important for several reasons. Despite some students requiring more support, some schools needing more interventionists and mental health provid-

FIGURE 8.2. Equality versus equity. Interaction Institute for Social Change (*interactioninstitute.org*). Artist: Angus Maguire (*madewithangus.com*).

ers, and having to assist some families more or differently than others, before we high-light what we're doing as schools, school districts, and educators, we should ask ourselves: What makes these actions necessary? Why do some students need more support? It's the fence of racism that disproportionately places less qualified teachers and instructional methods in front of REM students. Why do some schools require more mental health sup-port? It's the fence of redlining[2] and other discriminatory practices that unfairly places a significant number of students from marginalized backgrounds into a single school. Why do some families need more assistance than others? It's the fence of systemic oppression that prevents them from earning a livable wage, which leads to working multiple jobs and having less time to be meaningfully engaged in their children's schooling—not because they don't want to, but because they are balancing attending school-based meetings at 10:00 A.M. with providing for their families' basic needs. When educators overlook these and other systemic barriers, not only do we unintentionally reinforce deficit ideologies about students, families, schools, and communities, but we also perpetuate "savior" or "fixer" complexes about ourselves that are similar to Manifest Destiny (see Chapter 2). Moreover, we run the risk of thinking that the problem lies within the individual child, family, school, or community and shift the attention to what we are doing to help them.

As an individual who is short in stature, I used to say that there's nothing inherently wrong with me but that I would need more support (e.g., boxes) than those who were taller than me to see over the fence. Although on the surface this seemed like a reason-able explanation to not problematize the individual, it also didn't critique the fence that was obstructing my view and prematurely centered my personal circumstances. In other words, despite being short, I wouldn't need individual intervention if the fence wasn't there. More than being short, the fence was the problem.

Earlier in this chapter I mentioned the importance of educators modeling being life-long learners for their students. As I reflect on my own career, one of the biggest shifts in my thinking has been the importance of focusing on fences or policies. I used to believe that if we taught more about racism, implicit bias, privilege, and intersectionality because people legitimately didn't understand these concepts—in large part because they've never been exposed to them—they would do better by making better (more informed) decisions for their students. If we gave them more information, using clever analogies and metaphors, educators would see how their behavior, even unintentionally, was harm-ful to students and do better. As a psychologist and cognitive behaviorist, I had convinced myself, and at times tried to convince others, that we (educators) would change what we do (our behavior, actions) by first changing what we think and how we think. As much as this made logical or practical sense at the time, and despite being sincere in my beliefs, I was wrong.

---

[2]*Redlining* refers to policies by which banks and savings institutions refused loans to Black families in White suburbs and even, in most cases, to Black families in Black neighborhoods—leading to the deterioration and ghettoization of those neighborhoods (Rothstein, 2014).

A TRANSFORMATION: POLICY OVER PEOPLE

As lifelong learners, one of the most beneficial practices that we can engage in is to read beyond our discipline. Though the school psychology literature has taught me a lot, like other fields, it does not have the monopoly on what educators need to know to improve outcomes for their students. Learning from our colleagues in related fields can be invaluable to improving our knowledge base and what we eventually do for children and families.

Reading Ibram X. Kendi's *How to Be an Antiracist* helped me understand the role of policy in improving equitable outcomes for children. As I was doing, Kendi cautions against focusing on changing people's minds, what he calls "educational suasion" (Kendi, 2019, p. 208), either at the expense of or before changing the policies that are embedded in systems. Even the language Kendi uses shows where his actions are focused and where ours should be as well: *"Racist policy* . . . cuts to the core of racism better than *racial discrimination.* . . . Racial discrimination is an immediate and visible manifestation of an underlying *racial policy"* (pp. 18–19; emphasis added). As has been echoed throughout this book, when students are discriminated against, this is shown in inequities (inequitable outcomes), which are the by-products (the results) of policies and subsequent practices. But when we identify the underlying justice implications for disproportionality and address them, which often includes challenging systems and changing policies, we will improve equitable outcomes.

It's Not Cognitive

As Kendi (2019) contends that power ultimately rests in policies more than people, I have reached two conclusions. First, the reason for persistent inequities is not cognitive. A Navajo proverb says, "You can't wake a person who is pretending to sleep." The more I thought about some people's resistance to embracing social justice principles, I realized that their difficulty was not that they didn't understand what equity is and how socially just practices are necessary to improve outcomes for children, families, schools, and communities. In other words, equity is not a cognitively complex phenomenon. In its simplest terms, and as reflected in Figure 8.2, equity is ensuring that everyone has what they need to have meaningful access or opportunity. If anything is complicated, it's disrupting and dismantling systemic structures that marginalize certain groups. For reluctant and resistant educators, the challenge is that they are unwilling to do what is in the best interest of children.

Second, I've learned that everyone who talks about equity and social justice isn't really committed to doing what's necessary to embed these ideals into their (our) work as educators. As a result, policy is critical. To use principles of behaviorism, if the reason (the function) that educators aren't engaging in socially just practices isn't cognitive, then the intervention can't be more instruction, more professional learning, more teaching, or more workshops. Why? Because the intervention (what we do) must address the underlying reason (function) of the behavior.

Policy: The Relationship between Beliefs and Behavior

As I've often said while presenting about these ideas, policy doesn't change beliefs, but it does change behavior. Though I used to focus on changing what people believed, including what and how they thought about their students and families, shifting mindsets, especially adults' ways of thinking, is a monumental undertaking that requires their (not anyone else's) effort and commitment. And, quite frankly, we don't have the luxury of waiting for people to contemplate whether they want to change how they think at the expense of what can be done in the moment. So, as we're requiring our staff and colleagues to grow in their understanding through mandatory professional learning, we also need to hold them accountable for doing things differently in their day-to-day practices.

If you're reading this chapter, you might be thinking, "What does policy have to do with me? I don't make those decisions." But in many ways, policy simply means expectation or what people are required to do, whether they truly believe it or not. In life, if the policy (expectation) is that we obey the speed limit, whether we want to or feel (believe) that driving 55 miles per hour is necessary, we do it because we're held accountable (tickets, court dates) when we don't follow the expectation. For teachers, though it's not stated this way, lesson planning is a policy because it's expected. For school psychologists, evaluation standards that delineate the data that are necessary to make defensible eligibility decisions are policies because they are expectations, not options. As a building or central office administrator, what are you expecting from your teachers and staff to promote more equitable outcomes for children and families (Barrett, 2022)?

So What: Implications for Policy and the Five C's of Equity

It was Thursday, February 3, 2022, and I was sitting in an equity committee meeting. Though I had attended these monthly meetings since 2019, I began to think (and write) about equity in ways that I hadn't before. As I often do, I wrote a few ideas using the Notes app on my iPhone. In the closing pages of this chapter, I share them as reminders of what socially just practices should look like if we are truly working toward achieving equitable outcomes.

First, as mentioned in the Preface and earlier in this chapter, striving toward equity is both messy and uncomfortable. It's messy and uneasy. It's filled with missteps and sometimes mistakes. It's learning about ourselves, as individuals, and about the systems in which we live and work. Achieving equitable outcomes is also a dynamic process—one that's ever evolving and constantly shifting. And, as reflected in NASP's conceptualization of social justice, because it's a process and a goal (NASP, 2017), some of the uneasiness is learning to balance being comfortable, yet not complacent, in the many inevitable in-between stages. Though we might not be where we were, we're still not where we would like to be. It's growing pains that are filled with both sunshine and rain, triumphs and setbacks.

As previously discussed, social justice is far too important to be reduced to a series of steps on a checklist. But as a practitioner at heart, I also understand that concrete recommendations can be helpful to inform the day-to-day actions of teachers, school-based mental health providers, and administrators. In light of this chapter, but also the entire book, consider the following five ideas, also known as the Five C's of Equity (see also Appendix 8.4).

1. *Choose something to focus on.* In other words, get started. Don't know where to begin? Look at your data and the opportunities that disproportionate outcomes have given you. Nervous? Unsure? I know how you feel. Sometimes getting started is simultaneously the most important and the most daunting step that we can take toward accomplishing a significant goal. Though it is intimidating, after getting started by committing to focus on one inequity (outcome) in your school or school system, two things will happen. First, your efforts will lay the foundation and become the fuel for addressing additional inequities. Next, and perhaps more importantly, your work in a single area will take on a life of its own and provide the road map for your next steps. More than a person, the work will become your guide. More than a department, the work will become your compass. More than initiatives and committees, or slogans and hashtags that are shared on social media platforms, the work—an unflinching commitment to engaging in socially just practices—will lead you to your next steps in the process of achieving equitable outcomes.

2. *Commit to the work.* Having chosen an area of focus, commit to doing the work. And what is the work? The work is social justice. If equity is what we want to achieve (the goal) or where we would like to be, how we get there is social justice. The work is embedding socially just practices into our day-to-day roles and responsibilities. The work is not viewing social justice as separate from our teaching, our counseling, or our leading but as inextricably connected to everything that we do in the service of children, families, schools, and communities. Though uncomfortable, remember: Children are worth the commitment. Though it may be uneasy, children and families deserve our faithful attention to the issues that negatively affect their opportunities and access. Though messy at times, the health of our children, families, and schools depends on bold policy commitments that are reflected in changes in practice that ultimately become embedded in day-to-day expectations.

3. *Center marginalized and minoritized voices by building coalitions.* As echoed throughout this book, inequitable outcomes are often experienced by REM students and families, as well as individuals who have been marginalized for a variety of reasons. And

to effectively advocate for necessary practice and policy changes, not only do these voices and perspectives need to be amplified, but they also belong at the center of discussions. Rather than schools or school districts assuming that they know what a certain demographic of students and families need, they should partner with them by building collaborative coalitions. Whether it involves teachers working with individual students in their classes or broader school and districtwide initiatives to systemically and systematically improve access and opportunity for all children, being committed to the work includes continuously meeting with and listening to stakeholders. Though it may be time- and resource-intensive, being genuinely interested in the lived experiences of and actively listening to those who have been harmed, often in spaces that are conducive to authentic sharing, are invaluable to making strides toward equity goals.

4. *Communicate with stakeholders.* Coupled with centering minoritized and marginalized voices by building coalitions is a commitment to effective communication. To maintain the delicate balance between transparency and oversharing that school and school district leaders need to thoughtfully consider, staff, families, and community members should be kept informed of equity goals, priorities, and progress. Whether through posting periodic updates on school and school district websites or sharing information at school board meetings and through mail and electronic mail to staff, families, and community stakeholders, communication inspires trust.

5. *Celebrate the wins.* Last, no matter how big or small, celebrate the wins. From moving the needle in the right direction in a single area of disproportionality to taking the first steps toward revising a long-standing policy that has perpetuated inequities, celebrate the wins and communicate these with relevant stakeholders. In schools, the behaviors that we praise are likely to continue. When we want children to display appropriate behavior in the hallways, we positively reinforce them when they're walking appropriately. And so it goes for our equity work: We praise (draw attention to) the wins, knowing that we aren't finished and that there is more work to be done.

CHAPTER SUMMARY

Chapter 8 focused on advocacy, policy, and systems change. It began with an overview of the NASP Exposure Project as a model initiative for increasing diversity in various education disciplines. But as important as it is to recruit more people from REM backgrounds into school psychology, school counseling, school social work, and education, more work needs to be done. Although it is necessary, diversity is not sufficient for inclusion or equity, as we discussed in Chapter 7. In other words, hiring REM individuals into senior positions related to equity is not enough. Ultimately, the children, families, schools, and communities we serve deserve comprehensive systems and policy changes. Because the myriad issues facing American public education are significant, the remedies must also be systemic and not optional. Because it was legal (policy) to enslave Black individuals, a policy change (the Emancipation Proclamation) was necessary to free them. Because it was a matter of socially unjust policy that denied Black people the right to vote, a socially just policy alternative (the Voting Rights Act of 1965) was necessary to reverse its harm. And because one policy prevented Indigenous children from speaking their native languages or practicing their culture, another policy (the Religious Freedom Act of 1978) was necessary. Yes, there are individuals—teachers, principals, school-based mental health providers and central office administrators—who are committed to socially just practices that lead to equitable outcomes, but their ideas and practices must become systematized as the expectation for everyone.

As you focus on the fences that are preventing meaningful access and opportunity, being careful to choose where to start and what to focus on, remaining committed to the work, centering minoritized and marginalized voices, communicating with stakeholders, and celebrating wins, remember: More than the individual practices of people, social justice is about systems, structures, and policies.

RESOURCES FOR PROFESSIONAL LEARNING

1. To learn more about critical workforce shortages in school psychology, interested readers are referred to *Addressing Shortages in School Psychology: Resource Guide* (NASP, 2016), which can be accessed at *www.nasponline.org/resources-and-publications/resources-and-podcasts/school-psychology/shortages-in-school-psychology-resource-guide.*

2. If you are a school psychology faculty member, practitioner, or graduate student, you can make a meaningful contribution to addressing critical shortages and increasing diversity in school psychology. Please consider presenting at least once per semester to high school students or undergraduates in your area. All materials for the NASP-EP can be accessed at the following link: *www.nasponline.org/resources-and-publications/resources-and-podcasts/diversity-and-social-justice/cultural-competence/multicultural-affairs-committee/nasp-exposure-project-(nasp-ep)*

DISCUSSION QUESTIONS

1. How can the NASP Exposure Project serve as a model for recruiting more individuals to your respective profession?

    _____

    _____

    _____

2. Review data from your school or school district in the following areas: discipline, special education eligibility by category, graduation rates, gifted eligibility, and enrollment in advanced placement (AP) and honors courses. After reviewing these data, record whether disproportionality exists (yes or no) in the following table. Last, brainstorm with your classmates or colleagues possible reasons that are contributing to these disproportionate outcomes.

Category	Race or ethnicity	Gender or gender identity	SES	Disability status	Sexual orientation	Ideas to address disproportionality
Discipline: Suspension or expulsion						
Special education eligibility						
Gifted identification						
Enrollment in honors, AP, or IB (international baccalaureate) courses						
Graduation rates						

3. What is the significance of "Focus on the Fence" for your respective role as an educator? What are some fences that are negatively affecting students, families, schools, and communities? Brainstorm ways to address these fences and share your ideas with your classmates and colleagues.

   _____

   _____

   _____

4. In your respective role as an educator, how can you commit to remaining focused on policy rather than people?

   _____

   _____

   _____

Customizable NASP Exposure Project Principal Letter

The following letter can be helpful for school psychologists (e.g., practitioners, faculty, graduate students) who are interested in using NASP Exposure Project materials to introduce high school students to school psychology. Additionally, related disciplines (e.g., general and special education, school counseling, school social work) might find the letter helpful as they develop and plan their respective recruitment campaigns. Feel free to modify as appropriate.

Note: A similar letter should be developed for college/university professors.

[Date]

Dear Principal–

I am writing to you on behalf of the National Association of School Psychologists (NASP), the Multicultural Affairs Committee (MAC), and the African American Subcommittee. Consistent with NASP's strategic goals in the areas of social justice and workforce shortages, several multiyear initiatives are under way to recruit and retain school psychologists, especially those who are from racially and ethnically minoritized (REM) backgrounds. It is critically important that school psychologists reflect the students, families, schools, and communities they serve.

After a very successful pilot implementation during the Spring 2018 semester, NASP has launched the *Exposure Project* (EP) to introduce high school students to the field of school psychology. To measure success, we will be tracking the number of presentations completed and the number of students who attend each session.

As you are the principal of a high school, we invite you to support this initiative. With your permission, we would like **to present school psychology career information to your students. We envision school psychologists and/or school psychology graduate students offering a 30-minute presentation followed by the opportunity for questions and answers.** To accommodate school schedules, we are flexible in how these presentations occur (e.g., during certain classes and/or arranged through the career center/school counseling office).

If you are interested in supporting this exciting project that will shape the future of school psychology, please provide names and contact information of individuals who may be helpful in planning these presentations (e.g., career center director, school counseling director, school psychologist) at your earliest convenience.

If you would like additional information about the EP, please feel free to contact me [insert email address and/or telephone number].

I look forward to speaking with you in the very near future.

With respect and gratitude,

[insert your name or those of national leaders who can serve as sponsors for the project]

Customizable Supervisor Letter

The following letter can be helpful for school psychologists (i.e., practitioners) who are interested in using NASP Exposure Project materials to introduce high school students to school psychology but also need the support or permission of their coordinator, supervisor, or director. Additionally, related disciplines (e.g., general and special education, school counseling, school social work) might find the letter helpful as they develop and plan their respective recruitment campaigns. Feel free to modify as appropriate.

Dear [Coordinator, Supervisor, Director]

To address significant shortages in school psychology, the National Association of School Psychologists (NASP) has embarked on a multiyear initiative to expose high school students to the field of school psychology (please see *High School Exposure Project Principal Letter*).

With principals' permission, and working collaboratively with their staff, I will be supporting this project by offering a 30- to 45-minute PowerPoint presentation that has been developed and approved by NASP for this purpose.

I do not foresee any negative impact on my other job responsibilities.

Please let me know if you have any questions or concerns.

Thanks for your support as we raise awareness about school psychology.

[Your Name]
School Psychologist

NASP Exposure Project Checklist

The following checklist can be helpful for school psychologists (e.g., practitioners, faculty, administrators) and school psychology graduate students who are interested in using NASP Exposure Project materials to introduce high school students or undergraduates to school psychology. Additionally, related disciplines (e.g., general and special education, school counseling, school social work) might find the checklist helpful in developing and planning their respective recruitment campaigns. Feel free to modify as appropriate.

Number	Task	Relevant document	Comments
1	Contact a local high school or a high school in your school system.	Exposure Project high school principal letter	Customize the letter as appropriate. Ideally, presenters (e.g., school psychologists or graduate students) will already have a working relationship with high schools, which could increase the likelihood of principals agreeing to the presentation.
2	If necessary, send an email to your coordinator, supervisor, lead school psychologist, or director.	Exposure Project supervisor letter	Customize the letter as appropriate. The letter is not necessarily for their permission, but as a courtesy to inform them of what you are planning to do, why you are involved in this project, and NASP's support for the initiative.
3	After hearing from the principal, if necessary, offer to have a short meeting to explain the project.		You are supporting a NASP initiative to expose students to the field of school psychology. Relatedly, the larger goal is to help address significant shortages in school psychology.
4	Collaborate with the principal and/or others to determine the best way to offer the presentations.	Exposure Project high school presentation	The PowerPoint presentations should last between 30 and 45 minutes. If possible/available, AP psychology or psychology elective classes may be good options for offering the presentations.
5	Schedule the presentations.	Exposure Project high school presentation	Following the presentation, answer student questions. Also, leave your contact information (e.g., business card) with the teacher/school counselor, as well as NASP information about school psychology with the students or in the school counseling office (e.g., career center).
6	Collect the necessary data.	Google form	This is very important to track the number of schools, states, presentations, and students reached by this presentation.
7	Submit the data tracking form.	Google form	Please submit the data tracking form within 24 hours of each presentation.
8	Share, share, share!		Generate interest in the initiative by posting regular updates on various social media outlets (e.g., Twitter, Instagram, Facebook, LinkedIn) and using hashtags that represent the initiative.

The Five C's of Equity

To plan ways school- and district-based teams can use the Five C's of Equity by choosing something to focus on, committing to the work, centering marginalized and minoritized voices by building coalitions, communicating with stakeholders, and celebrating the wins, the following table can be used to brainstorm ways that you and your colleagues can engage in various activities that are aligned with these broad principles. For each principle, there are three columns for considerations and spaces to document your thoughts or ideas. Also, feel free to modify the considerations by adding or asking questions that are more significant to you and your team. The considerations provided are examples to help you think critically about each principle. Hint: you might refer to discussion question #2 for ideas related to the first three C's.

Principle	Consideration #1	Consideration #2	Consideration #3
CHOOSE something to focus on.	What problem are we trying to solve?	Why is this a problem?	How will solving this problem affect equitable outcomes for children, families, schools, or communities?
COMMIT to the work.	What specific behaviors will be used as indicators of commitment?		Which metrics will hold us accountable for remaining committed to the work?

(continued)

The Five C's of Equity *(page 2 of 2)*

Principle	Consideration #1	Consideration #2	Consideration #3
CENTER marginalized and minoritized voices by building coalitions.	For the problem that we've identified, which voices have been marginalized related to this issue?	How can we center the voices and perspectives of those who have been historically marginalized on this issue?	How can we build coalitions with communities that have been historically marginalized on the issue that we are trying to solve?
COMMUNICATE with stakeholders.	How regularly will we communicate with stakeholders?	What will be shared in our communication with stakeholders?	Which method(s) will be used for communication? Who will be responsible for facilitating communication with stakeholders?
CELEBRATE the wins.	What is one action that can be taken rather immediately that will likely lead to a small win?	How can the win be presented so that the work of historically marginalized voices is valued?	After each win, how can we build upon it for successive wins? Which action makes the most sense to pursue next based on our previous win?

CHAPTER 9

Social Justice and Me
The Formation and Evolution
of a Professional Identity

What Bro. Bruce modeled for me has informed most of what I believe about serving children: Love them unconditionally, support them unwaveringly, and advocate for them fiercely.

LEARNING OUTCOMES

After reading this chapter, you should be able to . . .

1. Identify personal experiences that have informed your perspectives about and approaches to serving children, families, schools, and communities.

2. Describe your formation and evolution as a social justice–oriented educator.

3. Identify your core values as an educator who is committed to infusing socially just practices into your respective role.

CHAPTER OVERVIEW

In the final chapter of this book, we focus on how personal experiences, including unique intersecting identities, produce educators who are committed to advancing socially just practices in schools and school districts. Having reviewed critical theories and concepts that are relevant to achieving equitable outcomes for children, families, schools, and communities, Chapter 9 also allows the reader to pause and reflect on how their lived experiences have informed their core values. And because it is impossible to separate who we are from what we do, the chapter shares autobiographical information to illustrate what has influenced our trajectories and continues to shape our beliefs and practices as educators.

INTRODUCTION

Although it may be a cliche, writing this book has been a life-changing experience. Among other things, I've learned a lot about myself, including recognizing and accepting some of my fears. It took me close to 1 year to begin drafting the manuscript. Despite thinking about the book every day, or almost every day, and saving short notes and ideas in my iPhone, almost 12 months passed before I actually started writing. I am a behaviorist, and while at home on a Sunday afternoon in November 2021, I finally realized the function of my behavior and the emotion that I was experiencing but couldn't articulate: fear.

Before this, I didn't fully grasp what it meant to engage in avoidance behaviors. Having served elementary, middle, and high school students as a school psychologist for 13 years and listening to teachers describe students as eloping from their classrooms, leaving their seats, making disruptive comments during lessons, or complaining of feeling sick so they could be sent to the nurse's office, I knew that these behaviors were clear examples of wanting to avoid challenging academic assignments or nonpreferred activities. Though some might say that I was procrastinating, which is a more sophisticated word for avoiding, procrastination detracts from what avoidance is and does not fully capture what I was feeling. For me, and especially related to this situation, avoidance is more emotive and paints a vivid picture of what was driving my behavior. For nearly 12 months, I was afraid to begin writing this book and avoided this project. But what was I afraid of?

Since elementary school, I've always enjoyed writing. I've won essay contests as a child, English is one of my undergraduate degrees, and writing has been a hobby for many years—bringing me much personal and professional satisfaction. Because phrases, paragraphs, and pages come relatively easily to me and this wasn't my first book or professional publication, what was I afraid of? Certainly, it wasn't the writing process. Having spoken or written about many of the topics in this book on numerous occasions, the content wasn't new to me, so that wasn't it, either. After some introspection, this is what I realized: Organizing a great deal of information and presenting it in a manner that others could not only understand but, more importantly, learn from simultaneously felt like the most daunting yet exciting feat of my career to date. I also believe that social justice is one of the most significant and relevant issues facing educators and the American public education system today. How would I effectively convey the information in a way that was not only beneficial to the reader but that would ultimately lead to positive and equitable outcomes for the children, families, schools, and communities that educators serve?

As in other areas of our lives, it's true that sometimes the most difficult part is getting started. For those who are in graduate programs, the hardest part of your next assignment is getting started. Writing your dissertation or master's thesis? I know it's overwhelming, but get started. Are you a teacher who needs to write lesson plans for next week's classes? Get started. Are you an administrator who needs to plan your school's or department's budget? Get started. As I began to write, as it always does, everything became clearer for me. The writing took on a life of its own and the information became even more real and meaningful. It was exciting.

But as much as this book is about social justice, equity, policy, and the professional practices of educators, it's also deeply personal. Not only do I write about racially and ethnically minoritized (REM) students and families, but I am a Black man. As such, these concepts, constructs, and ideas are more than theoretical. In many ways, they are a part of my daily life as a Black man who is married to a Black woman, the stepfather of a young Black man, the brother of Black men, the son of Black parents, and the uncle to Black nieces and nephews, most of whom attend American public schools.

WHO AM I?

As a child growing up in church (more about that later), reading the Bible was a significant part of my faith tradition. And as everyone does, I struggled (and still struggle) to understand certain passages. Although I don't remember who said this, it has helped me as a psychologist, teacher, presenter, and leader. Essentially, if we're reading a book, whether it's a novel or a textbook, and we have questions about the content, it helps to know a little about the author. Who are they? Where are they from? What do they believe? What are their core values? In an ideal situation, we would simply contact the author and ask them to clarify what they meant, but that's not always possible. As the next best alternative, I'll tell you how my lived experiences have made me who I am and formed my professional identity.

My parents are Jamaicans and emigrated to Brooklyn and Queens, New York, in the 1970s. I am the second of five sons (yes, I have four brothers), and we grew up in Freeport, New York, a suburban town on the South Shore of Long Island and east of New York City. Living among people from a variety of races, ethnicities, and language backgrounds, I was fortunate to attend Freeport Public Schools with children who were rich (at least I thought they were) and not so rich (me). My friends were Black, White, Asian, and Hispanic (Latinx). Some were Catholic, others were Protestant, and I attended my fair share of Bar Mitzvahs. Because this was my only reality, having lived in Freeport for close to 20 years and matriculating through its schools from pre-kindergarten through 12th grade, racial and ethnic diversity was not only normal for me, it was also comfortable.

A Lifelong Stutter

Between first and sixth grades, I had a significant stutter and received school-based speech therapy. Though I didn't know it at the time and having recently accepted that I have a lifelong stutter, this has become one of the most salient aspects of my identity.

> In my undergraduate and graduate courses, I require my students to speak in every class session. But because I stutter, I also intentionally, and quickly create a supportive environment that is conducive for students to feel comfortable sharing their ideas, asking questions, and responding to their peers and me. Because I stutter and know what it feels like to prefer listening rather than contributing verbally, I am sensitive to my English Learner (EL) students who may be self-conscious about their English proficiency. I am sensitive to shy students whose anxiety makes it difficult to present to their peers. Without a doubt, my perspective as a Black male who stutters has made me more patient because I wanted others to be patient with me. It has made me a better listener because I needed others to listen more intently when I was a youngster. It has made me a better psychologist—one who is slow to form impressions because all students deserve this from the adults in their lives. Having met with parents and students who stutter, I understand that they are quiet, not because they do not know the answer or want to contribute, but because they may be nervous. (Barrett, 2019, pp. 217–218)

As a child, stuttering was embarrassing. I didn't like it and didn't know why I was the only one of my brothers who stuttered. When my friends spoke quickly, I couldn't, and it bothered me. When I had to read aloud in class and couldn't predict when I would stutter, it bothered me. But more than 30 years later, and for the reasons I mentioned above, I can honestly say that stuttering is one of my best qualities because of how it has informed my perspective as a psychologist and educator.

A Racial Awakening: The College and Graduate School Years

After high school, I attended St. John's University in Jamaica, New York. Jamaica is a section of Queens, one of the five boroughs of New York City, that is also quite diverse in terms of race, ethnicity, and SES. It was primarily a commuter school at the time, and most St. John's students were from different parts of New York City—Brooklyn, Bronx, Manhattan, Queens, Staten Island—and Long Island. In many ways, my experience at St. John's wasn't much different from growing up in Freeport. I met a few people—some Black, some White, and some from other races. As it is the largest Catholic university in the country, many students were Catholic, but I also knew some who were Jewish or Muslim.

After college, I went to graduate school in pursuit of my PhD in school psychology. At 20 years old, I moved to Bethlehem, Pennsylvania, a relatively small city in the Lehigh

Valley, and attended Lehigh University. Unlike growing up in Freeport or attending St. John's in Queens, living in Bethlehem was a very different experience for me. For the first time, I was more aware of my identity: a Black man in America. Was it my maturation? Was my racial awakening beginning in my early 20s? Was it because Bethlehem wasn't particularly racially or ethnically heterogeneous? Was it because I was the only Black male in my graduate program, and one of a few Black students in the College of Education and Human Development? The answer is likely E: All of the above.

Having read "Just Walk on By," an essay by Brent Staples that was published in a 1986 issue of *Ms.* magazine, during my first semester of college, I found that living in Bethlehem gave this powerful piece of writing new meaning. Like me, Staples was a Black man living in America who became keenly aware of how his presence alters public space. When people saw him, they locked their car doors, and women clutched their purses. Eventually, Staples decided to adjust his behavior to make himself appear less threatening and others around him feel more comfortable. Whether walking slowly or even around the block a second time to allow people enough time to enter buildings rather than coming in directly behind them, whistling classical music while on city streets at night, or making the keys in his pocket particularly noisy to indicate that he had his own car and wasn't going to harm people in parking lots, these behaviors became a regular part of his existence as a Black man living in America. I must admit: Since reading Staples's essay, I've also adopted some of these behaviors.

While I was becoming more aware of being a Black man in America, though I didn't have the vocabulary at the time, I was also becoming interested in what I now know is social justice and how systems affect children. Even before I knew what school psychology was, I was genuinely curious about what I was hearing anecdotally from friends and family members: the overidentification of Black boys with ADHD and their subsequent placement in special education. Such curiosity led to my dissertation research (Barrett & DuPaul, 2018; see Chapter 5) and my current interest in examining the assessment practices that lead to diagnostic decisions for REM students.

WHAT DO I BELIEVE?

Coupled with being Black, faith, although it is not directly related to school psychology, is one of the most significant aspects of who I am and of my professional identity. Because it is deeply connected to everything I do and what I believe about serving people, I can't separate faith from who I am. Like many others, and perhaps you, too, my faith journey has taken me places that I didn't anticipate. My father is a minister and my grandfather pastored for many years, both in Jamaica, West Indies, and in Brooklyn, New York. Church, in the traditional sense for many Black people (e.g., attending services multiple times each week, including all day on most Sundays), was the epicenter of my existence for more than three decades. And though I appreciate much of what I learned and experienced in church, because life is about growing and evolving, I now have very different ideas about faith.

Growing up in church, I heard (and read) New Testament stories (parables) that were told from multiple perspectives. Notably, the writers, who were always men, accentuated what was salient to them about each event. And so it is for the equitable practice of school psychology: The words we use are a window into how we think (see Chapter 3). The words we use reveal what we believe and what we value. The words we use tell others what is and what isn't important to us as individuals and educators. The words we use not only show what we see but how we see. Whether we acknowledge systemic responsibility for the plight of children or prematurely focus on individuals and ignore derelict policies that perpetuate inequities, both are communicated by our words.

Though not necessarily reserved for faith-based settings, church was where I learned a word that has been transformative for my work as a school psychologist who is committed to social justice: *hermeneutics*. In short, hermeneutics means "perspective," or the lens through which someone views or interprets something else. Over time, I began to listen more intently, not only to what I heard in sermons but to the underlying hermeneutic that people used to formulate what they said. From whose perspective were they speaking? Whose voices and experiences were being centered? Was there any consideration of systems and structures that influenced their interpretation? As discussed in Chapter 2, the various theoretical orientations (e.g., behaviorist, cognitive behaviorist, psychodynamic) can be thought of as a person's hermeneutic. Ecological systems theory, the central framework for this text, is another hermeneutic or perspective that helps us understand the world in which we live.

The lessons learned through my faith journey are also applicable to my life's work as a psychologist and educator. Here's one of the biggest: Much of what we've been taught to accept as absolute (objective) truth are simply subjective interpretations. For students whom some staff describe as "bad," this is simply a subjective interpretation based on their hermeneutic or perspective. In fact, there are no bad children—just children who are communicating their wants and needs through behavior. There are no bad children; just children who have been subjected to chronic violence in their communities and attend schools that don't see or value their full selves. There are no bad children; just children who have not been taught to effectively manage their emotions—some of which are overwhelming based on what they've seen and encountered. Like other systems that we've read about in this book, organized religion, which is very different from loving our neighbors as ourselves or caring for the poor and those who have been placed in the margins of society, is yet another system that reinforces (perpetuates) harm for some while protecting the privileges of others.

Throughout the New Testament, parables (fictitious stories or fables) highlight important lessons. In other words, parables are an instructional strategy that makes information more accessible and learning more effective. You might be familiar with the parable known as the Good Samaritan. And though I've heard this story since I was a child, it wasn't until recent years that I realized that it was filled with microaggressions. The gist of the story is that a Jewish man was badly beaten and left to die on the side of a road. But rather than taking care of him, two religious people ignored the wounded man. A *despised Samaritan,* however, also known as the Good Samaritan, showed genuine love for the stranger by nursing his wounds and paying for his respite at a nearby inn.

As it relates to social justice, here's the question: Why was the Samaritan known as the Good Samaritan? While one plausible explanation is that *Good Samaritan* juxtaposes his compassion against the insensitivity of the religious people, from a historical, social, cultural, and political (systems) perspective, Samaritans were regarded as less than [Jewish] people. And because Samaritans were not expected to be good, the labeling of the man as such was not only offensive, but it also reinforced negative perceptions of the other (e.g., REM individuals). Because of his cultural background, the Samaritan wasn't expected to be good or to do good; therefore, his actions were made exceptional and noteworthy. Today, it's equivalent to comments about Black men and women being articulate when the same isn't highlighted for White people. When educators seem surprised that REM students have been accepted into competitive colleges and universities or that their parents have earned advanced degrees and are employed in certain industries, we expose our implicit biases and deficit thinking.

Through a growth process that led to new ways of reading and interpreting information, I've adopted a hermeneutic of justice that isn't reserved for faith. When I serve students and families who are living in low-income and economic marginalization (LIEM), a hermeneutic of justice leads me to not blame them for their circumstances but to interrogate the systems that led to such outcomes. When I serve REM students who have been referred for special education evaluations, though there is the suspicion of an educational disability, a hermeneutic of justice compels me to examine school and larger societal policies and practices that have contributed to their social, emotional, behavioral, and academic functioning.

BRINGING OUR WHOLE SELVES TO THE PROFESSION

As the son of Jamaican immigrants and having a lifelong stutter and deep roots in the Black church, my experiences inform both who I am and how I serve children, families, schools, and communities. I've often said that educators should bring their whole selves to what they do in their respective disciplines. Whether you're a teacher, counselor, principal, psychologist, social worker, or central office administrator, you can remember who you are, where you're from, and what informs your practice. Without knowing your story, I know that there are very real and deeply personal experiences that have brought you to where you are today. In fact, these aspects of our lives and intersecting identities can be powerful in our teaching, our counseling, our assessment, and our leadership.

In some of my school psychology graduate courses, students complete a Philosophical Orientation and Professional Schema assignment. Essentially, it's a brief paper and presentation that has them reflect on their emerging beliefs and professional positions as developing psychologists. Students write about why or how they entered the field of school psychology. They describe the populations that they are interested in serving. They discuss their theoretical orientations (e.g., behaviorist, cognitive behaviorist), research interests, and philosophical beliefs about school psychology and education. The assignment, which has been modified and is available in Appendix 9.1, is helpful because it allows students to identify what anchors them in a profession that will inevitably have challenging days, weeks, months, and sometimes years over the course of their careers. Without exception, students' personal experiences are significant to their philosophical orientations about the field. Some have shared their difficulties with having an educational disability, and others have written about encountering racism, whether in schools or the larger society. For some it was the experiences of siblings, cousins, neighbors, and friends that significantly influenced their decisions. Others were drawn to school psychology to be change agents in the areas of policy and practice.

THE FORMATION AND EVOLUTION OF A PROFESSIONAL IDENTITY

Without a doubt, my parents have been tremendous role models for me. From pre-kindergarten through graduate school, they were avid supporters and champions of my success in every area of my life. My parents, also known as Stuart and Patricia, were my first examples of not being afraid to challenge systems, including holding schools and educators accountable when they felt that my brothers and I weren't treated fairly. Despite not having a lot of money, they made tremendous sacrifices to ensure that we were exposed to experiences that were instrumental in our development. Though I didn't understand or appreciate it at the time, my parents were giving us access and opportunity. Every year, they took us on a family vacation. For 365 days, my brothers and I looked forward to 7 days of pure bliss, often during the last week of August. My parents made sure not only that we enjoyed ourselves but also that we were exposed to the world beyond Freeport and that we experienced life beyond what we typically saw in New York.

As we discussed in Chapter 7, schools and families are two of the most significant microsystems that can work together as partners in children's educational success. But for me, the mesosystem that was the product of church and family microsystems has been equally important. In addition to my parents, one individual significantly influenced my core values and the formation of my professional identity.

Reverend Bruce Ferguson (d. 2004), or as my peers and I affectionately called him, Bro. Bruce, was our youth leader. An educator himself, Bro. Bruce was a firm believer in young people and always gave us opportunities to grow. From public speaking to leadership, Bro. Bruce gave us a chance. Whether sports, music, or academic competitions, he was always interested in what we were doing and encouraged us to pursue our goals. Whether we placed in our elementary school's spelling bee, played in our first band or orchestra concert, won a track and field or swimming medal, or received a scholarship to an Ivy League university, Bro. Bruce had a way of making us feel that we could accomplish anything. The epitome of a servant leader, in good and not-so-good situations, he was there. His life was dedicated to supporting young people, helping their families navigate difficult situations with their children, and challenging schools and larger systems to do what's best for youth of all ages. What Bro. Bruce modeled for me has informed most of what I believe about serving children: Love them unconditionally, support them unwaveringly, and advocate for them fiercely.

CHAPTER SUMMARY

From growing up in a diverse community in New York, having a lifelong stutter, being the son and grandson of ministers, to becoming more aware of my race in graduate school, all of my lived experiences played a significant role in becoming the psychologist and educator I am today. And even when I didn't realize it, theological lessons in my childhood and having the greatest champion of young people and educational success as a mentor were some of the most pivotal experiences of my life and were instrumental in the formation and continued evolution of my professional identity.

Having read an entire book about the role of socially just practices in promoting equitable outcomes for children, families, schools, and communities, it would be unfortunate to focus only on the theoretical concepts while overlooking who we are as people—humans who interact with other humans in the pursuit of what's right and good for young people. Said another way, whether you are a teacher, dean, or principal; supervisor or director; assistant superintendent or superintendent; school counselor, school psychologist, or school social worker, don't allow what you do to overshadow who you are or the places and spaces that made you the professional that you are today. As children learn more from teachers with whom they have a relationship and staff members follow leaders that they connect to, allow others to know who you are regardless of your role. More than the degrees that we've earned that make us qualified to serve in various capacities, our effectiveness is wrapped in our authenticity as educators who are committed to serving people.

As this chapter focused on the autobiographical elements that made me who I am, what is your story? Who influenced you? What have you overcome? Or, like me and stuttering, what are you living with that makes you a better educator? Whatever our relationship to power and privilege, our intersecting identities, experiences with racism, the myriad challenges that we've overcome or are continuing to work through, or the lessons we've learned through our faith or upbringing, nothing is wasted or inconsequential. Rather, every aspect of our lives can be meaningful to what we endeavor to do on behalf of children: being committed educators who will advocate for socially just practices and challenge systems to promote equitable outcomes.

RESOURCES FOR PROFESSIONAL LEARNING

Please see Appendix 9.1 for a reflective activity that has been designed to reinforce important concepts from Chapter 9.

DISCUSSION QUESTIONS

1. In Chapter 9, I describe myself as someone with a lifelong stutter. In other words, this is something that I have not overcome but continue to experience daily. Think about something in your life that you have not overcome. How has this affected you as an educator?

   _____

   _____

   _____

2. In your respective role as an educator, what do you believe about children and families? What are your core values that influence what you do and how you do it?

   _____

   _____

   _____

3. One example of a mesosystem is the combination of school and home (family). In reflecting on your lived experiences, which microsystems (single settings) or mesosystems (a combination of microsystems) were influential in your life?

   _____

   _____

   _____

4. Reflect on your life as a child. What did you need to be successful in school? If you didn't receive these supports (including family support, unconditional posi-

tive regard, patience from teachers and administrators), how can you be the educator that you needed as a child?

_____

_____

_____

Philosophical Orientation and Professional Schema Worksheet

As described on page 170, the Philosophical Orientation and Professional Schema assignment is a brief reflection paper that encourages graduate students to provide a thoughtful analysis of their emerging beliefs and professional positions as developing school psychologists. The assignment, however, is applicable to all educators and disciplines. As a graduate student or someone already serving as an educator, use the following table to think about, fill in, and discuss the various sections with your classmates or colleagues.

Area	Comments and reflections	Why is this important to me?
What are my emerging beliefs about education (e.g., teaching, administration/leadership), school psychology, school counseling, or social work?		
How can my respective discipline support students, families, schools, and communities?		
Why did I choose to become a teacher, administrator, school psychologist, school counselor, school social worker, or other mental health provider?		

(continued)

Philosophical Orientation and Professional Schema Worksheet (page 2 of 2)

Area	Comments and reflections	Why is this important to me?
Are there particular students (e.g., age(s), grade level(s), race/ethnicity) that I am especially interested in serving?		
What skills are necessary for me to continue developing as an educator, administrator, or clinician?		
Which research should I learn more about to continue developing as an educator, administrator, or clinician?		

References

American Psychological Association. (2019). Guidelines for psychological practice for people with low-income and economic marginalization. *https://apacustomout.apa.org/commentPracGuidelines/Practice/LIEM_Guidelines.pdf*.

American Psychological Association Zero Tolerance Task Force. (2008). Are zero tolerance policies effective in the schools? *American Psychologist, 63*(9), 852–862. *www.apa.org/pubs/reports/zero-tolerance.pdf*.

Baba, H. (Host). (2020, August 10). A legacy of mistreatment for San Francisco's Black special ed students. [Audio podcast episode]. *Crosscurrents.* KALW Public Media. *www.kalw.org/podcast/crosscurrents-podcast/2020-08-10/a-legacy-of-mistreatment-for-san-franciscos-black-special-ed-students?fbclid=IwAR31YKXDDzRJ56nI9H82zqVGFnqsFXDAALDWHjGJZ-TqpO1_vHC2dS0YLRlo&fs=e&s=cl*.

Baldwin, J. (1962, January 14). As much truth as one can bear: To speak out about the world as it is, says James Baldwin, is the writer's job. *New York Times*, Section T, 11. *www.nytimes.com/1962/01/14/archives/as-much-truth-as-one-can-bear-to-speak-out-about-the-world-as-it-is.html*.

Barkley, R. A. (2015). *Attention-deficit hyperactivity disorder: A handbook for diagnosis and treatment* (4th ed.). Guilford Press.

Barrett, C. A. (2018). It's always about the children. *https://charlesbarrett.org/product/282554*.

Barrett, C. A. (2019). On stuttering and speech impediments: Stepping stones not speed bumps. In B. L. Wright, N. Bryan, C. Sewell, L. Yates, M. Robinson, & K. Thomas (Eds.), *Gumbo for the soul: III. Males of color share their stories, meditations, affirmations, and inspirations* (pp. 211–218). Information Age.

Barrett, C. A. (2020). *Today in school psychology: This is why a day without direct contact with students is wasted.* CAB Publishing.

Barrett, C. A. (2021a). A lexicon for social justice: New ways of knowing, new ways of seeing. *Communique, 49*(7), 30–31.

Barrett, C. A. (2021b). *Today in school psychology: This is why a day without direct contact with students is wasted* (Vol. 2). CAB Publishing.

Barrett, C. A. (2022). *Today in school psychology: This is why a day without direct contact with students is wasted* (Vol. 3). CAB Publishing.

Barrett, C. A., & DuPaul, G. J. (2018). Impact of maternal and child race on maternal ratings of ADHD symptoms in Black and White boys. *Journal of Attention Disorders, 22*(13), 1246–1254.

Barrett, C. A., Harper, E., Hudson, N., & Malone, C. (2020). The NASP Exposure Project: Using research in practice to advance strategic goals. *Communiqué, 48*(7), 12–14.

Barrett, C. A., Heidelburg, K., & Malone, C. (2019). The NASP Exposure Project: Addressing workforce shortages and social justice. *Communiqué, 47*(5), 8–10.

Barrett, C. A., Kendrick-Dunn, T. B., & Proctor, S. L. (2019). Low income and economic margin-alization as a matter of social justice: Foundational knowledge. *Communiqué, 48*(2), 1–21.

Black Lives Matter (n.d.). *Herstory. https://blacklivesmatter.com/herstory.*

Blandin, A. (2017). The home/school connection and its role in narrowing the academic achieve-ment gap: An ecological systems theoretical perspective. *Journal of Research on Christian Education, 26*(3), 271–292.

Bocanegra, J. O., Newell, M. L., & Gubi, A. A. (2016). Racial/ethnic minority undergraduate psy-chology majors' perceptions about school psychology: Implications for minority recruitment. *Contemporary School Psychology, 20*(3), 270–281.

Bottiani, J. H., Bradshaw, C. P., & Gregory, A. (2018). Nudging the gap: Introduction to the spe-cial issue "Closing In on Discipline Disproportionality." *School Psychology Review, 47*(2), 109–117.

Boyd, R. W., Ellison, A. M., & Horn, I. B. (2016). Police, equity, and child health. *Pediatrics, 137*(3), 1–3.

Bronfenbrenner, U. (1977). Toward an experimental ecology of human development. *American Psychologist, 32*, 513–531.

Bronfenbrenner, U. (1989). Ecological systems theory. *Annals of Child Development, 6*, 187–249.

Bronfenbrenner, U. (1995). Developmental ecology through space and time: A future perspec-tive. In P. Moen, G. H. Elder, & K. Luscher (Eds.), *Examining lives in context: Perspectives on the ecology of human development* (pp. 599–618). American Psychological Association.

Brown-Chidsey, R., & Steege, M. W. (2010). *Response to intervention: Principles and strategies for effective practice* (2nd ed.). Guilford Press.

Castillo, J. M., Curtis, M. J., & Tan, S. Y. (2014). Personnel needs in school psychology: A 10-year follow-up study on predicted personnel shortages. *Psychology in the Schools, 51*(8), 832–849.

Centers for Disease Control and Prevention. (2022). COVID data tracker. *https://covid.cdc.gov/covid-data-tracker/#datatracker-home.*

Chafouleas, S. M., & Iovino, E. A. (2021). Engaging a whole child, school, and community lens in positive education to advance equity in schools. *Frontiers in Psychology, 12*, 1–11.

Columbus, C. (Director). (1990). *Home alone* [Film]. 20th Century Fox.

Cook, C. R., Duong, M. T., McIntosh, K., Fiat, A. E., Larson, M., Pullmann, M. D., et al. (2018). Addressing discipline disparities for Black male students: Linking malleable root causes to feasible and effective practices. *School Psychology Review, 47*(2), 135–152.

Crenshaw, K. (2016). The urgency of intersectionality [Video]. TED Conferences. *www.ted.com/talks/kimberle_crenshaw_the_urgency_of_intersectionality*.

Crenshaw, K., Ocen, P., & Nanda, J. (2015). *Black girls matter: Pushed out, overpoliced, and underprotected*. Columbia University, Center for Intersectionality and Social Policy Studies.

Cummins, J. (1979). *Cognitive/academic language proficiency, linguistic interdependence, the optimum age question and some other matters*. Working Papers on Bilingualism, 19 (ED184334). ERIC. *https://eric.ed.gov/?id=ED184334*.

Cvencek, D., Meltzoff, A. N., & Greenwald, A. G. (2011). Math–gender stereotypes in elementary school children. *Child Development, 82*(3), 766–779.

de Ramirez, R. D., & Shapiro, E. S. (2005). Effects of student ethnicity on judgments of ADHD symptoms among Hispanic and White teachers. *School Psychology Quarterly, 20*, 268–287.

Delpit, L. (2012). *Multiplication is for white people: Raising expectations for other people's children*. The New Press.

Dorn, E., Hancock, B., Sarakatsannis, J., & Viruleg, E. (2020, June 1). *COVID-19 and student learning in the United States: The hurt could last a lifetime*. McKinsey. *https://tinyurl.com/y4ekuaps*.

DuPaul, G. J., Power, T. J., Anastopoulos, A. D., & Reid, R. (1998). *ADHD Rating Scale–IV: Checklists, norms, and clinical interpretation*. Guilford Press.

Eccles, J. S., & Harold, R. D. (1993). Parent–school involvement during the early adolescent years. *Teachers College Record, 94*(3), 568–587.

Eisenberg, M. E., Gower, A. L., Rider, G. N., McMorris, B. J., & Coleman, E. (2019). At the intersection of sexual orientation and gender identity: Variations in emotional distress and bullying experience in a large population-based sample of U.S. adolescents. *Journal of LGBT Youth, 16*(3), 235–254.

Every Student Succeeds Act, 20 U.S.C. § 6301 (2015). *www2.ed.gov/documents/essa-act-of-1965.pdf*.

Flores, N. (2020). From academic language to language architecture: Challenging raciolinguistic ideologies in research and practice. *Theory into Practice, 59*(1), 22–31.

Ford, D. Y. (2015). Multicultural issues: Recruiting and retaining Black and Hispanic students in gifted education: Equality versus equity schools. *Gifted Child Today, 38*(3), 187–191.

Ford, D. Y., Grantham, T. C., & Whiting, G. W. (2008). Culturally and linguistically diverse students in gifted education: Recruitment and retention issues. *Exceptional Children, 74*(3), 289–306.

Ford, D. Y., Harris, J. J., III, Tyson, C. A., & Trotman, M. F. (2002). Beyond deficit thinking: Providing access for gifted African American students. *Roeper Review, 24*(2), 52–58.

García, O. (2009). Education, multilingualism and translanguaging in the 21st century. In T. Skutnabb-Kangas, R. Phillipson, A. Mohanty, & M. Panda (Eds.), *Social justice through multilingual education* (pp. 140–158). Multilingual Matters.

Gilliam, W. S. (2005). *Pre-kindergartners left behind: Expulsion rates in state pre-kindergarten systems*. Foundation for Child Development.

Gilliam, W. S., Maupin, A. N., Reyes, C. R., Accavitti, M., & Shic, F. (2016). Do early educators' implicit biases regarding sex and race relate to behavior expectations and recommendations of preschool expulsions and suspensions? *Yale University Child Study Center, 9*(28), 1–16.

Goforth, A. N., Farmer, R. L., Kim, S. Y., Naser, S. C., Lockwood, A. B., & Affrunti, N. W. (2021). Status of school psychology in 2020: Part 1, Demographics of the NASP membership survey. *NASP Research Reports, 5*(2), 1–17.

Gregory, A., Skiba, R. J., & Mediratta, K. (2017). Eliminating disparities in school discipline: A framework for intervention. *Review of Research in Education, 41*(1), 253–278.

Gunn, D. (2019, February 26). Non-White school districts get $23 billion less funding than White ones. *Pacific Standard.* *https://psmag.com/education/nonwhite-school-districts-get-23-billion-less-funding-than-white-ones.*

Hallmark Media 254. (2018, June 3). Martin Luther King, Jr. explaining about slavery and Negro discrimination [Video]. *www.youtube.com/watch?v=QGPkLztG77I.*

Hammond, Z. (2014). *Culturally responsive teaching and the brain: Promoting authentic engagement and rigor among culturally and linguistically diverse students.* Corwin Press.

Hanford, E. (2018, September 10). Hard words: Why aren't kids being taught to read? *www.apmreports.org/episode/2018/09/10/hard-words-why-american-kids-arent-being-taught-to-read.*

Hart, B., & Risley, T. R. (1995). *Meaningful differences in the everyday experience of young American children.* Brookes.

Hart, B., & Risley, T. R. (2003). The early catastrophe: The 30 million word gap by age 3. *Education Review, 17*(1), 1–9.

Hawken, L. S., Crone, D. A., Bundock, K., & Horner, R. H. (2021). *Responding to problem behavior in schools: The check-in, check-out intervention* (3rd ed.). Guilford Press.

Holladay, J. R. (2000). On racism and white privilege. Learning for Justice. *www.tolerance.org/professional-development/on-racism-and-white-privilege.*

Hosp, J. L. (2006, May) Implementing RTI: Assessment practices and response to intervention. *NASP Communiqué, 34*(7). *https://digitalcollections.eku.edu/items/show/53293.*

Individuals with Disabilities Education Act, 20 U.S.C. § 1400 (2004).

Johnson, A. G. (2006). *Privilege, power, and difference* (2nd ed.). McGraw-Hill.

Kendi, I. X. (2019). *How to be an antiracist.* One World.

Klecker, M. (2020, August 7). Minnesota parents rush to create "learning pods" for distance learning. *www.startribune.com/minnesota-parents-rushing-to-set-up-distance-learning-pods/572032192.*

Landrine, H., & Klonoff, E. A. (1996). *African American acculturation: Deconstructing race and reviving culture.* Sage.

Lexia. (n.d.). LETRS. *https://www.lexialearning.com/letrs.*

Losen, D. J., & Orfield, G. (2002). *Racial inequity in special education.* Harvard Education Publishing Group.

Lott, B., & Rogers, M. R. (2011). Ethnicity matters for undergraduate majors in challenges, experiences, and perceptions of psychology. *Cultural Diversity and Ethnic Minority Psychology, 17*(2), 204–210.

McIntosh, K., & Goodman, S. (2016). *Integrated multi-tiered systems of support: Blending RTI and PBIS.* Guilford Press.

McIntosh, P. (1989, July/August). White privilege: Unpacking the invisible knapsack. *Peace and Freedom Magazine*, pp. 10–12.

Mooney, T. (2018, May 11). Why we say "opportunity gap" instead of "achievement gap." *www.teachforamerica.org/one-day/top-issues/why-we-say-opportunity-gap-instead-of-achievement-gap.*

National Association of School Psychologists. (2016a). Shortages in school psychology: Resource guide. *www.nasponline.org/resources-and-publications/resources-and-podcasts/school-psychology/shortages-in-school-psychology-resource-guide.*

National Association of School Psychologists. (2016b). Understanding race and privilege. *www.*

nasponline.org/resources-and-publications/resources-and-podcasts/diversity-and-social-justice/social-justice/understanding-race-and-privilege*.

National Association of School Psychologists. (2017). Strategic plan: 2017–2022. *www.nasponline.org/x41409.xml*.

National Association of School Psychologists. (2018). Implicit bias: Part 2. Addressing disproportionality in discipline: A prospective look at culturally responsive positive behavior intervention and supports. *www.nasponline.org/resources-and-publications/resources-and-podcasts/diversity-and-social-justice/social-justice/implicit-bias-a-foundation-for-school-psychologists/implicit-bias-part-2*.

National Association of School Psychologists. (2020). *The professional standards of the National Association of School Psychologists*. Author.

National Association of School Psychologists. (2021a). Social justice definitions. *www.nasponline.org/resources-and-publications/resources-and-podcasts/diversity-and-social-justice/social-justice/social-justice-definitions*.

National Association of School Psychologists. (2021b). Supporting Asian, Asian American, and Pacific Islander graduate students: Tips for graduate educators and students. *https://tinyurl.com/yh3wcpu2*.

National Center for Education Statistics. (2022). *English learners in public schools*. U.S. Department of Education, Institute of Education Sciences. *https://nces.ed.gov/programs/coe/indicator/cgf*.

National Reading Panel. (2000). *Teaching children to read: An evidence-based assessment of the scientific research literature on reading and its implications for reading instruction: Reports of the subgroups*. U.S. Department of Health and Human Services, National Institutes of Health, National Institute of Child Health and Human Development. *www.nichd.nih.gov/sites/default/files/publications/pubs/nrp/Documents/report.pdf*.

Nazario, S. (2007). *Enrique's journey: The story of a boy's dangerous odyssey to reunite with his mother*. Random House Trade Paperbacks.

Overstreet, S., Devine, J., Bevans, K., & Efreon, Y. (2005). Predicting parental involvement in children's schooling within an economically disadvantaged African American sample. *Psychology in the Schools, 42*(1), 101–111.

Pinto, E. (2010, November 15). Structural discrimination: The unequal opportunity race [Video]. *www.youtube.com/watch?v=vX_Vzl-r8NY*.

Proctor, S. L., Williams, B., Scherr, T., & Li, K. (2017). Intersectionality and school psychology: Implications for practice. *National Association of School Psychology, 46*(4), 1–19.

Puig, M., Lambert, M. C., Rowan, G. T., Winfrey, T., Lyubansky, M., Hannah, S. D., et al. (1999). Behavioral and emotional problems among Jamaican and African American children, ages 6 to 11: Teacher reports versus direct observations. *Journal of Emotional and Behavioral Disorders, 7*(4), 240–250.

Rogers, M. R., & Molina, L. E. (2006). Exemplary efforts in psychology to recruit and retain graduate students of color. *American Psychologist, 61*(2), 143–156.

Romney, L., Cusick, R., & Walters, P. (Producers & Hosts). (2019, June 7). G: The miseducation of Larry P. [Audio podcast episode]. Radiolab. WNYC Studios. *https://radiolab.org/episodes/g-miseducation-larry-p*.

Rosa, E. M., & Tudge, J. (2013). Urie Bronfenbrenner's theory of human development: Its evolution from ecology to bioecology. *Journal of Family Theory and Review, 5*(4), 243–258.

Rothstein, R. (2014, November 12). The racial achievement gap, segregated schools, and segregated neighborhoods: A constitutional insult. Economic Policy Institute. *www.epi.org/pub-*

lication/the-racial-achievement-gap-segregated-schools-and-segregated-neighborhoods-a-constitutional-insult.

Singleton, G. E. (2014). *Courageous conversation about race: A field guide for achieving equity in schools* (2nd ed). Corwin.

Skiba, R. J., Simmons, A. B., Ritter, S., Gibb, A. C., Karega Rausch, M., Cuadrado, J., et al. (2008). Achieving equity in special education: History, status, and current challenges. *Exceptional Children, 74,* 264–288.

Sonuga-Barke, E. J., Minocha, K., Taylor, E. A., & Sandberg, S. (1993). Inter-ethnic bias in teachers' ratings of childhood hyperactivity. *British Journal of Developmental Psychology, 11*(2), 187–200.

Staples, B. (1986). Just walk on by: Black men and public space. *www.ohlone.edu/sites/default/files/documents/imported/justwalkonbyblackmenandpublicspace.pdf.*

Stevens, G. (1981). Bias in the attribution of hyperkinetic behavior as a function of ethnic identification and socioeconomic status. *Psychology in the Schools, 18*(1), 99–106.

Strauss, V. (2014, August 21). For first time, minority students to be majority in U.S. public schools this fall. *www.washingtonpost.com/news/answer-sheet/wp/2014/08/21/for-first-time-minority-students-expected-to-be-majority-in-u-s-public-schools-this-fall.*

Sue, D. W., Capodilupo, C. M., Torino, G. C., Bucceri, J. M., Holder, A. M. B., Nadal, K. L., et al. (2007). Racial microaggressions in everyday life: Implications for clinical practice. *American Psychologist, 62*(4), 271–286.

Tervalon, M., & Murray-García J. (1998). Cultural humility versus cultural competence: A critical distinction in defining physician training outcomes in multicultural education. *Journal of Health Care for the Poor and Underserved, 9*(2), 117–125.

U.S. Department of Education Office for Civil Rights. (2014). Civil rights data collection: Data snapshot: School discipline (Issue Brief No. 1). *www2.ed.gov/about/offices/list/ocr/docs/crdc-discipline-snapshot.pdf.*

U.S. Department of Education, Office of Special Education Programs, Technical Assistance Center on Positive Behavioral Interventions and Supports. (2015, October 1). Positive behavioral interventions and supports (PBIS) implementation blueprint: Part 1. Foundations and supporting information. *https://assets-global.website-files.com/5d3725188825e071f1670246/5d79859de5f68d6b4d775c6f_PBIS%20Part%201%2018%20Oct%202015%20Final.pdf.*

Vespa, J., Armstrong, D. M., & Medina, L. (2018). *Demographic turning points for the United States: Population projections for 2020 to 2060.* U.S. Department of Commerce, Economics and Statistics Administration, U.S. Census Bureau.

Walcott, C. M., & Hyson, D. (2018). Results from NASP 2015 membership survey: Part 1: Demographics and employment conditions. *www.nasponline.org/Documents/Research%20and%20Policy/Research%20Center/NRR_Membership_Survey_2015_Walcott_and_Hyson_2018.pdf.*

Waters, A., & Asbill, L. (2013, August). Reflections on cultural humility. *CYF News. www.apa.org/pi/families/resources/newsletter/2013/08/cultural-humility.*

Welsh, R. O., & Little, S. (2018). The school discipline dilemma: A comprehensive review of disparities and alternative approaches. *Review of Educational Research, 88,* 752–794.

Zemeckis, R. (Director). (1994). *Forrest Gump* [Film]. Paramount Pictures.

Zhou, Z., Bray, M. A., Kehle, T. J., Theodore, L. A., Clark, E., & Jenson, W. R. (2004). Achieving ethnic minority parity in school psychology. *Psychology in the Schools, 41*(4), 443–450.

Index

Note. *f*, *n*, or *t* following a page number indicates a figure, note, or a table.

Teachers *(cont.)*
  responding to harmful behavior and language
    and, 50–56, 60–61, 62*t*–63*t*
  RIOT framework for assessment and, 98–101,
    104–105
  Semistructured Family and Teacher Interview
    Form, 106–107
  socially just assessment practices and, 99–100,
    106–107
  systems change and, 141–150, 145*f*, 149*f*
  training in handling behavior incidents and,
    46–47
  understanding families by, 109
Testing. *See* Standardized testing
Theoretical frameworks, 9–10
Tiered model of service delivery. *See* Multi-tiered
    system of supports (MTSS) frameworks
Trail of Tears, 19
Training for teachers, 46–47. *See also* Resources
    for professional learning; Teachers
Transgender individuals. *See* LGBTQIA+
    individuals
Transitions, 21–22
Translanguaging, 37–39. *See also* Language
Trauma, 114–115

U

Unconscious bias. *See* Implicit bias
Unearned advantages, 72, 74. *See also* Privilege

V

Violence, police, 75, 78, 113–115
Vocabulary, 35–36. *See also* Language; Word gap
Voiceless, 58–59, 62*t*–63*t*

W

We statements, 52, 55
Wealth, 72, 73*t*. *See also* Socioeconomic status
    (SES)
White individuals, 96–97, 97*f*, 143–144
White Privilege, 72–74, 82. *See also* Privilege
Word gap. *See also* Language
  discussion questions related to, 64
  overview, 34, 35–36, 37, 60
  schools and power and, 128
  socially just alternatives to, 36–39, 39*t*
Workforce shortages, 138–139, 141, 142–144, 155.
    See also Staff and staffing decisions

Z

Zero-tolerance policies
  discussion questions related to, 64
  macrosystem and, 20
  overview, 34, 44–49, 48*f*, 60–61, 66
  reserving for serious and severe behaviors, 49
  socially just alternatives to, 45–49, 48*f*